PELO

GROC'S C

GREECE

including
Patras, Korinthos, Nafplio, Argos, Tripoli,
Neapoli, Githion, Sparti, Kalamata & Killini
with excursions including the archaeological sites
of
Ancient Corinth, Acrocorinthos, the Sanctuary of
Epidavros, Tiryns, Mycenae, Tegea, Mantina,
Mistras & Olympia

For the package & villa holiday-maker,
backpacker & independent traveller,
whether journeying by air, car, coach, ferry-boat
or train

by
Geoffrey O'Connell

Published by

**Ashford, Buchan
& Enright**
31 Bridge Street
Leatherhead
Surrey KT22 8BN

CONTENTS

ILLUSTRATIONS

Readers must not forget that prices are given as a guide only and relate to the year in which this book was researched. In recent years, not only lodging and dining costs, but all transport charges have escalated dramatically. The increased value of most other currencies to the Greek drachma has compensated, to some extent, for these apparently ever-rising prices. On the other hand, the drachmae, being a controlled currency, is 'managed', and kept at a rather unrealistic value. In an effort to keep readers as up-to-date as possible, regarding these and other matters, the **GROC'S GREEK ISLAND HOTLINE** is available. See elsewhere for details.

The series is now in its eleventh year of publication, and I would appreciate continuing to hear from readers who have any additions or corrections to bring to my attention. As in the past, all correspondence (except that addressed to 'Dear filth', or similar endearments) will be answered.

I hope readers will excuse errors that barge their way into the welter of detailed information included in the body text. My only excuse is to hide behind the fact that in order to ensure the volumes are as up-to-date as possible, the period from inception to publication is often kept down to some six months, which results in the occasional slip up...!

The unique
'GROC's Greek Island Hotline'

Available to readers of the guides, this service enables a respondent to receive a bang up-to-the-minute update, to supplement the extensive information contained in a particular GROC's Candid Guide.
  To obtain these paraphrased computer print-outs, all that is necessary is to:-

Complete the form, enclosing a payment of £2.00* & a large SAE (50p) and send to:-
  Willowbridge Publishing, Bridge House, Southwick Village, Nr Fareham, Hants. PO17 6DZ.

  This only allows for postage & packing to a UK address.

Note: The information will be of no use to anyone who does not possess the relevant, most up-to-date GROC's Candid Greek Island Guide. We are unable to dispatch the Hotline without details of the guide AND the specific edition, which information is on the Inside Front Cover.

Clients who take out SURETRAVEL INSURANCE, at the same time as requesting a Hotline, will receive the Hotline Free of Charge.

Issue: Spring 1993

Planned departure dates.....................................
....

Mr/Mrs/Miss...
of..
....

I possess:		I require:
GROC's Greek Island Guides	Edition	GROC's Greek Island Hotline
to:............................	....	to:............................
....	....	....
....	....	....
....	....	....
....	....	....
....	....	....

and enclose a fee of £2.00 & a large SAE (50p).
Signature........................ .... Date........................
I appreciate that the 'Hotline' may not be dispatched for up to 7-10 days from receipt of this application.

GROC's Candid Guides
introduce to readers

Suretravel '93

A comprehensive, cost-effective holiday insurance plan that 'gives cover many other policies do not reach', to travellers all over the world, AND at a reduced cost to previous years! In addition to the more usual insurance, the

SURETRAVEL HOLIDAY PLAN

offers legal expenses, and up to double the cover in some categories. It also includes (where medically necessary) 24 hour world wide medical emergency service and, where appropriate, repatriation by air ambulance. Also incorporated are personal accident, medical and emergency expenses, EVEN while hiring a bicycle, scooter or car, as well as other wide-ranging holiday activities.

An example 1993 premium, for a 10-17 day holiday in Greece, is £16.00 per person.
Note: all offers & terms are subject to the Insurance Certificate Cover

For an application form please complete the cut-out below and send to: Willowbridge Publishing, Bridge House, Southwick Village, Nr Fareham, Hants. PO17 6DZ

Mr/Mrs/Miss..Age...........

of...

....

I request a **SURETRAVEL** application form

Date of commencement of holiday....................Duration.............

Signature...Date...........

FORWARD

This guide, **GROC's Candid Guide to The Peloponnese**, is the first edition, the area being a brand-new addition to the existing, extremely popular, well-proven series of nine Candid Guides to Greece and the Greek islands.

In spite of the extensive treatment given to the Greek islands, in general, for some obscure reason the Peloponnese has largely been ignored, by authors and publishers alike. And this, despite the enormous opportunities offered to each and every visitor, whichever direction it is that his, her or their interests might lie.

In spite of the sheer size of the area, the breadth of transport choices available enables travellers to reasonably easily cover the whole peninsula, as long as there is sufficient time to spare.

In order to cope with the problem of describing the Peloponnese, in detail, as would be expected from any GROC's guide, the basic format has been adhered-to, but adapted. Instead of having to particularise individual islands, in a chain, each principal settlement has been treated as if it were a major port or town, following the usual formula.

Hopefully, the considerations of all vacationers have been considered. If they are package hotel or villa holiday-makers, it is extremely important to have an unbiased and relevant description of the chosen resort and its surroundings, rather than the usual, extravagant hyperbole to be found in almost all sales brochures. On the other hand, independent travellers, arriving by air, coach, ferry-boat, hydrofoil or train, must have accurate, easy, instant, and specific information concerning their immediate whereabouts, as well as sleeping and dining opportunities, in addition to the availability of sundry other facilities, services and supplies. To cope with these differing requirements, factual and forthright location reports, combined with accommodation and eating out particulars, in addition to an A to Z, are coupled with detailed plans, as well as regional maps. The guide's make-up is designed to allow speedy identification in respect of these varying requirements, including their pinpoint location, as well as a swift and easy to read resume of the settlement's main quarters, itemised 'means of travel' timetables, and full regional narratives.

Most of the major archaeological sites are accompanied by a plan of the layout, a brief elaboration covering the main features, as well as particulars of relevant historical and mythological interest. The serious student should purchase one of the individual site guides, which are usually excellently illustrated and well produced, even if the English is sometimes rather quaint.

This particular GROC's guide, as are all the others in the series, is researched as close to the planned publication date as is possible. On the other hand, to facilitate production, it is not always feasible to wait for information only available in the year of publication. To overcome this awkward fact, as well as to keep an already produced guide up-to-date, year-on-year, any relevant alterations and changes in information, including current travel timetables, are 'punched' into a *Hotline* information pack, for particulars of which read on.

Part One introduces the Peloponnese to the reader, Part Two briefly introduces the transport alternatives, whilst Part Three heralds the individual chapters which cover the specific, major locations, be they a city, port or town.

As has become the routine, all general information about Greece, including travel, to and from the country, as well as the capital, Athens City, is covered in a separate guide. The necessary division of the material was first implemented in 1989, after which these preliminaries, and a thoroughly redrafted account of Athens City, still the hub for much Hellenic travel, were treated to an individual book. This decision had to be made to ensure the continued improvement and expansion of each guides' contents, as the sheer volume of information became rather unwieldy. Countless readers, who wished to take along two or three guides, were humping about hundreds of pages of duplicated information. Furthermore, in years gone-by, it was almost mandatory to include Athens in any Greek guide book, as the capital was pivotal to most forms of travel. With the ever-increasing number of direct destinations available, it is often feasible to reach a particular destination, without reference to Athens. Even if there isn't a convenient connection, many travellers' only sight of the capital will be the facilities and tarmacadam of the airport. And this only whilst transferring from the international to domestic airport, for the onward leg of a particular flight.

The exchange rate has, over the years, tended to gently slide in other currencies favour, with the Greek drachma constantly devaluing, but nothing like as much as it would, were it not a 'managed' money. At the time of writing the final draft of this guide, the rate to the English pound (£) was lurking in the region of 320drs. Unfortunately, Greek prices are subject to fluctuation, upward, with annual increases, in the last few years, exceeding 15/20%, and the drachma has ceased to devalue sufficiently to compensate for these uplifts.

Recommendations and personalities are almost always based on personal observation and experience, occasionally emphasised by the discerning comments of readers and colleagues. They may well change from year to year, and, being such individual, idiosyncratic judgements, are subject to different interpretation by others.

The series continues to incorporate two services, evolved over the years, one of which remains both innovative and unique. These are:
GROC's Greek Hotline: An unrivalled benefit available to purchasers of a particular, current GROC's Candid Guide. Application enables a reader to obtain a summary print-out listing all pertinent, relevant comments and information, that have become available, since the publication of that book. The Hotline is constantly being updated and revised, incorporating bang up-to-the-moment intelligence, not only culled from our own resources, but from readers correspondence. Completion of the form incorporated in the book, accompanied by the relevant fee and a SAE, is all that is required to receive the specific Hotline.
Travel Insurance: A comprehensive holiday insurance plan that 'gives cover that many other policies do not reach....' See elsewhere for further details.

The author (and publisher) are very interested in considering ways and means of improving the information contained in the guides, and adding to the backup facilities. In this connection, we are delighted to hear from readers with their suggestions.

Enjoy yourselves and 'Ya Sou' (welcome).

Geoffrey O'Connell 1993

ACKNOWLEDGMENTS

Apart from those numerous friends and confidants we meet on passage, there are the many correspondents who are kind enough to contact me with useful information, all of whom, in the main, remain unnamed.

One of the small, personal pleasures of life, is to note, over the years, that the list of those to be thanked has remained remarkably similar. As always, my constant travelling companion, Rosemary, who can unfailingly be relied on to add her often unwanted, uninformed comments and asides, requires especial thanks for unrelieved, unstinting (well, almost unstinting) support.

Although receiving a reward, other than in heaven, some of those who assist me, year in and year out, and more especially in the production of this book, require specific acknowledgement - if only for effort, far beyond the siren call of vulgar remuneration! These worthies include: Graham Bishop, who continues to draw splendid maps and plans; Ted Spittles who does clever things with the process camera, and the paste-up; Viv Grady, who now not only controls the word processor, but the laser printer - soon she will write the wretched things; and Richard Joseph, a long-standing friend, who encouraged me to 'put pen to paper', some fourteen or fifteen years ago, and continues to guide, help and encourage me. During those endless months, whilst this or that book is in the process of preparation, Viv's 'playmate' must wonder why she doesn't pick up her bed, and move into Bridge House!

Once again, I would like to include a general apology to chums, and more especially my Mother & Father, for the endless times I have had to forego an invitation or a visit... due to the time-consuming demands of authorship, and deadlines. In conclusion, I can only admonish Richard Joseph for ever encouraging and cajoling me to take up the quill - surely the sword is more fun?

The cover picture is of the reef-topping octagonal tower, or Turkish Bourzi, at the seaward end of the Venetian inspired, Methoni castle, and is reproduced by kind permission of GREEK ISLAND PHOTOS, Willowbridge Enterprises, Bletchley, Milton Keynes, Bucks.

Footnote. For details of the Symbols, Keys and Definitions used in the text, please refer to pages 216 & 217.

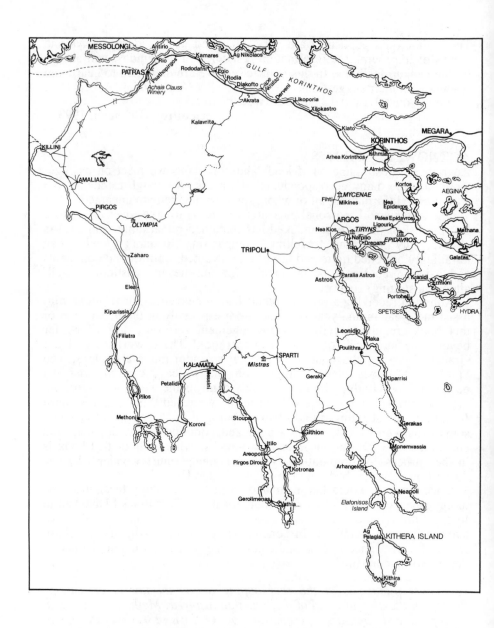

Illustration 1 The Peloponnese & Archaeological Sites

1 PART ONE
INTRODUCTION TO THE PELOPONNESE

Pragmatically speaking, this enormous peninsula might simply be considered as just one giant Greek island - and why not? Whilst making such a sweeping statement, this could be the appropriate point at which to dispel an oft-repeated, if totally untrue wisdom - that is, that the Peloponnese doesn't have any (sandy) beaches. This pronouncement is absolute nonsense, as there are some of the finest sweeps of sandy shoreline, anywhere in Greece, a number of them vying with the very 'best in the land'. The west coast is particularly blessed. A specific example is the huge sweep of Kiparissiako Bay, bordered for almost the whole of its length by a glorious stretch of wide, golden sand. Other locations that merit more than a passing mention include the golden sand beaches edging the large Egaleo peninsula, at the south-west corner, and the magnificent bay of sand on the south side of Elafonisos island, at the south-east corner of the huge land mass.

The Peloponnese is some 220km across, 220km from top to bottom, and has an overall area of 21,440 sq km - somewhat larger than Wales. The landscapes offers the widest possible variety of Hellenic scenery and panoramas imaginable, many of the most exciting archaeological sites in Greece, any number of stunningly attractive seaside locations, and some breathtakingly situated inland settlements. In fact the diversity and beauty of them is such as to make it difficult, if not impossible, to determine which is the more magnificent - the awe-inspiring countryside or the majestically ancient excavations.

The name of the region probably related to its association with the mythological character Pelops, after whom the land was named the *Island of Pelops*, or Pelopos Nisos. One or two of the civilisations achieved world-wide fame. These include the Mycenaeans (who between1500-1200 BC founded such city states as Mycenae, Pylos and Tiryns) and the Spartans. The latter dominated the Peloponnese, centred on an area spreading out from the modern-day town of Sparti, and the citizens spent some seven hundred years (5thC BC to the 2ndC AD) scrapping with the Athenians, for overall suzerainty. Such was the Spartans' renown, that apart from the more obvious affiliation with the modern-day adjective associated with austerity and frugality, the alternative name for their city state of Sparti (Laconica) has come down to our language as the adjective laconic. This latter root-link is due to the Spartans being renowned for brevity of speech (as well as supreme courage and self-discipline). There is no better illustration of these characteristics than the possibly apocryphal story of the Spartan mother who, as she passed her son his shield, is reputed to have advised him that he was to return carrying it - or on it! Another anecdote appertains to the warrior Phillip of Macedonia. He warned the Spartans that, if he was forced to move into Laconica to suppress them, he would raise it to the ground. They replied "If"!

After the Roman domination of the Peloponnese, the Byzantine Empire held a shaky sway, their reign being prone to depredations by pirates and various warrior tribes. The Byzantines were followed by two hundred years of Frankish rule, after which the Turks swept all before them, completing the job by 1460. This occupation finally came to an end after the Greek War of Independence (1821-1829).

It can be no surprise that the incredibly varied and lengthy history of city-states and conquerors has resulted in a wealth, almost an overwhelm of archaeological riches. And of all these, without question, Ancient Olympia, in the Nome or prefecture of Eleia, must rate as one of the most incredible excavations, splendidly situated in a valley between the Rivers Kladeos and Alfios. The glory of the Peloponnese archaeological sites is more than adequately borne out by the fact that Olympia's competition includes a number of truly outstanding locations. Amongst these are: the stunning Odeion at Epidavros, founded in the 6thC BC; Ancient Mycenae, enclosed by Cyclopean walls and possessing such 'jewels' as the Lions' Gate, the Grave Circles, and the Treasury of Atrius; as well as the fabulous city state site of Ancient Korinthos, and the adjacent Akrocorinthos Citadel, best known for its occupation by medieval soldiery. In fact, the area surrounding modern Korinthos is truly remarkable, with a further ancient site at Isthmia, once the venue of yet another pan-hellenic games. Remarkably, the starting line for the latter is still visible. Isthmia is quite close to the arresting Korinthos Canal, a deep, narrow cutting that allows sea passage between the Gulfs of Korinth and Argolikos. Surprisingly, the canal was only constructed as late as the 1880s, despite being planned as early as the 6thC BC. It should not be forgotten that the hedonism of the citizenry was so renowned, throughout the then acknowledged world, that St. Paul was moved to preach and dispatch his famous Epistles, or Letters to the Corinthians These missives were a vain attempt to persuade the citizens to adopt a more pure, godly way of life. Some hope! Another remarkable excavation is Tiryns, close to Nafplio, a Mycenaen city state hidden away behind an imposing wall. Apart from the to-be-expected Greek and Roman inspired remains, other civilisations also left their distinctive mark. Nowhere is this better evinced than close to Sparti, in the Nome of Laconia, where still stand (and lie) the outstanding ruins of the Byzantine city state of Mistras. Another Byzantine settlement is that of Old Monemvassia, the charming town draped over a mountainous promontory of rock, projecting into the eastern Aegean sea.

Almost the whole of the Sangias peninsula is taken up by an area known as the Mani. This has been inhabited, over the centuries, by a clan-like culture, dating back some 600 years, and only comparatively recently exposed to the curious gaze of the rest of the nation. In pursuit of their never-ending feudal battles, the natives of the Mani developed a series of tower fortified villages. This peninsula also has the eminently visitable Spili Dirou subterranean caves.

The Peloponnese boasts a number of splendid castles and forti-fications. Amongst these, the Venetian castle at Methoni is an unforgettable example of its genre, whilst the Palamidi fort at Nafplio is dramatically built over the edge of a mountain crag, a location allowing fantastic views. On the south-west coast is the visually arresting port of Pilos. The unique feature of this settlement is that it was almost entirely constructed in 1829, by the French, a lineage that has lost little of its freshness, down the years.

There are numerous other interesting archaeological and historical sites scattered about the Peloponnese, but happily these are not the only attractions. As would be expected, the many churches and monasteries have their adherents. Yet another diversion is to travel on the in-places rack and pinion branch railway line, from Diakofto to Kalavrita. Apart from the marvellous river valley scenery, the interestingly engineered route of the track, and the rather alpine town of Kalavrita, there is Mega Spileo Monastery. This is located half-way up the climb, from sea-level to the more mountainous heights.

Many of the seaside settlements remain splendidly rural in character, some being very reminiscent of those to found on the more distant, less easily accessible, and remote Aegean islands.

The Peloponnese traveller is fortunate to not only have the use of an extensive bus and coach network, but to have the option to utilise the almost circular, looping railway system that almost encompasses the large mass of land. This latter choice is a fortunate bonus, as the domestic airline possibilities are restricted to one airport, at distant Kalamata. Other intriguing (water-borne) transport alternatives are the ferry-boat and hydrofoil services. These call-in at a widespread number of large and small ports and harbours, spread out down the length of the eastern seaboard.

At the far, north-west corner of the Peloponnese is the international and domestic seaport of Patras. This accommodates Greco-Italian and the Ionian island ferries, the passengers of which can conveniently 'link-in' to the railway system or the widespread coach service, both with regular connections to Athens, and thus the rest of Greece. Furthermore, along the north shore of the Peloponnese, edging the Gulf of Korinth, are a number of small harbours from which ply ro-ro ferry-boats. These shuttle to and from the mainland Central Greek coastline.

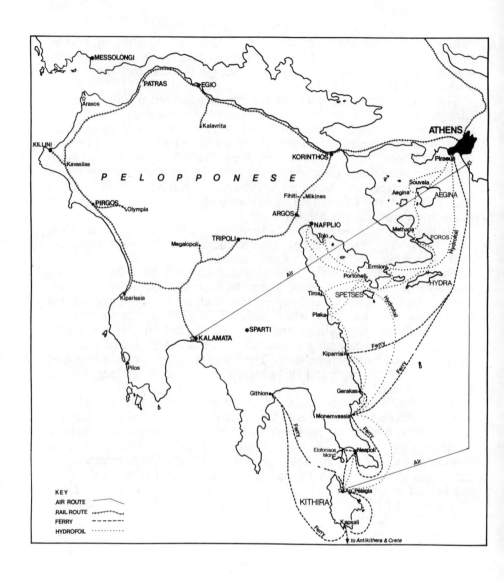

Illustration 2 Peloponnese Air, Ferry, Hydrofoil & Rail Links

2 PELOPONNESE CONNECTIONS

Strangely, the worst link is that offered by internal air flights, which, for the moment, only offer an Athens to Kalamata connection. But plans are afoot! Air travellers leaving Greece are to be charged a supplementary airport tax (equal to about £15), the proceeds of which are to be squirreled-away to finance an airport at Sparti. Rumour has it that the package holiday companies are absolutely delirious about this impost, which they regard as unnecessary, unlinked to their activities, and unjust. Well they would, wouldn't they?

Conversely, the Peloponnese has an almost circular, if very Greek 'in operation' railway system, which couples-up many of the peninsula's main centres and links to Athens.

As would be expected of a country wherein the bedrock of the transport system are buses, the Peloponnese is no exception. All the major cities and towns are tied into each other with an excellent and comprehensive network of bus and coach services. These scheduled timetables allow travellers to reach almost all of the Peloponnese locations, be they a major settlement or a remote hamlet.

Patras offers not only an Ionian island ferry-boat link, but is 'the' west coast, international liner port, with daily summer Italian services. Not to be left out, the ports spaced out down the length of the east Peloponnese coastline host an extremely efficient, daily hydrofoil service that sets out from, and returns to, Piraeus. These high speed craft are in addition to a less frequent ferry-boat connection that runs between Piraeus and Crete, calling in at a few of the selfsame ports as the hydrofoils.

For details of the specific services to and from each centre, Athens, and Piraeus, refer to the individual Peloponnese centres and *See* Illus. 2. I hope readers will appreciate that to cross-match timetables of the buses, ferry-boats, hydrofoils and trains of each major settlement, to the others, would have required a mainframe computer - of the sort of capacity that achieves moon landings! Unfortunately, even an Einstein of a Greek national cannot correlate them - what chance has a mere foreign mortal! I have to own up to allowing each centre to 'stand on its own', as it were. Cross-referencing will assist in determining some common factors, even if prices and times appear to differ.

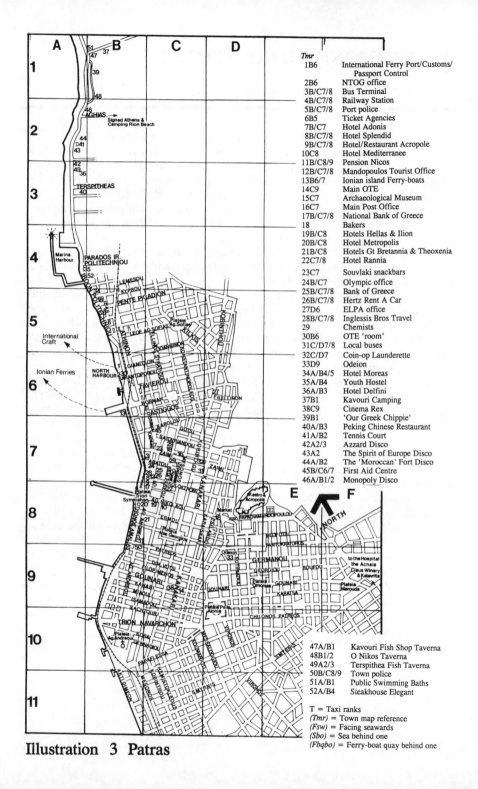

Tmr	
1B6	International Ferry Port/Customs/ Passport Control
2B6	NTOG office
3B/C7/8	Bus Terminal
4B/C7/8	Railway Station
5B/C7/8	Port police
6B5	Ticket Agencies
7B/C7	Hotel Adonis
8B/C7/8	Hotel Splendid
9B/C7/8	Hotel/Restaurant Acropole
10C8	Hotel Mediterranee
11B/C8/9	Pension Nicos
12B/C7/8	Mandopoulos Tourist Office
13B6/7	Ionian island Ferry-boats
14C9	Main OTE
15C7	Archaeological Museum
16C7	Main Post Office
17B/C7/8	National Bank of Greece
18	Bakers
19B/C8	Hotels Hellas & Ilion
20B/C8	Hotel Metropolis
21B/C8	Hotels Gt Bretannia & Theoxenia
22C7/8	Hotel Rannia
23C7	Souvlaki snackbars
24B/C7	Olympic office
25B/C7/8	Bank of Greece
26B/C7/8	Hertz Rent A Car
27D6	ELPA office
28B/C7/8	Inglessis Bros Travel
29	Chemists
30B6	OTE 'room'
31C/D7/8	Local buses
32C/D7	Coin-op Launderette
33D9	Odeion
34A/B4/5	Hotel Moreas
35A/B4	Youth Hostel
36A/B3	Hotel Delfini
37B1	Kavouri Camping
38C9	Cinema Rex
39B1	'Our Greek Chippie'
40A/B3	Peking Chinese Restaurant
41A/B2	Tennis Court
42A2/3	Azzard Disco
43A2	The Spirit of Europe Disco
44A/B2	The 'Moroccan' Fort Disco
45B/C6/7	First Aid Centre
46A/B1/2	Monopoly Disco

47A/B1	Kavouri Fish Shop Taverna
48B1/2	O Nikos Taverna
49A2/3	Terspithea Fish Taverna
50B/C8/9	Town police
51A/B1	Public Swimming Baths
52A/B4	Steakhouse Elegant

T = Taxi ranks
(Tmr) = Town map reference
(Fsw) = Facing seawards
(Sbo) = Sea behind one
(Fbqbo) = Ferry-boat quay behind one

Illustration 3 Patras

3 PART TWO

PATRAS (Patra, Patre, Patrai)
Illustration 3

VITAL STATISTICS Tel prefix 061. Pop. circa 115,000.

LOCAL RELIGIOUS HOLIDAYS & FESTIVALS include: the Patras Carnival, lasting some three weeks, from the middle of January - great goings on, and good fun; the International Cultural Festival - middle June-early Aug; 30th Nov - a feast to celebrate St Andrew, the city's patron saint.

GENERAL The modern city was rebuilt to a grid layout, in the 1820s, after the Turks had razed it to the ground, in 1821.

Patras is the third largest city in Greece, as well as being a major commercial centre, international seaport and railway terminal. Thus, it is not surprising that the large settlement has a traffic-busy, industrial, cosmopolitan, bustling, noisy ambiance.

The outskirts are a chaos of urban sprawl, spawning an ever-increasing number of international ferry-boat ticket vendors, as well as the to-be-expected rash of garages, tyre firms, furniture warehouses, dusty olive grove patches, pottery stores, billboards, all skirted by dumps of rubbish and building materials. Incidentally, the true 'professional' can determine, at a glance, which are piles of rubbish, and which are new construction sites!

It is quite possible that a visit to Patras will only occur in order to embark, disembark or switch between bus, ferry or train. The key to the city is the Esplanade, named Odhos Othonos Amalias (*Tmr* B6, B7 & B8), which is across the way from, and runs parallel to, the waterfront quay wall, and beside which the railway line also runs. To add to the general confusion, and the seemingly continuous stream of traffic, a shunting train shares the carriageway with the tangle of cars and humans. Keep an eye open, and ears cocked.

Alongside the Esplanade are ranged the majority of a traveller's immediate needs. For instance, it sweeps past the International Ferry Port and NTOG office (*Tmr* 1 & 2B6), the main Bus terminal (*Tmr* 3B/C7) and the Railway Station (*Tmr* 4B/C7/8). The latter is almost adjacent to Plateia Trion Symmahon, about 20m to the north of which is conveniently located a Tourist police 'cabin'.

Plateia Trion Symmahon is a palm-tree'd and paved square at the hub of waterfront Patras, edged by cafes, restaurants and newsagents. After dark the square comes alive, some families strolling around, whilst others sit beneath the spreading branches of the trees, drinking coffee or ouzo at one of the many small cafes. Unfortunately, the almost ceaseless flow of traffic, that bludgeons its way along the Esplanade and lower side-streets, has all but ruined the waterfront for a pleasant perambulation. Once beyond the marina and boat harbour (*Tmr* A4), to the north, the ambiance is less frantic, much calmer and quieter, if rather 'new-suburb' clinical and uninteresting.

From the far, south-east side of Plateia Trion Symmahon, Odhos Ag Nikolaou (*Tmr* C8) gently climbs, straight and true, to the bottom of a very steep flight of steps that 'pants' all the way to 'old' Patras and the Kastro.At the top of the steps, on the right is a drinking water fountain and a small taverna. The Kastro dominates the left-hand hillside and is circumscribed by a narrow twisting lane.

Returning to the bottom of the steps, from the 'top' end of Ag Nilolaou St, Odhos Sotiriadou bends round to the right (*Sbo*), past an extensively restored Odeion (*Tmr* 33 D9). After which, the main road turns to the left on to the interestingly arcade-lined Odhos Germanou, and up through the older city heights, also to the Kastro.

THE ACCOMMODATION & EATING OUT

The Accommodation There are a profusion of pensions and hotels in the area radiating out from the Railway station, but hereabouts the streets are somewhat canyon-like and the traffic noise intrusive. Furthermore, being an epicentre for travellers, room rates tend to be rather expensive.

Many owners of accommodation raise prices to the 'height of summer' rates, or more, for Carnival weeks (Jan/Feb).

The Tourist police and NTOG staff supply accommodation details, but ..."No Rooms, only hotels".

A last point to bear in mind, is that the streets and buildings of Patras are on a large scale. On the plan a distance might appear a few paces, but may well prove to be a twenty minute trudge.

Diagonally across the, busy Esplanade from the Railway Station are the:
Hotel Splendid (*Tmr* 8B/C7/8) (Class D) 28 Ag Andreou   Tel 276521
Directions: As above, but with the entrance in the next street back.

Splendid it may have been, but not now... Rather a 'sleazy', despite which the *Splendid* is not inexpensive any more. A single room costs 5600drs & a double 7670drs, both sharing the bathrooms, and an en suite double 10430drs. And the:
Hotel Acropole (*Tmr* 9B/C7/8) (Class C) 39 Othonos Amalias   Tel 279809
Directions: As above.

All rooms have en suite bathrooms, with a single charged from 3400drs & a double 5300drs.

Hotel Rannia (*Tmr* 22C7/8) (Class B) 53 Riga Fereou   Tel 220114
Directions: From the Railway station, turn left (*Sbo*) on the Esplanade, as far as the corner with Koloktroni St. The *Rannia* is in the third block along Koloktroni St, on the right.

All rooms have en suite bathrooms, with a single room priced from 5700drs & a double 9100drs.

Hotel Adonis (*Tmr* 7B/C7) (Class C) Zaimi/9 Kapsali Sts   Tel 224213
Directions: Behind the main Bus terminal, alongside the English church of Ag Andreas.

Clean, modern, and all rooms have en suite bathrooms, with a single room costing from 4500drs & a double 5100drs.

Hotel Delphi (Class D) (*Tmr* B/C8) 63 Ag Andreou   Tel 273050
Directions: Bordering Plateia Trion Symmahon and, depending on one's viewpoint, unclean and noisy, or dirty and downright clamorous!
Rooms all share the bathrooms and cost about 2000drs for a single & 3500drs for a double.

Hotel Hellas (*Tmr* 19B/C8) (Class D) 14 Ag Nikolaou   Tel 273352
Directions: On the right (*Sbo*) of the street that climbs from Plateia Trion Symmahon.
Another 'down at the heel', and thus inexpensive hotel. Single rooms cost 2500drs & doubles 3500drs, all sharing the bathrooms.

Hotel Ilion (*Tmr* 19B/C8) (Class D) 10 Ag Nikolaou   Tel 273161
Directions: As for the *Hellas*, from which it is separated by a cinema, the Cine Elite, but nearer the waterfront.
Much as for the *Hellas*.

Hotel Mediterranee (*Tmr* 10C8) (Class C) 18 Ag Nikolaou/Riga Fereou Sts
Tel 279602
Directions: As for the *Hellas*, but the next block up the street.
Well appointed, comfortable and all rooms have en suite bathrooms. A single room costs 3670/5360drs & a double 5850/8430drs.

Hotel Metropolis (*Tmr* 20B/C8) (Class D) Trion Symmahon Sq   Tel 277535
Directions: On the south side of the square.
A single room costs 2000drs & a double 3500drs, all sharing the bathrooms.

Hotel Gt Bretannia (*Tmr* 21B/C8) (Class E) 95 Ag Andreou   Tel 273421
Directions: From Plateia Trion Symmahon, proceed south-west along Ag Andreou St, which parallels the Esplanade, but one back.
As befits a Patras E class hotel, rather decrepit, if clean. Strangely, it is more expensive than look-alike D class hotels, with all rooms sharing the bathrooms.

Hotel Theoxenia (*Tmr* 21B/C8) (Class D) 97 Ag Andreou   Tel 222962
Directions: As for the *Gt Bretannia*.
Despite being adjacent to the *Gt Bretannia*, priced at about the same rates as the *Hellas*.

Pension Nicos (*Tmr* 11B/C8/9) 3 Patreos/121 Ag Andreou Sts   Tel 276183
Directions: South, or right (*Sbo*) from Trion Symmahon Sq, along Ag Andreou St, and on the corner of the third turning to the left.
Possessing an ethnic, somewhat forbidding, hostel atmosphere. Callers find themselves in a gaunt, dark brown coloured, high roofed hallway, decorated with a couple of huge travel posters. From the rear ascends a broad flight of stairs. A sign instructs enquirers to ring the bell for assistance. Any inclination to proceed to the upper floors is stopped short by a 'charming' sign which declares ..."It is strictly forbidden for those who are not resident to stay or come upstairs according to the 976028134012,19,77 decision of the Department of Law and Order". It is so nice to be made welcome, isn't it? The cost of a bed for the night kicks off from some 1000drs per head. Oddly enough, the patron accepts payment by *Visa*.

To the north, bordering the Esplanade, are a number of swish, more up-market hotels. These include the:
Hotel Moreas (*Tmr* 34A/B4/5) (Class A) Iroon Politechnou/Kyprou Sts
Tel 275981
Directions: As above.
Extremely smart, despite which, the en suite room prices are a not outrageous 4860/5835drs for a single room & 6760/8115drs for a double.

Hotel Delfini (*Tmr* 36 A/B3) (Class C) 102 Iroon Politechnou/Terspitheas Sts
Tel 421001
Directions: Further north, beyond the marina harbour.
All rooms are en suite, with a single costing 3500/4500drs & a double 5000/6500drs.

Youth Hostel (*Tmr* 35A/B4) 68 Iroon Politechnou   Tel 427278
Directions: Turn left (*Sbo*) on leaving any ferry and proceed along   the quayside north-eastwards, for between 1-1½km, depending on the   point of outset. The solitary building is set in its own grounds, on the right, across the Esplanade from the marina harbour. The sign is rather small, so if you reach the marina restaurant, you have gone too far.
The old, but restored Victorian style house was once used by the Germans as an HQ, during the Second World War. The architectural style is..., well, try castellated baroque, with the stonework picked out in white. Inexpensive, if a bit of a squeeze, with cheap snacks and breakfasts, as well as laundry facilities available. A dormitory bed costs from 800drs, but guests must bring their own sheets, or be prepared to hire them for 60drs. Breakfast in the common room-cum-cafe-bar costs a very reasonable 200drs, and there is a most informative notice board. 'Outsiders', or more politely, non-residents, may avail themselves of the shower facilities at a cost of 100drs.

Camping
Kavouri Camping (*Tmr* 37B1)   Tel 422145
Directions: This site is some three kilometres from the centre of Patras, north-east along the Esplanade. Alongside the turning to the campsite is the *Kavouri 'Fish Shop' Taverna*. A few metres beyond the junction is the 'town' swimming pool covered in by a   semi-dirigible envelope - all straining posts and wire hawsers. Across the shore road here, is a pebbly, narrow, not so clean seashore, with an acceptable swimming beach still further to the north. Bus No 1 turns up Terspitheas St, where passengers should alight, but this only saves about half the leg-work.
Prices at the well-shaded, neat site range from: 500drs per head; children 250drs; a tent 250drs; a car 120drs; a caravan 500drs; and electric hook-up 200drs. The site is open April-Oct.
There are also campsites at: *Rio Camping, Rio George* and *Rio Mare*, all in or around nearby Rio (*See* Route One).

The Eating Out Any number of tavernas and restaurants are spaced out along and around the Esplanade, Odhos Ag Nikolaou and Plateia Trion Symmahon (what isn't?). Despite the competition, the average cost of a meal tends to be expensive, especially those served by the establishments lining the dusty, dirty Esplanade, some of which are 'proper' greasies. Typical of the 'frontage' establishment is the:

Restaurant Acropole (*Tmr* 9B/C7/8)
Directions: In the ground floor of the *Hotel Acropole*, diagonally across from the Railway Station.
   A typical 'special' is meatballs in savoury sauce, served with roast potatoes, a cucumber & tomato salad, 'fresh' bread, a soft drink 'of your choice', all from 1200drs.
   Two or three restaurants advertise 'A, B & C' set menus, one of which number is the *Marco Polo*.

There are a pair of souvlaki pita snackbars (*Tmr* 23C7) across the road from each other, in the narrow street behind the *Hotel Adonis*. I prefer the one on the hotel-side corner of the road, an excellent 'stool and counter' establishment. This is the:
Snackbar Bon Appetit.
Directions: Turn right (*Railway station behind one*) off the Esplanade, once past the Bus terminal, and climb Zaimi St. As above, with a *Hotel Kentriko* sign above the two storey building.
   The pleasant staff serve one of the best souvlaki pita's it has been my 'wont' to salivate over. The constituents include a dash of potatoes, onions, tzatziki and tomato, all for some 120drs. Other offerings available take in Greek style fried eggs, chicken livers, potatoes, meatballs, hamburgers, gigantes and fried aubergines. An Amstel beer costs 150drs.

For those prepared to wade past a plethora of cocktail bars and expensive restaurants, there is a 'jewel in the newspaper', namely:
'Our Greek Chippie' (*Tmr* 39B1) No 50.
Directions: Follow the wide Esplanade, north-east, past the marina harbour, and the side turning, Odhos Terspitheas. The taverna shack is down a roadside bank, on the right.
   It has to be admitted that the cafe is short on the fripperies, niceties and trimmings, but is very long on inexpensive, edible quantity. The menu is limited, but the offerings are piping-hot. In fact, limited is a fairly wide-ranging adjective, to encompass a range of dishes that solely comprises fish or kalamares! Side dishes include tomato & cucumber salad, feta cheese, and saute style patatas. Liquid refreshment embraces kortaki retsina and bottles of Amstel beer, as well as various 'fizzies'. A meal for two of tasty kalamares (300drs a head), a huge plate of patatas (70drs a head), a reasonable sized salad (300drs), retsina (200drs), bread and service, costs some 1300drs. We were unable to clear our plates, the establishment is packed with locals, and the service is so fast, it is almost unbelievable.

The 'Greek Chippie' has some adjacent competitors. Beyond it is the *Kavouri 'Fish Shop' Taverna* (*Tmr* 47A/B1), whilst to the south are the *Terspithea Fish Taverna* (*Tmr* 49 A2/3), as well as *O Nikos Taverna* (*Tmr* 48B1/2).

It may be of interest to a few, that on the way to 'the Chippie', the route passes by Odhos Terspitheas, on the right of which is the:
Peking Chinese Restaurant (*Tmr* 40 A/B3)
Directions: As above, and open every day 1230-1530hrs & 1900-0100hrs.
   Serves lunches and dinners, is air conditioned and accepts credit cards and Eurocheques. As the wide-ranging menu is unpriced, it is difficult to ascertain if carrying 'our friendly plastic' is a wise precaution..., but all my instincts suggest it might be! One of the dishes rather caught my fancy -*wanton soup*.

Incidentally,   this company also has restaurants in the Athens suburbs of
Kifissia and Glyfada.

Closer to the city waterfront centre is another establishment that might appeal
to the 'traditional' Englishman, who eschews ...'that   foreign mishmash',
and considers Calais part of the 'far-flung'! This is the *Steakhouse
Elegant* (*Tmr* 52A/B4). Mmmh!

THE A TO Z OF USEFUL INFORMATION

AIRLINE OFFICES & TERMINUS There is an Olympic office (*Tmr* 24B/C7)
set in the rear of the *Hotel Astir* building, on the corner of Aratou and Ag
Andreou Sts. Only open usual weekday office hours.

BANKS The **National Bank of Greece** (*Tmr* 17B/C7/8), where they change
Eurocheques, is conveniently situated across the Esplanade from the Railway
station. The **Bank of Greece** (*Tmr* 25B/C7/8) is to the left (*Sbo*) of the
Railway station, on Odhos Andreou, one street back and parallel to the
Esplanade. There are any number of banks scattered along the length of the
Esplanade, Othonos Amalias, and the parallel streets of Ag Andreou, to the
right (*Sbo*) of the Railway Station (*Tmr* 4B/C7/8).

BEACHES None in town, it being necessary to travel about three or more
kilometres north-east along the coast road, past the shore-mounted navigation
light, in the direction of Agia (Patron). The gritty, pebbly beach undulates
along the sea's edge, with, at the wider sections, shady groves of tamarisk
trees. The beach showers 'don't'!

BICYCLE, SCOOTER & CAR HIRE I'm (still) not sure about bikes and
scooters, but car hire is available, for instance, from: **Hertz Rent A Car** (*Tmr*
26B/C7/8), on the left (*Sbo*) of Odhos Koloktroni; **Avis** at No 11 Othonos
Amalias; and **Inter Rent** at No 10b Ag Andreou St.

BOOKSELLERS One, **Papachristou** is at 16 Ag Nikolaou St (*Tmr* B/C8) and
another, **Calitas**, is on the parallel Ermou St.

BREAD SHOPS There is a Baker, **To Zalogoon** (*Tmr* 18C7), on the left
(*Sbo*) of Odhos Zaimi, at No 17. **Patisserie Pakalos** is a very good shop,
located on the nearside of *Hotel Ilion* (*Tmr* 19B/C8), at the outset and on the
right (*Sbo*) of Ag Nikolaou St. There is a fruit and vegetable grocer, that sells
bread rolls, in the same building as the *Hotel Metropolis* (*Tmr* 20B/C8). For
those at the top end of the city, there is a **Baker** (*Tmr* 18D8) on the right (*Sbo*)
of Ag Nikolaou St. Those to the north-east, might turn off the Esplanade
along Odhos Kyprou, wherein is a **Baker** (*Tmr* 18A/B4/5), on the right.

BUSES Apart from the main routes to Athens, Ioannina, Volos, Thessaloniki,
and down the west coast of the Peloponnese (for Killini, Pirgos, Pilos and
Kalamata), there are any number of local services, with one, for instance, to
Rio. The journey to Killini is direct and connects with the ferry to the Ionian
island of Zakynthos.
   The major Bus Terminal (*Tmr* 3B/C7) is situated on the far side of the
Esplanade, opposite the point at which the quay takes a left turn. Apart from
a mini-market, toilets and the usual grubby snackbar, there is an information

office located in the large building. This latter opens daily at 0700hrs, and some of the staff speak basic English.

Local buses 'terminus' along the 'port' side of Odhos Kanakari (*Tmr* 31C/D7/8), between the lateral streets of Zaimi and Koloktroni (as distinct from the long distance services that arrive and depart from the Esplanade bordering the main terminal (*Tmr* 3B/C7)). There is a bus ticket hut, and local bus schedules include:

No 1 to Aglikas, via Terspitheas St.
No 4 to Ovria village (south of Patras).
No 7 to Saravali village & Achaia Clauss Winery.

Bus timetable

Patras to Athens (Tel 5136185)
Daily   0530, 0615, 0700, 0800, 0900, 1000, 1100, 1230, 1330, 1400, 1500, 1630, 1730, 1830, 1930, 2030hrs.
Return journey
Daily   0615, 0715, 0815, 0900, 1045, 1130, 1230, 1330, 1455, 500, 1545, 1645, 1745, 1830, 1930, 2030, 2130hrs
One-way fare 2400drs; duration 3½hrs.

Patras to Ioannina (NW Greece)
Daily   0815, 1430hrs
Return journey
Daily   0800, 1430hrs
One-way fare 2800drs; duration 4 hrs.

Patras to Kalamata (S. Peloponnese)
Daily   0700, 1430hrs
Return journey
Daily   0700, 1430hrs
One-way fare 2700drs; duration 4 hrs.

Patras to Killini (NW. Peloponnese)
Daily   0800, 1445hrs
One-way fare 600drs; duration 1½hrs.

Patras to Pirgos (W. Peloponnese)
Daily   0530, 0700, 0900, 1000, 1100, 1330, 1500, 1700, 1830, 2030hrs
One-way fare 850drs.

Patras to Thessaloniki (NE Greece)
Daily   0830, 1500, 2100hrs
Sat   0830, 1500hrs
Return journey
Daily   0830, 1515, 2030hrs
Sat   0830, 1515hrs
One-way fare 5500drs; duration 9½hrs.

Patras to Volos (E. Thessaly)
Thur, Fri   1500hrs
Sun   2100hrs
Return journey
Mon, Fri,   1315hrs
 & Sun.
One-way fare 3550drs; duration 6 hrs.

Patras to Psathopirgos (N. coast Peloponnese)
Daily   0645, 0800, 1200, 1300, 1900, 2015hrs

Patras to Egio (N. coast Peloponnese)
Daily   0700, 0800, 0900, 1000, 1100, 1200, 1300, 1345, 1415, 1500, 1600, 1700, 1800, 1900, 2015, 2215hrs

Patras to **Kalavritra** (inland, SE of Patras)
Daily   0530, 0710, 1310, 1530hrs
One-way fare 750drs.
Patras to **Tripoli** (inland Peloponnese)
Daily   0710, 1400hrs
One-way fare 1950drs: duration 4hrs.
Patras to **Vrourasio**
Daily   0600, 0650, 1410, 1600, 1700, 1800hrs
Patras to **Metochi** (west of Patras)
Daily   0600, 0900, 1100, 1315, 1515, 1900, 2030hrs
Patras to **Santomeri & Portes** (south, south west of Patras)
Daily   0530, 1315hrs
Patras to **Kalogria** (coastal, west of Patras)
Daily   0900, 1100, 1315, 1515, 1700, 1900hrs
Patras to **Kato Achaia** (coast, west of Patras)
Daily   0415, 0545, 0715, 1100, 1130, 1200, 1410, 1900, 2000, 2115, 2215hrs
Patras to **Rio** (east of Patras, ferry port for Antirio, whence other buses for
                                                      Central Greece)
Daily   0615, 1000, 1300, 1715hrs
Patras to **Eliso**
Daily   0715, 1200, 1410, 1900, 2215hrs
Patras to **Petes**
Daily   0615, 1000, 1300, 1715hrs
Patras to **Krinos & Mirtos**
Daily   0600, 1000, 1300, 1715hrs
Patras to **Arla**
Daily   0615, 1245, 1730hrs
Patras to **Spata & Vernitses**
Daily   0530, 0615, 1245hrs
Patras to **Varda**
Daily   0650, 0800, 1000, 1200, 1410, 1600, 1800hrs
Patras to **Araxo**
Daily   0545, 0715, 1030, 1200, 1445, 1900hrs
Patras to **Mazaraki & Metopoli**
Daily   0615, 1330, 1645hrs
Patras to **Mazaraki**
Daily   0615, 0830, 1330, 1645hrs
Patras to **Filakes**
Daily   0830, 1645hrs
Patras to **Verianou & Moireika**
Daily   0630, 1330hrs.
Patras to **Axiako & Lousika**
Daily   0630, 1315hrs
Patras to **Vassiliko, Isomar & Tharrai**
Daily   0530, 1200, 1300, 1630hrs.
Patras to **Agrinia**
Daily   1300hrs
Patras to **Sterakori**
Daily   0530, 1300hrs.
Patras to **Ag Dimitrio**
Daily   0530, 1300hrs.
Patras to **Kalana, Tsa & Kalouzi**
Daily   0530, 1300hrs (Kalana & Tsa).
Patras to **Moirani**
Daily   1300hrs.

Patras to Karpita, Eremanthia & Skiala
Daily   0500, 1230, 1630hrs.
Patras to Drossia
Daily   0430, 1200hrs.
Patras to Roubakia & Kalfa
Daily   0500, 1230hrs.
Patras to Dathni
Daily   0630, 1400hrs.
Patras to Leivarsi
Daily   1400hrs.
Patras to Supoto & Oriania
Daily   1400hrs
Patras to Piditsa
Daily   1615, 1420, 2000hrs.
Patras to Liontio
Daily   1230hrs
Patras to Lakomata
Daily   1230hrs.
Patras to Souli & Moira
Daily   1330hrs

Note that **OSE** (that is the Railway company, as compared to **KTEL**) also runs bus services to major city centres, from outside   the Railway station (*Tmr* 4B/C7/8). For instance, they operate some 20 buses a day to Athens, as well as 4 a day to Methoni (1850drs).

CHILD CARE There aren't any specific agencies, and the only facilities are some kiddies' swings, close to the Tennis Court (*Tmr* 41A/B2), in the region of the 'rash of discos'.

CINEMAS The **Cine Elite** separates the *Hotels Ilion* and *Hellas* (*Tmr* 19B/C8), whilst the **Cinema Rex** (*Tmr* 38C9) squats on the right (*Sbo*) of Gournari St.

COMMERCIAL SHOPPING AREA The main district (*Tmr* C7/8) is that bounded   by the main streets of Zaimi, Korinthou, Ag Nikolaou and the Esplanade, with a clutch of offerings spaced out around Plateia Trion Symmahon (*Tmr* B/C7/8). There is a concentration of Fruit & Vegetable, Fish, and Butchers shops on, or close to, the crossroads of the streets of Zaimi and Riga Fereou (*Tmr* C7).
    In the same building as the *Hotel Metropolis* (*Tmr* 20B/C8) are a General Store and a Fruit & Vegetable shop, which supply most items. Peripteros are plentiful, especially around the main squares.

CONSULATES From the Railway station (*Tmr* 4B/C7/8) turn right (*Sbo*) for some six blocks and on the left is Odhos Dim Votsi, the street on which the office (*Tmr* B/C8/9) of the United Kingdom vice-consulate is located. Minimal office hours!

CUSTOMS (*Tmr* 1B6) Customs and passport control are both located in one single storey block, towards the north end of the main waterfront, where the international ferries berth. To either side of the entrance gateway are an NTOG office and a small OTE office, inside the gates are toilets and a drinking water fountain, whilst parked close-by, outside the entrance is a Post Office caravan, open seven days a week (*See* Post Office).

DISCOS As is often the way, they are bunched together, in this case north along the Esplanade, beyond the marina harbour. The first is the **Azzard Club** (*Tmr* 42A2/3), the next **The Spirit of Europe** (*Tmr* 43A2), and the last is located in a garish 'Moroccan Fort' inspired building (*Tmr* 44A/B2) - yes, a Moroccan... Beyond Odhos Aghias is the **Monopoly Disco** (*Tmr* 46A/B1/2). The usual hours, entrance fees and drink charges.

ELPA (*Tmr* 27D6) The office is situated close to the crossroads of Filellinon, Astiggos and Korinthou streets.

FERRY-BOATS International craft dock (*Tmr* 1B6) on the north side of the main quay, whilst the Ionian ferry-boats berth (*Tmr* 13B6/7) at the southern end of the main quay.

Ferry-boats & timetables

Day	Departure time	Ferry-boat	Ports/Islands of Call
International			
Daily			Ancona(Italy), Brindisi(Italy), Bari(Italy)
(Summer months)			
Weekly			Limassol(Cyprus), Ortona(Italy).
(Height of Summer months)			
Domestic			
Daily	1330hrs	Kefalinia	Sami(Cephalonia), Vathi(Ithaca).
	2200hrs	Ionis/Ionian	Poros(Cephalonia), Vathi(Ithaca),
		Glory	Gaios(Paxos), Igoumenitsa(M), Corfu.

One-way fare:	Patras to Cephalonia	1500drs; duration circa 3½hrs
	Ithaca	1500drs; " " 5½hrs
	Paxos	2300drs; " " 9hrs
	Corfu	2300drs; " " 10¼hrs.

Remember that international departure involves a 1000drs port tax. A general note to bear in mind is that ferry-boat timetables are subject to a number of year to year variables which include the season, the availability of boats and changes in planned schedules. It is necessary to check, double-check and check again.

FERRY-BOAT TICKET OFFICES These 'gather' along the Esplanade, mostly in the stretch between the Railway station (*Tmr* 4B/C7/8) and the North Harbour (*Tmr* B6), and are open early morning to late at night. Some of the offices appear to be run with a total disregard for the ferry-boat companies' life blood, that is the welfare of the passengers.

A particularly helpful business is:

Mandopoulos Tourist Office (*Tmr* 12B/C7/8) 35 Othonos Amalia   Tel 223621

Directions: To the south side and adjacent to the junction of Odhos Koloktrioni with the Esplanade.

Apart from ferry-boat tickets and exchange facilities, they deal in European railway matters,

A more typical, take-it-or-leave-it set-up is **Inglessis Bros** (*Tmr* 28B/C7/8 - tel 277776), a little further to the north of the Railway Station. Another Inglessis, Nikos, has a rather hole-in-the-wall office, further on than the International ferry-boat quay, beyond the **Kabouris Agency** and Odhos 28th October, which advertises details of the Githion ferries, but appears to be always closed. It is almost quicker to go to Githion!

If planning to use a ticket office for exchange purposes, it is worthwhile combining the task with the purchase of ferry-boat tickets, as some firms will not carry out money transactions only. And it is a bit late to discover that little detail, after tickets have been purchased from an office that doesn't deal in exchange matters! One other warning is to bear in mind that shopping around should not result in finding cut-price tickets. One ferry-boat company may be less expensive than another, but tickets sold below face-value will result in their confiscation at the point of departure. You have been warned.

HAIRDRESSERS Search the streets radiating out from Plateia Trion Symmahon.

LAUNDRY There is a coin-op (*Tmr* 32C/D7) at No 49, on the left (*Sbo*) of Odhos Zaimi. It opens Mon-Sat., between 0900-2000hrs, and operates a pleasant if 'relaxed' service with a machine-load and dry costing 800drs.

LUGGAGE STORE *See* the Railway station (*Tmr* 4B/C7/8).

MEDICAL CARE
Chemists & Pharmacies. There are a couple (*Tmr* 29C7) towards the north end of Riga Fereou St, whilst others are spaced along the streets radiating out from Plateia Trion Symmahon.
First-aid Centre (*Tmr* 45 B/C6/7). On the right (*Sbo*) of Odhos Karolou, opposite the junction with Odhos Ag Dionisiou.
Hospital. The city's hospital (*Tmr* F9) is almost immediately beyond the right-hand fork, on the main Kalavrita road, from the top of Odhos Gounari.

NTOG (*Tmr* 2B6). The smallish office is on the left of the main gateway into the International ferry-boat complex. The staff are most helpful, speak excellent English and 'man' the desk (actually more often 'woman' the desk) seven days a week, from about 0800hrs to 2100hrs.

OTE The main office (*Tmr* 14C9) is on the corner of Odhos Gounari and Kanakari, and is open daily, between 0830-2200hrs. There is a very convenient OTE 'room' (*Tmr* 30B6), with a row of booths, to the right of the International ferry-boat gateway (*opposite the NTOG*), which opens Mon-Sat, between 0800-2200hrs, and Sunday afternoons.

PETROL Plentiful.

PLACES & EVENTS OF INTEREST
The Kastro (*Tmr* D/E8). At the top, south-east end of Ag Nikolaou St are a steep flight of steps, which climb to upper Patras - the Chora. The large castle area dominates the hilltop, to the left. Those not prepared to walk can catch a taxi. The site was an ancient Acropolis with a sanctuary dedicated to Zeus and Artemis. Being perfectly located for fortifications, the Byzantines started construction of a castle, in the 9thC AD. In the early Middle Ages the Venetians continued the work, which the Turks completed. Thus, on the northern side is a Byzantine wall, whilst the main entrance gate, at the eastern end, is topped by a Turkish tower. The enclosed area has been made into a park. Open daily 0800-1900hrs.

The Odeion (*Tmr* 33D9). To the south-west of the Acropolis and rediscovered in the 1800s. From the top end of Ag Nikolaou, signs point the way. The small 'perfectly formed' theatre has been the subject of extensive restoration. This was necessary, it is said, due to the acquisitive nature of local builders, who used much of the original stonework for their own jobs! Although a Roman construction, it seems to me that the restoration has been carried out in a brickwork reminiscent of the Byzantine period, although some of the lower stone seating has a more Greco-Roman appearance. The staging is startling modern, but this is required, as the facility is pressed into use to produce performances, more especially during the summertime Patras International Festival. Around the walls are scattered unconnected archaeological finds. Open daily, entrance is free.

Museums

Archaeological Museum (*Tmr* 15C7). Situated three blocks back from the Esplanade, on Aratou St, edging Plateia Olgas. Not outstanding. Open daily 0830-1500hrs, but closed Mondays.

Churches & Cathedrals

The Church of Ag Andreas (*Tmr* B10) The Orthodox Cathedral overlooks Plateia Ag Andreou, towards the far, south-west end of the city. A large, modern, but colourful church, with small cupolas attractively dotted about, and dedicated to St Andrew. He was martyred on a crucifix erected in the form of an X, and the church is the repository of his gold and silver encased head. Apart from services, the building is open daily 0900-1700hrs, but visitors must dress conservatively.

The International Cultural Festival. An annual 'arts and freedom' jamboree that takes place from about the middle of June to early August. Shows, events and exhibitions featuring, for instance, flamenco, choirs, contemporary jazz, photography, orchestras, a film week, traditional dances, opera and recitals. These are staged at various venues which include the Odeion (*Tmr* 33D9) and Rio Castle (*See* Route One).

POLICE

Port (*Tmr* 5B/C7/8). In Ag Andreou St, one back and parallel to the Esplanade, in the area of the Railway station.

Town (*Tmr* 50B/C8/9). The main 'cop-shop' is close to the junction of Agiou Andreou and Patreos Sts.

Tourist. There is a smart 'cabin', about 30m north of the Railway Station (*Tmr* 4B/C7/8).

POST OFFICE (*Tmr* 16C7). The central office is located on the corner of Odhos Zaimi, and Mesonos St. Open the usual hours. There is a very convenient Post Office caravan sited close to the gates of the International Ferryboat terminal (*Tmr* 1B6). This opens seven days a week, during the height of season months, Mon-Sat, between 0800-2000hrs, & Sun 0900-1800hrs.

SPORTS FACILITIES

Swimming There is a large, 'tent' covered, public pool (*Tmr* 51A/B1), a few kilometres to the north along the Esplanade.

Tennis In amongst an outcrop of discos is a Tennis Court (*Tmr* 41A/B2).

TAXIS (*Tmr* T). Rank at various 'hot spots' around the town, including the Bus terminus and Railway station.

TELEPHONE NUMBERS & ADDRESSES
Bus Terminus (*Tmr* 3B/C7)	Tel 222164
Festival office. PO Box 1184, 26110 Patras.	Tel 278730/278206
Hospital	Tel 222812
NTOG (*Tmr* 2B6)	Tel 420304/5
Olympic office (*Tmr* 24B/C7) 16 Ag Andreou.	Tel 222901
Police, tourist	Tel 220902/3
United Kingdom Vice Consul, 2 Votsi St.	Tel 277329

TOILETS There are facilities at the Railway Station (*Tmr* 4B/C7/8), the International Ferry-boat terminus (*Tmr* 1B6), and the main Bus station (*Tmr* 3B/C7).

TRAINS
Railway Station (*Tmr* 4B/C7/8). The rather functional, 1930s style building is bounded on one side by the quayside and on the other by Odhos Othonos Amalias, and is diagonally across the way from Plateia Trion Symmahon. Facilities include: an information office, inside the booking hall (open daily, between 0800-1300hrs), where the young lady speaks reasonable English; a bus office; toilets; a periptero; and a left-luggage office. The latter costs 95drs per piece, for up to 24hrs storage, after which the charge is increased to 190drs. Luggage must be removed 20 mins prior to a train's departure. Close to the station is an old tank-engine, on static display. This is a common practice, in the locality of many main railway towns.

Train timetables
Patras to Kavasila Junction (for Killini Port), Pirgos (for Olympia) & on to Kalamata
Daily dept.	1120,	1220,	1445,	1745,	1955,	0155,	0620,	0720hrs
Pirgos	1342,	1406,	1655,	1950,	2219,	0405,	0835,	0945hrs
Olympia	-	1449,	-	2036hrs				
Kiparissi	1507,	-	1818,	2103,	-	0523,	1007,	1106hrs
Kalamata	1702,	-	2013,	-		-	0717,	1210hrs

Patras to Athens
Daily dept.	0200,	0630,	0837,	1118,	1237,	1408,	1600,	1815,	1910,	2050hrs
Egio	0246,	0704,	0923,	1156,	-	1456,	-	1854,	1952,	2128hrs
Diakofto	0304,	-	0944,	1216,	-	1515,	-	1909,	2014,	2145hrs
Xilokastro	0353,	-	1035,	1300,	1404,	1607,	1720,	-	2104,	2229hrs
Korinthos	0428,	-	1110,	1335,	1433,	1646,	1748,	-	2145,	2305hrs
Athens	0628,	0953,	1309,	1523,	1608,	1900,	1922,	2143,	2342,	0045hrs

One-way fares Patras -	Pirgos	480drs;	duration 2hrs 10mins.
	Kalamata	990drs;	5hrs 30mins.
	Korinthos	670drs;	2hrs 10mins.
	Athens	970drs:	4hrs 40mins.

TRAVEL AGENTS & TOUR OFFICES Inextricably mixed in with the Ferry-boat ticket offices (*Tmr* 6B5) that line the Esplanade (*See* Ferry-boat Ticket Offices). There aren't any businesses selling local excursions.

YOUTH HOSTEL *See* Accommodation.

EXCURSIONS
Excursion to Achaia Clauss Winery (some 10km). Take the No 7 bus, which might be signed 'Krines', or follow the brown signs to the top of Odhos Gounari - where they disappear! No problem, simply select the

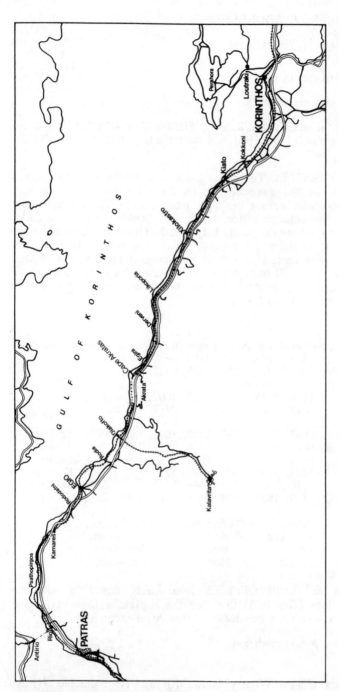

Illustration 4 Route One

right-hand fork at Plateia Marouda, for (distant) Kalavrita, past the
Hospital. The signs, which head in the direction of Saravali village,
reappear in time to save the traveller proceeding to the right, in the
direction of Kalavrita and Tripoli. The road crosses over the perfectly
ghastly river-bed running down the Glafkos valley, to pass through the
village of **Petroto**, beyond which, to the left, are the gates for:
Achaïa Clauss Winery (10km from Patras). Open during the summer
months, between 0930-1730hrs. The entrance allows access to a steep,
winding, tree-lined and shaded dual carriageway. This climbs up to the
'eagles eyrie' - actually part Bavarian, part castle style buildings,
attractively flanked by cypress trees. The place is squeaky clean, with
even the driveway being swept hourly.
   Not only is admission 'on the house', but there are two free tours
around the 'works' - between 0930-1200hrs & 1500-1730hrs. Visitors
can partake of a complimentary cup of one of the selected wines, often
Mavrodaphne. Apart from the more classy offerings, the 'chateau' is
responsible for *Demestica*.
   The 'beer-kellar' ambiance is quite possibly due to the founder being a
German, one Baron Von Clauss. He alighted on the spot in or around
1861. There is a possibly apocryphal story that the wine *Mavrodaphne* is
named in memory of a local girl who the Baron loved, and lost!

ROUTE ONE (Illus. 4).
To Korinthos via Diakofto & Kalavrita (about 140km). For almost the
whole of the route the New National Highway parallels the Old National
road, both running along the north coast. They cross over each other,
and the railway line, all the way from Patras, almost as far as Korinthos.
   To the left, the other, north side of the ever-narrowing waters of
Patras Gulf, are the dramatic, granite-like hills that contour along the
coastline of Central Greece. The upper slopes are so bare that they
almost appear to be snow-covered.

A turning to the left, opposite a large hospital, decends to:
Rio (Rion)(8½km from Patras) Tel prefix 061. Nowadays, really no
more than a very busy ferry-boat way station for the Gibraltar-like, 2km
crossing to **Antirio** (Antirion), on the opposite, Central Greece shore.
   The historical importance of the site is indicated by, to the right (*Fsw*),
the still moated remains of the Venetian **Castle of the Morea**, built in
1400, and buttressed by a Turkish sultan, in 1499. On the opposing,
mainland bank, at Antirio, is the **Kastro Rumelis**, dating from the 17thC.
   Rio is constructed on a messy promontory, over which is spread olive
and bamboo groves, and housing. It cannot come as a surprise that the
fortress remains are rather overshadowed by the frenetic comings and
goings caused by the vehicle and landing-craft style ferry-boat traffic, as
well as the dusty industrial activity.
   Accommodation includes the: *Georgios* (Class C, tel 992627), with en suite
singles priced from 2760drs & doubles from 4800drs; *Rion Beach* (Class C,
tel 991421), where en suite single rooms cost from 4500drs & double rooms
from 6000drs. Numerous signs indicate *Camping Rion* (tel 991585, open May-
Sept). There is also *Rio Mare Camping* (Tel 992263, open all year round).

Ferry-boat Timetable
Rio to Antirio & vice-versa: 0700-2300hrs, every 15mins; 2300-0130hrs, every 30mins; 0130-0630hrs, once an hour.
One-way fare per person 76drs; vehicle & driver 781drs; duration 15mins.

East of Rio, hereabouts the Old National Road is some 150m from the shore of the Gulf of Korinthos, and interweaving with the railway line. It passes through the ribbon development of **Ag Vasilios** and then the more rural, rather smarter 'strip' of **Arahovitika,** where are the *Patras Bay Villa Hotel* and a fish restaurant, both on the left.

Filling stations are spaced out along the route. Ruining the view of the Gulf, in the area of the **Drepano** turning, and a cafe-bar, is a substantial *Titan* cement works, and a concrete pipe spinning factory. They are incongruously, but pleasantly complemented by donkeys statuesquely shading themselves from the sun's rays, beneath a straggle of tree branches. Despite some maps indicating water skiing, it is hardly worth following the side road, then path, between the two industrial sites. But if you must..., it tracks through a repair and coal yard, to a most uninviting stretch of seashore, edging a dirty, pebble bottomed sea-bed. To the right is a 'sort of pierhead', and a spur of land covered in bamboos and waste building materials. A few boats there may be, but no water skiing! A narrow stony path edges the backshore to the left, advancing to a pebble of land, and a quite pretty, castellated building, alongside a lighthouse.

The Old Road crosses over a wide, dry, stony river-bed, a sign to the left indicates a railway halt, and then, with the New Highway to the right, a side-turning bridges the railway line, leading to:
PSATHOPIRGOS (18km from Patras) Tel prefix 061. A pleasant, pretty, neat, rather self-contained 'Patras-away-from-it-all resort'. This borders a shallow bay, off the main Gulf, and in the waters of which are a number of moored caiques. There is a clear likeness to an island port, with the crescent-shaped, main body of the village to the left. The sea-bed is pebble, the sea water clear - clear enough to spot and date the occasional yoghurt carton(!), in amongst some wind driven seaweed. A few makeshift piers stretch into the sea and, if pushed, I would liken the location and its rather exclusive ambiance to one or three of Evia's island resorts.

At the outset of the approach road is the *Hotel Florida* (Class B, tel 931279), the grounds of which stretch all the way down to the waterfront, and where all rooms have en suite bathrooms, a single costing 6000drs & a double 9000drs, with suites a princely 18,000drs.

At the junction with the well-organised, concrete Esplanade, to the left passes by at least five tavernas, interspersed by mature tamarisk trees, prior to petering out alongside a sea wall edging a boulderous sea-bed, and swathes of stony pebble.

To the right, along the Esplanade, are a few 'railway coach' beach chalets, a 'little bit' of pebbly shore, beyond which the thoroughfare runs out, leaving the shoreline to continue on round a bluff.

Casual callers are not really encouraged, and there isn't any evidence of *Rooms.*

Psathopirgos is almost immediately succeeded by the very much smaller settlement of:
KATO RODINI (20km from Patras) Tel prefix 061. The tree shaded, very narrow pebble shore is approached from the Old Road, by yet another slip road over the railway line. Away to the west and separated from it by a scrubbly little bay is the aforementioned Psathopirgos.

Accommodation is present in the shape of the *Rodini Apartments* (Class B, Tel 931300), with suites from 6850/1100drs and the *Hotel Aphrodite* (Class D, tel 931450), at which en suite doubles priced at 4000drs.

In the main, the strip of land between the main road and the narrow, rocky/pebbly shoreline is amply planted with olive and fir trees, in amongst which are some soldier-like cypresses. The seaward edge borders a series of small, curving coves, split up by headlands. From above they appear extremely pretty, but in places are actually rather scrubbly.

At about 23km from Patras, a sign points to the left, which, if followed, leads over the railway track, past a well established rubbish pile, to a large, circular, paved quay - possibly once a ferry-boat dock, surrounded by clear sea-water. To the right is an interesting section of the original, narrow, winding coastal road which undulates past a jetty to the gates of:

Camping Arion Beach (Tel 0691 31301) A pleasantly relaxed - alright, rather laid-back site. It is draped over a pine tree shaded, low headland, on which caravans and tents lurk, and which falls away to a narrow, pebble shoreline. Prices are: adults 500drs; children 250drs; a car 250drs; trailer 500drs; trailer tent 400drs; trailer car 550drs; small tent 350drs; large tent 450drs; small bus 300drs; big bus 350drs, motorcycle 150drs; bicycle 100drs; electrical connection or sleeping bags 150drs. There is another, more direct entrance off the Old Road, on the far, east side of the site. A further 3km or so, to the east is:
Solis Camping A well shaded, reasonably organised, pretty, if locals-flavoured site, with a number of 'permanently' located caravans, and a mock windmill at the entrance.

LAMBIRI (28km from Patras) Tel prefix 0691. A pleasant, parochial, off-the-beaten-track, seaside village. The presence of a *Club Mediterranee* holiday camp has resulted in a scattering of French style signs, advertising various local services, as well as some Gallic specialities on restaurant menus. There are a number of tavernas, with a few shack-like ones spread along the concrete edged, tree shaded shore, as well as some *Rooms*, a mini-market and a couple of filling stations. A number of fishing caiques are anchored close inshore.

There are two Class C hotels, the *Avra* (Tel 31271) and the *Galini* (tel 31231), all en suite rooms, with a single priced at 3500drs & doubles 3750/5000drs.

Immediately beyond Lambiri, the Old Road, bordered mainly by olive tree groves, passes beneath the New Highway to **Kamares** (29km), a ribbon development, boasting a cafeteria/pizzeria, filling station, and a drinking water fountain. At the outskirts of the railway-halt **Nea Erineo**s, a wide, summer-dry river-bed is bridged. To the left is a turning to the homely, mature, 'no concessions' village of Longos, wherein the road squiggles around a small plateia, traditionally bordered by a spreading plane tree, and a large church. Local buses call.

Back on the Old Road, the route advances to yet another quiet, neat, ribbon-spread settlement, that of:

SELIANITIKA (34km from Patras) Tel prefix 0691. Edging the High St are a supermarket, filling station, bread shop and a large church. At either end of the village are turnings signed to the beach (*Paralia*). Following the latter leads to the waterfront of a very Hellenic, busy, Greek holiday-maker popular, seaside resort. This is typical of a now 'familiar' Corinth Gulf pattern - a narrow, pebbly sea-shore (here with stretches of fine shingle), and a ashphalted Esplanade snaking along the backshore. In this case, the latter is bordered by hotels, cafe-bars and tavernas, some of which have tables and chairs edging the strand. At the right-hand end the shore widens and is well shaded by trees. A few of the spaced-out shower heads work, some do not.

As might be expected, there is a scooter hire firm, whilst accommodation includes the: *Pension Panayotic* (Class B, tel 71840), with en suite single rooms costing 2290/3100drs & doubles 3370/4450drs; smart *Hotel Kanelli* (Class C, tel 72442); *Hotel Kyani Akti* (Class C, tel 72202); and the *Hotel Plage* (Class C, tel 72206), where en suite single rooms are charged at 3550/4500drs & doubles 4000/5500drs.

Leaving Selianitika, the countryside is dominated by vines and olives. After a couple of kilometres, an unsigned, 'unintentional' turning, to the left, 'ducks' beneath a fairly low bridge of the New Highway, only to spill out on to the west end of a large cove, in which a pleasant number of fishing boats are moored. This is a similar location, if much less developed, to that of previously detailed Selianitika. To gain the 'proper' access, continue along the Old Road, past an inland pointing sign indicating Piantana to a signpost to:

Akoli Beach The location of several ethnic, well-shaded campsites, including *Akoli Beach* (Tel 71317) and *Korali Beach* (Tel 71558), a *Rooms* (but only by the week), a bakery (well at least a sign for one), several rural tavernas, a cocktail bar, complete with a swimming pool, some beach showers, and a smidgin of sand, towards the left-hand side of the shore.

The Old Road crosses over the railway line on the outskirts of:
RODODAFNI (30km) A rather spaced out village, as are many of these Old Road settlements, with a to-be-welcomed lack of traffic, probably due to the New Highway. Mind you, the paucity of vehicles has not discouraged the construction of four filling stations.

Beyond Rododafni are the outskirts of:
EGIO (41km from Patras) Tel prefix 0691. Actually two distinct towns. The western end is a small, once active, industrial quarter, with a Victorian ambiance, and ferry-boat quay, boasting a cross-Gulf summer months

connection to **Ag Nikolaos** (Eratini), on the coastline of Central Greece. The ferries depart from Egio to Ag Nikolaos, daily, at 0730, 1330 & 1700hrs, for the 45mins voyage, with craft returning from Ag Nikolaos at 0830, 1530 & 1830hrs. Passenger fares cost 386drs, whilst a car & driver is 1875drs.

The ferry-boat quay is so large as to indicate that there were further plans afoot, once upon a time. The railway halt breaks out into sidings, and warehouses border the Old Road. There is an effort being made to beautify the strip of land between the waterfront and the roadway. In addition to three restaurants, there is a *Playboy Club*, yes, a ..., as well as indications of a tennis club. There are very few shops and only one hotel, the *Hotel Helmos* (Class E, tel 22514), an old-fashioned, two storey building wherein the bedrooms share the bathroom.

A sign on the dirty, pebble beach advises that the 'Water is Polluded' (*sic*), which I am quite prepared to believe. One or two pipes that arrow out to sea certainly give one food for thought (sorry).

A concrete thoroughfare continues along the backshore, for quite some distance, terminating at a surprisingly wide, unattractive, shadeless stretch of pebble beach. Here is an unbelievably smart cocktail bar, as well as beach showers, and another beach bar, which appear to cater for locals who can catch a town bus out here. Prior to the road branching away from the shore, around a salt-bed, there are a pair of bright yellow, tardis-like lavatories. The bamboo bordered road curves back to terminate alongside a similarly pebbly, busy shore, at a pan-handle dead end, alongside which is the garden *Taverna Eliki*, and another pair of 'Dr Who' loos.

The traditional, eastern, main town Egio has a pleasant mix of shops & bakeries, a post office, banks, a large bus station, with a taxi rank adjacent, but few, if any *Rooms*.

Listed hotels include the: *Galini* (Class B, tel 26150), wherein en suite single rooms cost 5300/5800drs & doubles 6800/7500drs; *Telis* (Class C, tel 28200), with en suite singles priced at 3400/3700drs & doubles 5200/5800drs; and *Lory* (Class E, tel 27771), where double rooms sharing the bathrooms cost 3600drs & doubles en suite 4000drs.

Out on the headland bulging into the gulf, to the east of Egio's outer environs, are:
TEMENI Really nothing more than a pleasant, sprawling and mature suburb of Egio. In amongst the more modern houses are some late Victorian dwellings.
And 5km from Egio:
VALIMITIKA Once over the railway line, which may sport the occasional chair-seated chap, lounging on the track, there is evidence of a separate village, with one or two shops, prior to the road running out on the undeveloped coastline.

To the right of the pebble shore, edging a pleasant, if flat, bay, is a football playing field. There are no concessions to tourism, apart from one or two souvenir shops, a few signs in French, and the *Hotel Eliki* (Class C, tel 91301, with en suite singles costing 6400drs & doubles 8000drs).

Instead of continuing east along the coast, monastery enthusiasts might

consider an interesting, and picturesque detour. This can be undertaken by following the signposts inland for, say, Mavriki, up the Selinous River valley, towards the:
Monastery Pan. Taxiarhon (11km). Similarly to that of Amorgos island, the original monastery was impossibly clagged-on to a seemingly vertical, east river bank cliff face, cave-pocked most of the way up to a tree and shrub capped plateau. When, in the 17thC, it suffered from a fire, the still extant brotherhood decamped to an alternative, close-by, but less altitudinous, more easily approachable location.

Back at the coast, on the Old Road, some 5km from Egio, is:
NIKOLEIKA (46km from Patras) Tel prefix 0691. This village radiates out from a simple main square. At the outset of the settlement of Nikoleika is the *Hotel Themisto* (Class C, tel 81888), whose en suite singles cost 4800drs & doubles 6500drs, a *Pension* (tel 24058), a few restaurants and, opposite a local taverna, and a butcher, a side road to the left signed *Hotel Poseidon Beach*.
    This turning crosses over the railway line, passing by a possibly abandoned disco, one or two villa apartments, a taverna or two, prior to spilling on to the backshore of a reasonably wide swathe of pebble beach. Despite the presence of trees, they are well set back, so the shore is rather shadeless. This is quite a popular location, with a glass fronted, fast-food place alongside the junction of the access road and the backshore, as well as two or three tavernas.
    The *Hotel Poseidon Beach* (Class B, tel 81400) is not easily observed, but offers en suite singles from 3400/4900drs & doubles 4200/6300drs.

Continuing along the Old Road, after passing what appears to be a successful taverna and swinging over a bridge, there's a side road to the left, in the direction of:
RODIA & Rodia Beach Serviced by local buses. A large, paved main square, part shaded by very mature trees, is at the centre of this old, quintessentially Hellenic village. Edging the plateia is a children's play-ground and a cafe-bar cum taverna - at which 'a roast of lamb or pig' can often be found 'on the spit'.
    The road continues on over a swathe of inland 'bundy', to the right-hand side of a shallow bay, and an 8m wide, pebble shore. There are some 'polite' apartments/*Rooms*, and the smart, three storey, avant garde *Pension Rodia* (Class B, tel 81195). There is some shore-shade and a few beach showers, at the west end of the bay. Close by a 'No Camping' sign are a clutch of camper-vans and long-stay tents, the latter almost tethered to the damned notice, proscribing their presence!

Back on the Old Road, almost immediately, to the left, is yet another side road signposting a campsite, apartments and:
Eleona Beach A surprisingly large, extremely busy, old-time railway halt community, straddling the tracks. To the far side of the lines are a cinema, and a taverna, followed by the well-shaded backshore road, which services

quite a large, informal spread of typically rustic, Greek resort development. Any number of taverna tables and chairs are spread along the edge of the reasonably wide sweep of fine shingle, and there are beach showers. Proceeding to the right (*Fsw*), in the direction of the campsite, passes a *Hyde Park Pizza Spaghetti House* (yes, a ...), and a huge taverna. Towards the far end, the surrounds become rather doo-hickey, if not scrubbly, with some chalets and small huts scattered about, past which the roadway winds by the *Annabella Disco*, to the entrance of the *Eleona Beach Campsite*. Another turning off the Old Road leads down to *Eleona Beach* and the next, similarly flat bay, also edged by a (not so wide) pebble beach. Inshore are anchored a few fishing boats. To the left is the modernish, four storey *Pension Beach Demitropoulos*, followed by a taverna, after which the shore peters out alongside a small, concrete quay, jutting into the sea.

Back on the Old Road, the next settlement is:
DIAKOFTO (55km from Patras) Tel prefix 0691. An old-fashioned, busy, delightful, if disorganised and messy railway halt village. It is one of the north coast Peloponnese delights, with the added attraction of a branch line, part rack-and-pinion, to the inland, mountain village of Kalavrita.

Diakofto is really two places - inland 'railway junction' Diakofto, and 'seaside resort' Diakofto. At the outset to Diakofto 'proper' is a sign pointing to the left, to the Post Office. Other services and supplies include a National Bank and the railway station, the lines of which divide the centre of the village, blocking off the straight-line progress of the High St. In fact, approaching from the south, it is necessary to follow the street that rambles round the dinky main railway buildings, over a level-crossing, to get to the far side. To one side of the terminus, is the static display of an old-time 'Thomas the Tank Engine'. The squashed up Main Square, bounded by the railway on the north side, doubles-up as a bus turn-round, and a taxi rank (Tel 41402). Close by are a couple of constantly running drinking water fountain heads. The cafe-bar, alongside the junction of the square and the road down from the main road, charges a reasonable 100drs for a Nes meh ghala. A restaurant advertises that English is spoken.

The air-conditioned *Hotel Chris Paul* (Class C, tel 41715) has en suite single rooms at a cost of 3900drs & doubles 6500drs, whilst the old-fashioned *Hotel Chelmos* (Class D, tel 41236), where all rooms share the bathrooms, offers singles priced at 2200drs & doubles 3000drs.

Once the other side of the tracks, the shortish, straight High St passes by a taverna and, on the right, the *Hotel Lemonies* (Class D, tel 41229), where an en suite single costs 2500drs & a double 3500drs. Several apartments advertise *Rooms*, but probably only by the week.

At the junction of the High St and the waterfront is the popular *Fish Restaurant Koxyli*, and across the way, half-right, the caique harbour. To the left (*Fsw*) stretches away a nicely shaded Esplanade, topping a low sea-wall on one side, and boxed in by the boundaries of various properties, on the inland side. The sea-bed is pebble whilst further west are some teeny stretches of pebble shore, which eventually become crescents of pebble beach. It is worth noting that the shallows are home to sea-urchins.

A meal at the *To Koxyli Taverna* can be a nail-biting, wearisome experience. That is not to deny that the food is plentiful and tasty, and the initial service speedy, but attracting the attention of a waiter, in order to amend or add to an order, or even to pay, is almost impossible. One evening, when admittedly rather tired, the wait was so protracted that we both fell asleep, face down on the tabletop. And I don't mean tired, as in *Private Eye* 'tired and emotional', simply whacked! A meal for two of 1 tzatziki (175drs), 2 plates of the most scrumptious chicken (550drs each), with a large plate of chips, an excellent Greek salad (550drs), a bottle of retsina (150drs), bread & service (35drs each), cost 2045drs - but we were charged 1950drs. Spit roast chicken 'bits & pieces' are a house speciality.

Other Diakofto hotels, not mentioned in the text, include the *Acropole* (Class D, tel 41226); the *Panorea* (Class D, tel 41216); and the *Hotel Panorama* (Class D, tel 41614), where singles sharing are charged at 2400/3400drs, doubles sharing 3200/4500drs & en suite 4200/6000drs.

One of the main reasons for Diakofto's importance, to the excursion-lover, is the referred-to branch-line climbing to the alpine-like village of Kalavrita. The technology that originally made the ascent possible was the rack and pinion, and lengths of the track utilise the technique. Its presence, combined with the wild, natural beauty of the route's scenery, makes it very popular with Greeks, and tourists alike. In fact, such is the renown of the branch-line, that, if at all possible, it is best to avoid weekends, and start out early. Another tip is to bear in mind that the best views of the journey are seen from the front or rear compartments, which are 1st class. The *hoi-polloi* have to travel in the crowded, chaotic, 2nd class carriages.

Branch line timetable
Diakofto to Kalavrita
Daily   0700, 0905, 1025, 1148, 1550hrs
Return journey
Daily   0820, 1020, 1213, 1320, 1720hrs
One-way fare: 2nd class fare 270drs; duration 1hr 10mins.

Long-standing Grecophiles might be puzzled that the locals should be capable of constructing this (at the time) advanced concept. It will be a relief to realise that the line was built, under licence, by the Italians, in the 1890s. Ah, that explains all!

The first half of the track cuts along the Vouvraikos Gorge, down which courses a summer running river. Once the rack and pinion has been engaged, the climb becomes very steep, with the line cutting in and out of tunnelled portions of the mountain, and criss-crossing the river-bed, in one or two places at waterfalls. Menacingly, the route passes by several railside shrines! Further up, the scenery is similar to the Black Falls in North Wales, or for that matter, the Valley of the Butterflies, Rhodes. After about half an hour, a passing point heralds the outset of another section of rack and pinion, at a more open, greener section of the gorge.

Fifty minutes into the journey, the first halt is encountered, namely: **Zahlorou/Mega Spileo** Tel prefix 0692. A lovely mountain hamlet, whereat the obligatory railway hotel/taverna, the *Romantzo* (Class D, tel

22758 - double rooms, sharing, cost 3500drs & en suite 4000drs). About 100m distant is the *Restaurant/ Rooms Messinia*.

Some forty five minutes hike from this settlement is the:
Monastery Mega Spileo (or Great Cave) The present, modern, rather hostel-like building was constructed, in the 1930s, flat up against the smooth, vertical cliff-face, once again beautifully, sited, overlooking the river ravine. The recent rebuild, the last of inumerable reconstructions necessary over the centuries, was due to an explosion and fire in 1934, caused by the self-ignition of a quantity of explosives, reputed to date back to the time of the War of Independence. Despite the conflagration, many of the artifacts, relics and treasures where saved. The monastery nomenclature is derived from an adjacent rock chamber, and the still working order is reputed to be, not only one of the richest, but one of the oldest in Greece. These chronicles reach back to the discovery, in the cave, in AD362, of a wooden icon of the Virgin Mary, attributed to St Luke. The museum exhibits reflext this depth of history and riches.

Beyond Zahlorou, the countryside flattens out a little, if remaining mountainous with a profusion of maple trees, chestnuts and conifers, with some grassland. There is yet another little railway halt, **Kerpini**, after which the scenery softens even more, with rolling, grass-covered slopes, rich in trees and copses. As the climb continues, the River Vouraikos diminishes in size and strength, to become more a stream - or rivulet.

KALAVRITA Tel prefix 0692. An alpine-like village, with sparklingly clear air, compared to the coast. Despite the rather unhappy, comparatively recent and tragic events, there is a milieu of wealth.

In and around the railway terminus buildings are a station cafe, some unisex squatty loos (in a mind-boggling state), a drinking water fountain, set into a main wall, and a mural acclaiming the 'Hands of Friendship'. The latter is a poignant reminder of a Second World War act of madness, when the Nazis exacted a grim and terrible reprisal on the citizens of the town. Some 1400 males, men and children, were put to death and the town razed to the ground, by fire. The mural's caption advises that Kalavrita is a 'fully paid-up' member of the 'Union of Martyred Towns'. To the far side of the Railway station square is a sign showing the direction of the tomb to the fallen.

But Kalavrita was no stranger to suffering at the sharp end of invaders' weapons. Oh no! Leaving out early historical events, the settlement vies with Kalamata (*See* Chapt. 11) as the first town to be liberated at the outset of the Greek War of Independence (1821-1829). Despite this, the Turkish Pasha retook Kalavrita twice, in 1826 and 1827, prior to the cessation of hostilities. Once may be regarded as misfortune, twice as carelessness' (to misquote Oscar Wilde).

In fact, the uprising centred on the **Monastery Ag Lavras**, which is some 6km to the south-west, along a metalled road. The institution dates back to AD961 when a hermit took up residence. His humble beginnings expanded into a monastery, which incurred any number of disasters, causing it to be rebuilt on many occasions. Despite the present building being constructed in 1839, within is a church dating back to before the War of Independence.

Returning to the present. Immediately to the front of the ticket office entrance is the 'Station' Square, whereon taxis rank. The nicely shaded, part-pedestrianised High St, Odhos 25th March, makes off from the far side of the square. Around to the right (*Railway station behind one*) is a fenced-off steam engine and carriage display. Perhaps the fencing is in case somebody attempts to 'steal the train'.

Close to the station is the *Hotel Kalavrita*, and a souvenir shop. Note, the farther one is from the Railway Station, the less expensive are postcards to purchase.

Progressing up the gently climbing High St passes by a taverna, then, on the right, the *Hotel Maria* (Class C, tel 22296 - en suite singles 3600/ 5600drs & doubles 4800/7800drs). A chemist (and they are plentiful) is followed by another hotel, the school, a supermarket, a branch of the National Bank of Greece, in an imposing building, and a local taverna, all prior to the large, tree-shaded Main Square. To the right of the latter is the Post Office, close by which is another taxi-rank. To the right is an attractively decorated twin-tower church, each tower having a clock face, the left-hand one supposedly recording, forever, the exact time of the German's mass execution.

At the far right of the square is an underground public toilet, also unisex, and also filthy. Most High St shops, which include a yoghurterie, a speciality cheese shop, and a baker, open seven days a week. On the whole, the restaurant schlepping is half-hearted.

To the right of the Main Square is a lateral side-street, beside which is the modernish *Hotel Filoxenia* (Class B, tel 22422 - en suite single 4860drs & a double 7060drs). Further along, 'Odhos Filoxenia' 'junctions' with a parallel street to the High St, beside which are a number of local tavernas and a cinema, and on which terminus the Patras buses. Cutting back to the Railway station passes by the *Pub Playboy* - oh dear!

Kalavrita possesses a hospital, which I suppose is not surprising, considering the bloodthirsty recent past. Prior to a closing comment, attention should be drawn to the north coast's most impressive, and highest mountain, Mt Helmos, which tops 2341m, and is some 9km east-south-east of Kalavrita. The approach to this, and other delights, is best from coastal Akrata, for details of which read on. The closing comment? Just to report on the overall lack of tour buses. How nice.

From Kalavrita an almost circular route can be followed by heading south-east past the War Memorial, on an unsurfaced track, towards Mt Helmos. At a crossroads, prior to the Helmos Ski Centre, select the turning in the direction of the mountain settlements of **Ano** and **Kato Lousi,** and on to **Kastria** (circa 19km from Kalavrita). Here is **Spileo ton Limnos** (Cave of Lakes), a series of underground waterways. Continuing south, past a turning to the left, which angles back to a quartet of mountain settlements, advances to **Kato Klitoria** (circa 27km from Kalavitra). From this bustling village, the route 'clockwises' round through, for instance, **Kastelli** and **Priolithos,** the source of the River Vouraikos, and back to Kalavitra, a round trip of some 57km. For those wishing to return to Patras, there can be no better choice of route than to proceed from the western outskirts of Kalavrita, past the northern slopes of Mt Erimanthos, through vineyards, to **Halandritsa**, and on to Patras.

Returning to the coastal Old Road, east of Diakofto, at the 75km Korinthos 'milestone' mark, is a sign to the left to the *Fish Taverna Mekelis*. This leads to a 'day-trip' pebble beach. The 20m wide shore, which suffers from some seaborne rubbish, runs away to the right (*Fsw*) and is shadeless, but the backshore has been planted with saplings. A surfaced track edges the beach, and windsurfers are for hire, close by the access junction with the backshore track. About where the surfacing runs out, there is a taverna, on the inland side, whilst the now stony track continues on past a few private homes and villas, scattered about in a patchy development. The shore narrows down, crossing a summer-dry river-bed, *en route* to a small spit jutting into the Gulf.

The Old Road crosses the railway line to parallel the Gulf shore in the region of a slip road, bordering the rocky coastline, which proceeds to: **PARALIA PLATANOU** (circa 62km from Patras) There is a *Rooms*, a few fishing caiques drawn up on the foreshore, a smart-looking fish taverna, beyond which the shore widens out a little, advancing by another 'swept-up' taverna. Much of the old village has disappeared under a 'landslip' of snappy, seaside villa development. Towards the east end of Platanou is another fish taverna, and the water's edge is bounded by a tree planted sea-wall, prior to the slip road drifting back to rejoin the Old Road.

Much of the immediate coastline is rugged (in the area of the Korinthos 68km 'milestone'), with a few seaward turnings off the Old Road (one very acute, immediately after passing over the railway line) which drops down to a man-made harbour.

Next along is the fairly acceptable *Krionery Camping* (Tel 0696 31405, open April-Oct).

To the left is **Cape Akratas**, a large chunk of cultivated land projecting into the Gulf, with a 'bit of a winery' beside the roadside, near the sign heralding Akrata. Hereabouts the road crests the brow of a hill, and close to a summer-dry river, is a turning down to a campsite. This track borders a wide river-bed, from which building materials are torn. The well-shaded *Akrata Beach Camping* (Tel 31378, open April-Oct) is along a right-hand fork, and appears to be a favourite with long-stay caravans. The access road peters out, up against the backshore of an extremely pebbly, long sweep of featureless shore, stretching away to either side, and surrounded by rather unattractive environs. The only shelter is a grove of trees set back from the backshore, on the left (*Fsw*).

Returning to the Old Road leads to:
AKRATA (about 68km from Patras) Tel prefix 0696. The presence of this large village/small town, is heralded by some new, four and five storey apartments, over to the left.

At about the heart of the settlement is a pointer indicating *Lemon Beach Camping* (Tel 31639), which is a short way down towards the water's edge. Following this, once at the Esplanade, there are a plethora of signs. Surprisingly, this uncompromising, seaside resort sports a sign in English advertising 'Flats for Rent'. To the left (*Fsw*) 'flows' the nearside bank of the previously described Krathis River, *en route* to which passes by a number of modernish, but not garish developments. In amongst these is the *Akrata Beach Hotel* (Class C, tel 31180, where en suite single rooms cost 4150/5100drs & doubles 5400/6700drs). The 10m wide pebble shore hereabouts is bounded by a 4m high sea wall, up against which are lined the tables and chairs of one or two tavernas based on the inland side of the street. As the backshore widens out, the buildings thin out, and the strip is nicely planted with tamarisk trees. Towards the far, western end, some of the wide-open spaces are being developed, in a style reminiscent of the Costa Brava. A few camper vans 'lurk', the buoys of a water-ski schoolbob about in the shallows, of the now fine shingle foreshore, and a few pedaloes 'idle'. Prior to bumping into the eastern river bank, the apparentlyspacious *Lemon Beach Camping* (Tel 31639, open April-Oct) is surrounded by groves of lemon trees, in generously watered orchards. Incidentally, for the moment, this campsite is not crowded out with long-stay, home-grown caravans, as are so many Peloponnese sites.

A roadway heads back inland, along the river bank as far as the main road, where it is signed 'No Entrance', thus completing a large, rectangle of a one-way system.

From Akrata, the inland trek up the narrow valley formed by the River Krathis, advances, via the hamlets and villages of **Pirgos**, beyond which the road is unsurfaced, **Valimi**, **Agridi**, and **Solos**, to:
Mt Helmos (circa 42km). Height 2341m. From the last mentioned, near depopulated, mountain-slope hamlet, if not already on foot - it is from hereon. The trek takes about 5/6hrs. Follow the signs for abandoned **Gounarianka**, beyond which continue trekking to the impressive drop of the Mavroneri waterfall and River Styx ravine, from whence the waters disappear underground. Mythology dictates that the Styx flows 'nine times round the infernal regions' or hell! So that's where marriages are made.

Returning to the coast, the next location of any note is:
EGIRA (about 71km from Patras) Really nothing more than a rather lifeless High Street strip, from which branch a number of short, 50m long access streets to an asphalted, waterfront Esplanade. The latter is edged by a one metre high sea wall, bordering a very narrow strip of pebble, boasting a number of beach showers. There are few, if any, facilities.

Beyond the limits of Egira, is a small 'boulder of a headland' as well as a fishing boat harbour. The coastline of this pretty, if not lovely, section of the route becomes rocky and boulder-strewn, whilst the countryside is dominated by lemon groves. The Old Road drops down alongside a pebble shoreline, prior to passing through a 'strip of village', with just enough room for small houses between the road and the sea, close to the 59km

Korinthos 'milestone'. A 3m wide, large pebble shore continues on, passing through random villa country, where old and new housing are mixed in with farmland and clusters of bamboo. From the foot of a headland are glimpses of the fairly large **Petalou**, another shoreline village, through which the road rumbles. Old, red ridge tiles to some of the houses, new buildings here, a stretch of beach there, piles of crates, and the occasional scratching chicken - pleasantly Greek and scrubbly.

Proceeding eastwards progresses to the sign for:
DERVENI (about 76km from Patras) Tel prefix 0743. The same mix as before, if possessing a slightly wider street, so it is a bigger and nicer village, with some young tamarisk trees planted along the sea wall of the backshore. There is a filling station as well as a nice little chapel beside the road. The road narrows down into what is probably the original, pleasant core of the village. There isn't an Esplanade, just a number of short streets down to the sea. What shoreline is available, is pebble, and not very wide.
The hotels include the *Evrostini* (Tel 31223) and the *Kyma* (Tel 31441).

Across a summer dry river-bed, the Old Road winds about, keeping quite close to the shoreline. The buildings of yet another unmarked, old village are pleasantly strung along the roadside. At the 54km Korinthos 'milestone', is:
LIGIA (about 81km from Patras) The settlement is spaced out beside the High St, with most of the narrow block of houses to seaward. At a junction is an inland turning in the direction of **Pirgos**.
The small seashore, on which are beached a few little boats, is pebbly and kelpy, and an outcrop of trees provides some shade. The next stretch of houses are on the south side, old and new alike, and two or three storeys high. Towards the east of Ligia, the mainly rocky, boulderous coast is broken up by outcrops of tamarisk tree shaded, pebble beach, littered with some kelp.

The completion of Ligia, marks the outset of the ribbon development of **Stomio**. Beyond the latter, the Old Road turns away from the coastline, exposing a quite wide, not unattractive, swathe of shore, with a skeletal lighthouse plonked down on a spit of pebble. A grove of tamarisk trees edges the backshore, on which there is, more often than not, an enclave of camper vans. The actual foreshore is very fine pebble and gritty sand. Some unshaded taverna tables and chairs are clustered together on a part of the shore known as **Saradaphiotika**.

Beyond a river-bed, in which some summer month water flows, is:
LIKOPORIA (about 87km from Patras) Tel prefix 0743. A fishing boat village, the houses of which are strung along both sides of the High St, with a few kafeneions here and there. In amongst the backshore is some messy, pebble 'beach'. There are a few tourist apartments, and a rather old hotel, the *Alkyon* (Class C, tel 51221 - shared bathroom singles cost 3200/3900drs, shared doubles 4000/4600drs, & en suite doubles 4750/5750drs). A length of 3m or 4m wide, not very appealing shore

is followed by a Post office, at about the 48km Korinthos 'milestone' mark, whilst on the inland side, an OTE is signposted, as is a Railway station, and the village of Kallithea.

Stunted tamarisk trees edge the backshore, bounded by a low breeze-block sea wall. The right-hand side of the Old Road is subject to a 'ribbon', a disparate mix of villas, houses and apartments, seemingly rolling-on forever, but which were probably a number of separate little hamlets, now run into each other. Here and there is a very old house, and, every so often, a spindle windlass remains projecting from the beach - lonely reminders of the fishing fleets of yesteryear. In a cluster of restaurant/tavernas, beyond the 46km Korinthos 'milestone', is a *Rooms*, followed by the eastern limit of Likoporia

Once over a narrow, grotty stream, the settlement of Kato Pitsa is encoun- tered, for which repeat the previous description, noting it is even more scrubbly, if that is possible. The Old Road bridges another equally nasty, little, summer-dry river-bed, the route continuing to be lined, on the inland side, by ribbon development, though it does thin out somewhat, being supplanted by a scattering of old bits of agriculture, and a boulderous sea's edge. The Korinthos 'milestone' reads 44km.

One and a half kilometres further on is Kato Loutro, whereat an inland turning to Vrisoules. Set in the rugged coastline, close to the Korinthos 42km 'milestone', across the Old Road from a church, is an extremely kelpy, smelly, triangle of filthy beach. This parish's boundaries are marked by a summer-dry river-bed. This is yet another source of con- struction materials, and in order to bridge the gulch, the road loops inland.

The approach to Kamari is marked by some messy industrial buildings. As heretofore, the houses ribbon along the road, but Kamari appears to have a rather more interesting atmosphere than most of the previous settlements. It has to be admitted that the reasons for this judgement are difficult to define, but the ambience is better - it could hardly be worse! The 'High St' is only one plot distant from the seashore, glimpsed along the narrow alleys between the various buildings, some of which are *Rooms*. The narrow, pebble shore has been graced with the nomenclature 'beach', by one cartographer. I presume he, or she, has relations hereabouts, as it would have required a generous dollop of artistic licence to describe this tree-bestrewn, building rubblle littered shoreline and sea's edge, as a beach.

At the Korinthos 39km 'milestone', alongside which is an older, carved sign listing 129km (probably for Athens), the Old Road cuts inland, prior to passing over a narrow river defile, beyond which the roadside develop- ment almost peters out, making way for groves of olive and lemon trees.

Where the Old Road merges, once again, with the waterfront, is the far-flung outset of:
XILOKASTRO (about 101km from Patras) Tel prefix 0743. The sweeping road borders a mostly shadeless, dirty, kelpy, pebble beach. The latter narrows down to almost nothing, prior to broadening out to a width of

some 10m. Where the main body of Xilokastro lines the road, the thoroughfare swings away from the seafront, past a rebuilt, castellated tower, alongside a fairly modern church. A branch turning heads inland for Trikalon, whilst the 'High St' bridges a river-bed, prior to the *Hotel Apollon* (Class B, tel 22239 - en suite single rooms cost 5307/6200drs & doubles 7975/9440drs).

A side-street advances to the typical resort waterfront, where a wall holds back the sea. An Esplanade stretches away to the east, whilst to the west is a spacious, man-made harbour, and a tiny, 30m long patch ofpebble beach - surely enough for some map-maker to splash the fact with enormous symbols! The Esplanade is pleasant, the sea-edge being bordered by a wide, tree-shaded pavement, along which are spaced-out a number of restaurants and tavernas' tables and chairs. Apart from the beach, there is a small quay from which it is possible to swim. The *Hotel Arion* (Class A, tel 22230) is rather smart, only offering en suite double rooms at a cost of 6760/9800drs. A forest of pine trees edges a cove of clean, 5m wide, pebble beach where another side-street makes a junction with the Esplanade, opposite a popular cafeteria restaurant. Hereabouts many of the buildings are seven storeys high.

Following the Athens' signpost passes an unfinished church, an open-air cinema, and an OTE.

On the right is the oldish, 2 storey *Hotel Hermes* (Class D, tel   22250), wherein rooms share the bathrooms, with a single priced at 2300/2700drs & a double 2900/3300drs. Bordering the same road are the: tremendously ritzy *Rallis Hotel* (Class B, tel 22219), where en suite singles cost 5275/6345drs & doubles 7535/9395drs; the as-smart looking *Hotel Miramare* (Class B, tel 22375), where singles sharing are 2600/2900drs, doubles sharing 3370/4000drs, & en suite doubles 4600/6000drs. Other Greek tourist accommodation includes the: *Hotel Fadira* (Class B, tel 22648), with en suite singles costing 4785drs & doubles 7000drs; *Hotel Periandros* (Class C, tel 22272), en suite singles 4515drs & doubles 5200drs; *Hotel Villa Kreoli* (Class C, tel 25360), with en suite singles at 4945/5715drs & doubles 5800/7205drs; *Hotel Kyani Akti* (Class D, tel 22225), where en suite double rooms cost 4000/7500drs; and the *Hotel Kentrikon* (Class E, tel 22223).

From the eastern side of Xilokastro, an inland road courses through Kesari, skirting the flanks of Mt Killini, to the village of Stimfalia (circa 34km from Xilokastro). Close by are the unexpected ruins of a medieval Cistercian abbey. A few kilometres further on are the reedy wetlands of Stimfalian Marshes, home for various varieties of birds, many uncommon elsewhere. Continuing on round the mountain slopes, through Kateri, leads to the old, mountain settlement of Kastanea.

Back at the coast, the road east of Xilokastro skirts a very large pine parkland, on the left. Sikea is almost a suburb of Xilokastro, whereabouts the Old Road rejoins the high, sea-walled coastline, and ribbon development lines the inland side of the route. Steps descend to the up-to-10m wide, pebble beach, from the tamarisk tree shaded pavement. The shore narrows down, as the road progresses around the curve of the cove, only to completely disappear, where a small spit projects into the sea, at the far, east side.

Beyond the 31km Korinthos 'milestone', the Old Road edges away from the coast, through rather scrubbly countryside, spotted with villas, taverna tables spread about, some camper vans 'anchored', piles of building materials, bits of rubbish and then a length of varying width, kelpy pebble shore at:
MELISSI (About 111km from Patras) Tel prefix 0743. The western limits are heralded by a few shacks, close by a dirty, pebble shore, to befollowed by some small villas, and then 'traditional' ribbon development. The *Hotel Lido* (actually furnished apartments) is succeeded by the *Hotel Makis* (Class D, tel 61262).

There is a fairly pleasant, if 'Kosta' ambiance about the place - perhaps the gum trees make the difference. Meanwhile there is another length of pebble shoreline, hidden from view by a line of backshore villas, after which the road squeezes up to the beach in a messy area. The *Hotel Xylokastron Beach* (Class C, tel 61190 - en suite singles 3500/4100drs & doubles 5000/6000drs) is followed by a 'campsite of sorts', a restaurant, and then a rubbishy, scrubbly, landscape. This is occasionally 'totally despoiled' by an outcrop of industry, a broken-down disco, building plots-to-be, as well as small outcrops of 'this, that and the other', and depressingly dusty olive groves.

The Old Road jinks away from the coast leaving room for a spotting of stylised, 'jelly mould' villas. Signs indicate the presence of **Diminio**, whereat low-key, single storey development, to the left and right, beyond which is:
KIATO (Some 126km from Patras) Tel prefix 0742. A quite large town, noticeable and memorable for the nice skeletal clock towers that accompany a number of the churches. The first encountered is on the right and pleasantly shaded by a palm tree.

As the build-up of Kiato commences, an 'intrusion' of fast food establishments and neon signs is experienced, even if the buildings are fairly low profile. There are some 'No Parking' signs on a broad section of shore, to which are almost tethered a few German camper vans. Typical! The backshore hereabouts is quite attractive, due to the presence of a band of pine trees.

The High Street, blessed by a few trees, is paralleled by a resort waterfront. The up-to-10m wide, pebble beach is edged by a low-rise Kosta, which, despite the trees, remains forgettable. The tables and chairs of a 'litter' of tavernas and cafe-bars are spaced about, in addition to pedaloes, water skiing, speedboat rides and kiddies swings. The westerly beach Esplanade comes to an abrupt end, up against the *Disco Superstar*, even if the pebble shore bumbles on, and on.

Towards the centre of Kiato, marked by a splendid church, are one or two "We speak Deutsh" and "Breakfasts served" signs. Close by is a large, 'proper job' harbour, not some footling caique mole, the right-handend (*Fsw*) of which is reserved for yachts, private craft and small fishing boats. There is a beach within the harbour walls, at the west-end, and despite the disparaging remarks of my companion, the sea-water appears clean. Beyond this facility, going east, the unattractive coastline becomes a series of breakwaters, interspersed by tiny patches of shore between.

Accommodation takes in the hotels: *Triton* (Class B, tel 23421), where en suite singles cost 5000/6000drs & doubles 6000/7000drs; *Galini* (Class C, tel 22207), with en suite singles priced at 3000/3500drs & doubles 4500/5500drs; *Pappas* (Class C, tel 22358), where en suite singles cost 4800/5800drs & doubles 6000/6800drs; and the *Pefkias* (Class C, tel 28650).

In the town, ancient site buffs might look-out for the inland signpost indicating Sikion, nearby which are the picturesque archaeological remains of Sikyon.

At the eastern outskirts of Kiato, the Old Road first passes through an industrial sector, in amongst which is a sports ground, and then farmland. The route bridges a deep river-bed, host to stagnant water, and passes by the 18km Korinthos 'milestone'.

The spacious main road 'charges' through Velo, nuzzling up to the railway line, and which offers a Rooms, a hotel, filling station and a cafe-bar or two.

Immediately beyond the 16km indicator is a side-turning, enlivened by various signs, one of which is for the *Hotel Kokoni Beach* (Class C, tel 33108), and the outset of:

KOKONI (Some 133km from Patras) Tel prefix 0742. A lively railway halt. The aforementioned branch road passes by some smart, two storey villas, and the *Garden Pension Rooms*, prior to spilling on to the back-shore, alongside the *Hotel Karava's Village* (Class B, tel 32091 - en suite double rooms cost 4600/5400drs). This is a very long stretch of up to 10m wide, pebble beach, lacking any tree cover, an absence that is sorely missed, as the shady arboreal presence would immeasurably improve the location. The inland side is an 'informal' resort development, with a hint of Greek package tourism, possibly backed-up by weekend coach parties, intent on patronising the smart, bouzouki playing restaurants. The shore is cleanish, with some kelp on the foreshore, and pedaloes are for hire. The *Kokoni Beach* is a four storey high, smart cube of concrete, with bolt-on balconies. Towards the east-end, the shore becomes extremely rocky, with small pockets of shingle, hemmed-on within the confines of moles of boulders. Hereabouts, inland of the backshore is mainly agricultural, in amongst which are scattered villa outcrops - and the certainty that the area will be completely overbuilt - in time. Korinthos City is easily discernible in the distance, as is the very dramatically positioned Gerania peninsula lighthouse, so vividly described by Dilys Powell, in her - oh so readable and evocative book 'An Affair of the Heart'.

From Kokoni, the Old Road heads slightly inland, still parallelling the coastline and passing through an absolute mishmash of 'Hellenic Canvey

Island' development. At **Vrahati**, suspended above the roadway, is an inexplicable, decorative symbol. Beyond the east limit of the latter settlement, is the 12km Korinthos 'milestone'. At some distance from the coastline, and beyond the farmland which borders the road on the coast side, is a swathe of low-rise villas. The road rumbles by the occasional two storey development, filling station, bamboo outcrop, groves of olives and lemons, to **Assos**. This location is memorable for being some sort of lorry park, with what appears to be a *Chicken Shack*, alongside the main crossroads. After bridging a river, notable for its filthiness, the route leads to **Perigiali**, where a singularly tall tower is adjacent to a newish church. Here is an OTE, and a few oldish houses still standing, with little of the new construction rising above three storeys. Perigiali is not very large, despite indications to the contrary on many maps. It is almost immediately followed by **Leheo** (Tel prefix 0741), which once again appears to boast an informal lorry park, at the outset. A strip of shops include a chemist, supermarket, a PASOK office, ouzeries, a snackbar, another new church (not to be outdone by the one about 100m back up the road), filling stations, a bakery, a tyre outfit, a souvenir shop, and a video outlet. Actually Leheo is larger than Perigiali, with, at the east end, a rather squalid mess of marble factories, scrapyards, a paint spray and vehicle repair garage, and a woodchopper's enclosure, in amongst which are the occasional 'grove of something or other', struggling to survive, and a car dealership. There just has to be some chickens, scratching away, somewhere in here!

At the eastern end of Leheo is a sign to the left for *Blue Dolphin Camping* (Tel 25766/7) - 'on the beach'. The side-turning curves back on itself, to proceed in a westerly direction, actually running parallel to both High St and the coast, for a time, prior to curving back to advance towards the sea, crossing over the railway and arrowing through a hopeless mishmash of farmland, from which jut skeletal frameworks of to-be-finished buildings. The coastline is awful, the undulating pebble shore appearing to be the beneficiary of most of the waste bamboo terracing, in all of Greece! Definitely 'polluded'! God knows where the campsite has gone, and after a good look down here, I'm sure most readers would not want to find the location. There are more signs to the Blue Dolphin. Back on the Old Road and at the eastern limits of Leheo, where the railway line is to the right, on the left is an enormous steelworks.

Beyond the turning signed for Ancient Korinthos (*See* Excursions To Korinthos Surrounds), is a long stretch of 10m wide, steeply shelving, pebble beach, appallingly litter bestrewn in places, but from which people swim. There are any number of campsites hereabouts.

At the 3km sign, Korinthos is manifestly 'looming large', with a really unpleasant build-up of disparate, unplanned development. Immediately beyond the 'milestone', the Old Road enters the suburbs of Korinthos.

I don't think he will catch many here! Elafonisi island

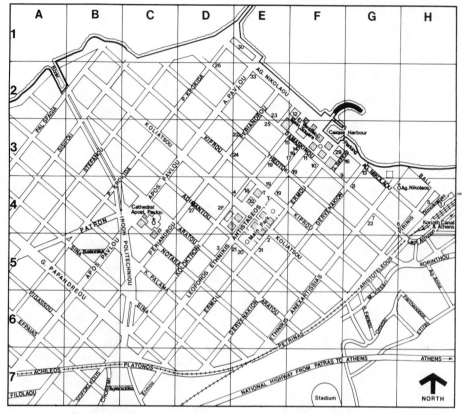

Tmr
1H4	Railway Station
2E4/5	Athens Bus Terminus
3D5	Peloponnese Bus Terminus
4D/E4	Local Bus station
5H4	Hotel Byron
6G/H4	Hotel Apollon
7G4	Hotel Acropolis
8F/G3/4	Hotel Konstantatos
9F/G3/4	Hotel Korinthos
10F3	Hotel Belle Vue
11F3	Hotel Akti
12E/F2/3	Hotel National Nederlanden
13G3/4	Cafe-bar Averoff
14E/F3	Restaurant Pantheon/Tea Room
15E/F3	Greek Food Takeaway
16F/G3	Taverna Theodorakis
17E/F3	Town Hall
18E4	Palace of Justice
19	Banks
20D/E5	Post Office
21D/E5	Liberopoulos Motor Rent
22	Bakers
23E2/3	Cine Lais
24D/E3	Central Market
25E2/3	Cafe Mordillo/Sound & Light Pub
26D1/2	Borsalino Club

27D4	Ladies Hairdresser's
28D/E4	OTE
29F/G3	Historical & Folklore Museum
30D/E1/2	Port police
31E5	Town police
32E4	Public toilets
33E1/2	Mykonos Piano Bar

† Church
T = Taxi rank
(Tmr) = Town map reference
(Fsw) = Facing seawards
(Sbo) = Sea behind one
(Fbqbo) = Ferry-boat Quay behind one

Illustration 5 Korinthos

4   KORINTHOS (Corinth)

Illustration 5

FIRST IMPRESSIONS: Rather barren appearance.

SPECIALITIES: Currants; sultanas.

VITAL STATISTICS: Tel prefix 0741; Pop. 16,0000.

HISTORY: Apart from particularly convoluted, mythological associations, Korinthos and its environs are steeped in a long, long history. In fact, Ancient Corinth was one of the most important of all the Greek city states, reaching its peak, its eminence between the 8th-4thC BC, boasting a population of ¾ million.

In the 8thC BC the city founded two western colonies, Syracuse and Corcyra. This highlighted the difficulty of spanning the isthmus on which Ancient Corinth was built, with the Gulf of Corinth to the west, leading to the outer Mediterranean, and the Aegean Sea to the east. To overcome this, and to maintain their nautical supremity, sometime in the 6thC BC, the Corinthians devised the scheme to build a canal. Hey, ho! So, nothing is new, only rehashed ideas! The cost and practical difficulties dissuaded them, as it did the Roman Emperor Nero, hundreds of years later, when he revived the scheme, in AD67.

Not to remain disadvantaged by the geography, the state caused to be constructed a paved track, or *Diolkos*, in the stones of which were cut parallel grooves. The latter were to guide the wheels of the 'transporters'. This 'railway', which stretched diagonally north-west to south-east, across the isthmus, enabled the fleet to be launched to the east or to the west, as required. It was the Corinthians who were supposed to have perfected the legendary *Trireme*, and it was these fighting ships that were loaded on to wheeled platforms, to be pulled along the *Diolkos*. Thus the navy could make equal use of the western port of *Lechaeum,* or the eastern facility at *Kenchreia*. It is interesting to note that, some 2000 years later, the surveyors of the existing canal settled on a line that almost exactly mirrored that of the ancient 'boatway'.

During the Peloponnese Wars (431-404BC) Ancient Corinth sided with Sparta, only to change sides, to Athens, in 395BC, thus starting the Corinthian Wars (395-387BC). The Macedonians conquered the state in 335BC. In 146BC Corinth was destroyed by the Romans, despite which Julius Ceasar subsequently caused it to be rebuilt, in 44BC. This reconstruction heralded a second period of great importance, during which Corinth was famed for its hedonistic ways, especially sexual excesses! Perhaps this led to St Paul preaching to the inhabitants, in about AD54, as recorded in the Apostle's Letters to the Corinthians.

Emperor Hadrian expended even greater amounts of state cash in erecting more magnificent buildings, between AD117-138, only for an earthquake to destroy much of the infrastructure, in AD357. This devastation was 'complemented' by invading Goths, who razed the city to the ground, in AD395. Nature finished off the job with an earthquake, in AD551. The area then lay dormant for some 500 years, until the Byzantine period, when the governor of the Peloponnese ensconced himself at (the now named) Korinthos. The revitalised city endured attacks from various 'passers-by', including the Normans, Franks, and Knights of St John, prior to the Turks sweeping all before them, in 1458. The Knights returned in 1612, and threw the Turks out, but were, in their turn, expelled by the Venetians, in 1687, who were then ousted by the Turks! The latter held sway until 1822, when, during the War of Independence, the Greeks finally recovered the site.

GENERAL The wasteground appearance of some of the waterfront may have a lot to do with the fact that the city has suffered from a series of major earthquakes, over the centuries. The most recent occurrences were in 1858, 1928 and 1981.

Much of the rebuilding has, of necessity, been carried out to the design parameters required to achieve quake-proof construction. Practical, but not pretty! On the other hand, the city is extremely spacious, if not inconveniently so, for those without transport. The streets are, in the main, laid out on a grid basis. The main avenue, a dual carriageway, is the tree-lined Leoforos Ethnikis Antistaseos. This is flanked, by the Palace of Justice (*Tmr* 18E4), on one side, and the Main Park (*Tmr* E4/5), on the other side. Lucky passers-by might observe, across the road from the Palace of Justice, one of those glorious, Victorian-old, all wood and tripod, pavement mounted cameras.

Readers must not be fooled by some of the cartographers romantic visions of the city's river. In actuality, it courses along a wide, concrete trough, all the way to the sea, but in the summer months the watercourse is dry. The quayside Main Sq, Plateia El Venizelou, is almost a piazza, bounded on the sea side by the caique harbour. A number of the 20m high, palm trees seem rather naked, their trunks starkly bare, all the way up to the topmost 'hair-piece' of shoots.

Truthfully, there is little reason to visit Korinthos, were it not for the nearby 'mega' attractions of the Korinth Canal, as well as the remains of Ancient Corinth and the hillside site of Acrocorinthos. If these were not sufficient unto the day thereof..., also in the area are other, if lesser historical sites. These encompass Ancient Isthmia, close by modern-day Isthmia, and Lechaeum Port (Lechaion), at Leheo.

ARRIVAL BY BUS Korinthos is a pivotal terminus for buses. Apart from daily services to and from Athens, it is a 'major' passenger distribution point for the Peloponnese. It is unfortunate that the three bus terminals serving, respectively, Athens, the Peloponnese and the city suburbs, are rather distant from each other, and the Railway station.

ARRIVAL BY FERRY Strangely, bearing in mind the focal transport positioning of Korinthos, there are no international or local services.

ARRIVAL BY TRAIN The Athens-Peloponnese railway line conveniently routes via the city, even if the Railway station is set apart from the centre of things.

THE ACCOMMODATION & EATING OUT

The Accommodation There is a pleasant mix of old and new hotels. They are scattered about the waterfront environs, and the lateral main streets, with a typically 1950s 'effort' close to the Railway station. As would be expected, the three bus stations are circled by the 'busiest' concentration of choice.

Across the wide road alongside the Railway Station (*Tmr* 1H4) is the:
Hotel Byron (*Tmr* 5H4) (Class D) 8 Dimokratias   Tel 22631
Directions: As above.
     A classic 1950s, two storey hotel, wherein all rooms share the bathrooms, with a single room costing 1620drs & a double 1870drs.

A block south along Odhos Pirinis, and to the right, immediately prior to the main road, is the:
Hotel Apollon (*Tmr* 6G/H4) (Class D) 18 Pirinis   Tel 25920
Directions: As above.
     Despite the classification, all the bedrooms have en suite bathrooms with singles priced at 2220/2490drs & doubles 3460/3990drs.

At the next junction to the west, along Odhos Damaskinou, and on the left, at the corner with Odhos Ethnikis Anexartissias, is the:
Hotel Acropolis (*Tmr* 7G4) (Class C) 25 E. Anexartissias   Tel 26568
Directions: As above. Prospective guests should note that this is a very noisy location, due to most of the Athens buses, as well as private traffic being routed along a one-way system, around this corner.
     All bedrooms have en suite bathrooms, with a single room costing 4500/5300drs & a double 5400/6300drs.

Still further west, actually north-west, is the:
Hotel Konstantatos (*Tmr* 8F/G3/4) (Class C) 3 Dervenakion Tel 22120
Directions: As above, in a modern block, and on the right (*Railway Station behind one*), close to the nearside of the junction of Damaskinou & Dervenakion Sts.
     An en suite single bedroom is priced at 7000drs & a double room 8500/10000drs, per night.

In the next block, west along Damaskinou St, and also on the right, is the:
Hotel Korinthos (*Tmr* 9F/G3/4) (Class C) 26 Damaskinou   Tel 26701
Directions: As above.
     All bedrooms have en suite bathrooms, with a single charged at 4800/5800drs & a double 6200/7400drs.

Further north-west, with the caique harbour away to the right (*Railway Station behind one*), and on the left of Odhos Damaskinou, are two older-style, two storey high hotels, the:
Hotel Belle Vue (*Tmr* 10F3) (Class C) 41 Damaskinou   Tel 22068
Directions: As above, at the nearside of the block.
     All rooms share the bathrooms, with doubles only charged at 4500/5400drs.

And the:
Hotel Akti (*Tmr* 11F3) (Class D) 1 E. Antistaseos   Tel 23337
Directions: In the same block as the *Belle Vue*, but the far side.
All bedrooms share the bathrooms, with singles costing 1600/1800drs &
doubles 3200/3500drs.
Incidentally, between the *Belle Vue* and the *Akti* is a 'dead' cinema, perhaps
another victim of the increased availability of television and videos. Still
closer to the quayside, on the west side of El Venizelou Sq, is the package
holiday *Hotel National Nederlanden* (*Tmr* 12E/F2/3).

The Eating Out The smartest, as well as the most disreputable bars and
take-away joints are littered along the Esplanade and Damaskinou St,
many concentrated across the way from the waterfront Main Square
(*Tmr* F3). In amongst these are the:
Restaurant Pantheon/Tea Room (*Tmr* 14E/F3)
Directions: As above, and a smarty, whitewashed, old-fashioned,
high-ceilinged establishment with a very large floor area - rather Athens-like.
Despite the old-world appearance, the prices are modern enough, with
chicken costing 420drs, a dish of macaroni 650drs, macaroni pie 700drs, as
are spiced meatballs, veal with green peas are priced 920drs, and string
beans 520drs.

At the far corner of the same block, and in strict contrast, is an especially
Hellenic, ladies-popular, *Greek Food Take-away* (*Tmr* 15E/F3) with a blind-
shaded patio across the street, and serving giro pita, as well as chicken.
Fairly close by, on the west side of the waterfront Main Square, is a large,
single storey building, dominated by the fairly popular *Hambro Restaurant*,
wherein the decor is 'Neon 1930'.

A true, 'dyed in the retsina', ethnic little rural number, is the:
Taverna Theodorakis (*Tmr* 16F/G3)
Directions: From the landscaped quay, to the left (*Sbo*) of the caique harbour
is extensively used as a lorry and car park. The taverna is on the left of Odhos
Seferi, edging a large plot of bombsite wasteland. The dining room is old-
fashioned, low-ceilinged and cellar-like, with the traditional, summer-dead,
stove pipe heater prominent.
An excellent, very palatable, piping hot meal, for two, of Greek salad
(500drs), kalamari (scrumptious, 800drs), a plate of chips (200drs), a
water-bottle full of apo vareli (open wine - 200drs), bread and tip (150drs),
cost a total of 2650drs. And regulars may well receive an 'on the house' small
bottle of retsina.

Close to the Local Bus station (*Tmr* 4D/E4) is a nice man serving stick &
bread souvlaki, whilst across the street, on the reverse side of the Palace of
Justice (*Tmr* 18E4), is a pleasantly cool, tree shaded area whereon are strung
out tables and chairs serviced by nearby kafeneions.
Incidentally, as would be expected, both the Peloponnese (*Tmr* 3D5) and
Athens Bus stations (*Tmr* 2E4/5) have a cafeteria incorporated within their
ticket office halls. Also close to the Peloponnese bus office, a metre or two
north along E. Antistaseos St, is a small, dark, hot, but more than welcome
(and welcoming) *Souvlaki Cafe-bar*, where it is possible to sit down. They
serve kortaki retsina.
It almost goes without writing, that the lifeless Railway Station (*Tmr* 1H4)
possesses a cafeteria.

THE A TO Z OF USEFUL INFORMATION

BANKS No shortage, with seemingly dozens present, and at least four of the 'heavyweights' grouped together. These include the **National** (*Tmr* 19E/F3/4), close to the corner of E. Antistaseos and Theotoki Sts, the **Commercial** (*Tmr* 19E3/4), alongside the junction of E. Antistaseos and Kiprou Sts, and, across the avenue, the **Bank of Crete** (*Tmr* 19E/F4). There is yet another 'Eurocheque bank' next door to the Post Office (*Tmr* 20D/E5).

BEACHES No town beach, so (*See* Routes One & Two).

BICYCLE, SCOOTER & CAR HIRE As might be expected of a 'one-stop', way-station of a city-halt, there aren't many establishments.

Liberopoulos Motor Rent (*Tmr* 21D/E5) 27 E. Antistaseos St   Tel 72937
Directions: On the left (*Sbo*), beyond the Main Park, and established in 1934.
     In fact, the friendly proprietor, who may well be found repairing one of his steeds at the roadside, if not the gutter, only hires scooters. The doors open between 0830-1330hrs & 1730-2030hrs. A Vespa/scooter costs 3000drs a day, with a 10% discount for a minimum of 3 days hire.
     In order to hire a car it is only necessary to cross the road, and walk a few paces to the south to **Grig Lagos Rent A Car**, at No 42   (Tel 22617). If the shop appears closed, simply wander down the alley to one side. The hours appear to be roughly the same as those of *Liberopoulos*.

BOOKSELLERS To purchase English language newspapers and books, it is necessary to travel the 7km to the Korinth Canal.

BREAD SHOPS Considering the size of Korinthos, there are not many about. There is a **Baker** (*Tmr* 22G4/5) alongside the *Hotel Acropolis*, and yet another **Baker** (*Tmr* 22D/E3) the other side of the street to, and north of the Market (*Tmr* 24D/E3).

BUSES As already advised, there are three Bus stations. The **Athens Terminus** (*Tmr* 2E4/5) also serves the surrounding area, up to 35km distant, mainly to the south and south-east of Korinthos.

Bus timetables
(a) Athens Terminus (*Tmr* 2E4/5)
Korinthos to Athens (Tel 25645)
Daily   0600-2130hrs, every hour.
Return journey
Daily   0530-2100hrs, every hour.
One way fare 1000drs; duration 1½hrs.
NB The bus from Athens can be caught for the north coast journey to Patras.
Korinthos to Ancient Corinth (Arhaea Korinthos)
Daily   0710-2110hrs, every hour
Return journey
Daily   0730-2130hrs
One-way fare 120drs (tickets on the bus); duration 20mins
Korinthos to Loutraki (north of the Canal)
Daily   0600-2100hrs, every half-hour, 2210hrs
One-way fare 150drs; duration 20mins
Korinthos to Nemea (south-west of Korinthos, for Ancient Nemea)
Daily   0720, 1000, 1215, 1330, 1530, 1900, 2100hrs
One-way fare Nemea 390drs; Ancient Nemea 360drs

Korinthos to Sofiko (south-east of Korinthos)
Daily   0730, 0900, 1100, 1200, 1300, 1400, 1700, 1830, 2000hrs
Korinthos to Athikia (south of Korinthos)
Daily   0615, 0845, 1030, 1200, 1400, 1600, 1800, 2000hrs
Korinthos to Klenia (south of Korinthos, for ruins of Tenea)
Daily   1130, 1215, 1330, 1700, 2000hrs
Korinthos to Katakali (south-east of Korinthos)
Daily   1400, 1830hrs
Korinthos to Ag Ioannis (south of Korinthos)
Daily   0615, 1815hrs
Korinthos to Angelokastro (south-east of Korinthos)
Daily   1700hrs
Korinthos to Spathovouni (south-west of Korinthos)
Daily   1330hrs
Korinthos to Limnes (south of Korinthos)
Daily   1330, 1700hrs
Korinthos to Korfos (south-east of Korinthos)
Daily   1400hrs
Korinthos to Isthmia (east of Korinthos)
Daily   0930, 1200, 1300, 1630, 2000hrs

(b) Peloponnese Terminus (*Tmr* 3D5, tel 24403) is rather incongruous.
Korinthos to Nafplio, via Fichtio (for Mycenae) & Argos
Daily   0700-2130hrs, every hour.
One-way fares   to Fichtio 380drs; duration 45mins
                            to Argos   470drs;   "   1hr
                            to Nafplio 600drs;   "   1¼hrs
Korinthos to Sparta, via Tripoli
Daily   8 connections a day.
One-way fares   to Tripoli 1100drs; duration 2hrs
                            to Sparta 1550drs;   "   3hrs.
Korinthos to Kalamata
Daily   7 connections a day.
One-way fare 1900drs; duration 4hrs.

(c) **The Local Bus Station** (*Tmr* 4D/E4) services the city suburbs and outlying destinations to the west.

CAMPING The two competing campsites, **Camping Corinth** and **Blue Dolphin Camping** are 'big on signs' at the Railway station. These conveniently detail which buses to catch.
    Camping Corinth (Tel 25767), some 3km distant, reckons it is the biggest and nearest to the city, whilst Blue Dolphin Camping (Tel 27967), similarly distant, is of the opinion that it is the only one 'on the beach', and for which catch the Leheo bus. Rates are averagely 550drs per head and 450drs for a tent. Both are to the west, where the Old Highway edges the outer suburbs shoreline, which, in places is quite wide, if mainly pebble and disfigured with rubbish. Some of the beach is fine, gritty sand, close to the water's edge, but it is hard not to come to the conclusion that the sea is rather polluted.

CHILDCARE Not surprisingly, there aren't any baby-sitting services. The Main Park is a pleasant area, with an aviary, whilst, to the left (*Fsw*) of the quayside Main Sq, beyond the *Hotel National Nederlanden* (*Tmr* 12E/F2/3), is a children's playground.

CINEMA Close to the outset of the western end of Damaskinou St, and on the right (*Main Sq behind one*), is the **Cine Lais** (*Tmr* 23E2/3).

COMMERCIAL SHOPPING AREA In addition to the usual stores, there are a number of smart shops scattered about the city, but fortunately there is a modest Central Market (*Tmr* 24D/E3).

DISCOS The canyon-like, west end of Damaskinou St is 'rock-music alley' with, on the left (*Main Sq behind one*), the *Cafe Mordillo* and adjacent *Coffee Sound & Light Pub* (*Tmr* 25E2/3), the last named located on the building's first floor, whilst the ground floor seems to be permanently closed. Although they both appear 'dead by day', as dusk falls these establishments absolutely throb with sound, and Greek youth, the latter spilling out over the pavement in a human tide of bodies. For those of a sporting instinct, next door is a pinball arcade! Also in this street, grouped close to the junction of Damaskinou and P. Krokida Sts, are the: *Grasshopper Pub/Cocktails*, on the right; the neon-light flashing *Oneiro*; and the *Ouzerie Barnecko*. The *Mykonos Piano Bar* (*Tmr* 33E1/2) edges the parallel street of Odhos Ag Nikolaou, immediately to the east of the Port police/Customs building. Continuing back towards Plateia El Venizelou, is the popular *Porto Rico*, where they serve bottled *Henninger*, and a few paces further on, at a 'bit of a jink' in the street, is the *Anaximanda Pub/Cafeteria* - 'We speak Englich (*sic*), French and German', followed by a childrens' playground. A sample of the prices, in these juke-box thumping, disco-beat establishments, are as follows: orange juice 250drs; Chivas Regal whisky 850drs; Cutty Sark Whisky, Tequila, Drambuie and Tia Maria, all 600drs; 3 Star Greek Brandy 300drs; French brandy 750drs; French champagne 4950drs a bottle; and special cocktails 700drs. Mmh!

ELPA The office of this Hellenic equivalent of the UK Automobile Association/RAC is distantly located, beside the National Highway, on the left-hand side of the eastern, Athens bank of the Korinth Canal.

HAIRDRESSERS As usual, the chaps are adequately looked after. There is at least one **Ladies Hairdressers** at No 59 Adimantou St (*Tmr* 27D4).

LAUNDRY The 'proper' launderette, **Krenos**, 77 Koliatsou St, appears to have been 'thoroughly' closed, but there is a conventional **Dry Cleaners** in the same block as the Peloponnese Bus Terminal (*Tmr* 3D5), on Leoforos E. Antistaseos.

LUGGAGE STORE There is one at the Railway station (*Tmr* 1H4).

MEDICAL CARE
Chemists & Pharmacies Plentiful, and apart from one or two edging Odhos Koliatsou, there is a **Chemist** (*Tmr* E/F3/4) on the left (*Fsw*) of Leoforos E. Antistaseos, in the block bounded by the streets of Theotoki and Kiprou.
Dentists There are any number, including one at No 59 (*Tmr* D5/6) Leoforos E. Antistaseos, south of the junction with Odhos Notara.
Hospital About one kilometre east of the Railway station, on the left of Leoforos Athinon, *en route* to the Korinth Canal.

MUNICIPAL TOURIST OFFICE/NTOG None!

OTE (*Tmr* 28D/E4) Bordering Kolokotroni St. The doors are open daily, between 0700-2400hrs.

PARKING No problem, in such a spaced out city as this, with a conveniently landscaped park-cum-car park, to the immediate right (*Fsw*) of the caique harbour (*Tmr* F/G2/3).

PETROL Although there aren't many city filling stations, there are any number alongside the approach roads.

PLACES & EVENTS OF INTEREST Most of these are covered in Excursions to Korinthos Surrounds.
Churches:
Apostolou Pavlou Cathedral (*Tmr* C4). Possesses a separate, rather splendid clock tower on which all four clock faces show the same, and correct time.
Ag Nikolaos (*Tmr* G/H3/4) To the east of the quayside parking. A rather grand church with an adjacent set of bells roofed over with a corrugated iron roof.
Museums
Historical & Folklore (*Tmr* 29F/G3) A very smart, five storey high, designer-building, on an island site, towards the right-hand (*Fsw*) end of the Commercial quay, close by the caique harbour. Exhibits reflect the title, plus traditional costumes and crafts. Open daily between 0830-1300hrs, except Mondays.
Park, Main (*Tmr* E4/5) The elongated gardens are pleasantly landscaped, with any amount of seats, as well as a wired-off aviary enclosing some rather beady eyed birds.

POLICE
Port (*Tmr* 30D/E1/2) At the far, west end of the port quayside.
Town (*Tmr* 31E5) The cop-shop looks out over the Main Park. There is supposed to be a Tourist police department, but... There is a telephone number.

POST OFFICE (*Tmr* 20D/E5) The modern building boasts safety deposit boxes, and faces north along the Main Park.

SPORTS FACILITIES The local football club might give a visitor a game, and might not.

TAXIS (*Tmr* T) The main rank is either side of Leoforos E. Antistaseos, about where the avenue is straddled by the Palace of Justice and the north end of the Main Park.

TELEPHONE NUMBERS & ADDRESSES
Hospital   Tel 25711
Taxis (*Tmr* T)   Tel 24844
Tourist police (*Tmr* 31E5) 51 Ermou St   Tel 22143

TOILETS Apart from the facilities at the Railway station (*Tmr* 1H4), there is a block (*Tmr* 32E4) alongside Leoforos E. Antistaseos. The latter are quite clean, combining both squatties and seatless sit-downs. The Bus termini also have their own 'offerings'.

TRAINS The Railway Station (*Tmr* 1H4) is in a lifeless, downtown neck of Korinthos - no tourist office, nor souvlaki snackbar. This pivotal Peloponnese terminus passengers to catch the west-about, or east-about route to Kalamata.

Train timetables
Korinthos to Kalamata (west bound)
Daily dept   0848, 1200, 1333, 1533, 1708, 2326hrs.

Xilokastro	0926,	1235,	1403,	1606,	1746,	0041hrs.
Diakofto	1015,	1329,	-	1646,	1835,	0052hrs.

(for Kalavrita)

Egio	1033,	1347,	1455,	1704,	1856,	0111hrs.
Patras	1117,	1445,	1528,	1744,	1954,	0154hrs.
Pirgos	1342,	1655,	-	1950,	2219,	0405hrs.

(for Olympia).

Kiparissia	1507,	1818,	-	2103,	-	0523hrs.
Kalamata	1702,	2013,	-	-	-	0717hrs.

Korinthos to Kalamata (east bound)

Daily dept	0922,	1111,	1623hrs.
Mikines	1011,	-	1714hrs.
Argos	1022	1210,	1726hrs.
Tripoli	1147,	1327,	1855hrs.
Kalamata	1438,	1549,	2148hrs.

Korinthos to Athens

Daily dept	0402, 0428, 1110, 1159, 1335, 1433, 1552, 1646, 1748, 2035, 2145, 2305hrs
Athens	0543, 0628, 1309, 1355, 1523, 1608, 1742, 1900, 1922, 2219, 2342, 0045hrs.

Return

Athens dept	0650, 0730, 0930, 1000, 1200, 1340, 1430, 1503, 1700, 2128hrs.
Korinthos	0848, 0923, 1111, 1200, 1333, 1533, 1623, 1708, 1830, 2336hrs.
One-way fares	to Athens 910drs
	to Patras 1150drs
	to Olympia 1500drs
	to Argos 480drs
	to Tripoli 1050drs

TRAVEL AGENTS & TOUR OFFICES Although some are listed, they are rather noticeable by their lack of brouhaha. Three or four firms are grouped on Damaskinou, Leoforos E. Antistaseos and Koliatsou Sts.

EXCURSIONS TO KORINTHOS SURROUNDS (Illus. 6)

Excursion to the Korinth Canal (circa 7km). Travellers who arrive by train, at Korinthos, should bear in mind that it is a long, hot, dusty walk to the Canal. Furthermore, the way is mostly besides a very busy, unattractive stretch of highway, and the first kilometre or so is uphill. You have been warned. Why not catch the bus?

The route along Leoforos Athinon passes by the city's hospital, a bus depot of sorts, where there is a restaurant, as well as a stick and bread souvlaki hut, a 'mess' of car and lorry repair yards, oil change pits, tyre outfits, scrapyards, garage and service sheds, souvenir shops, boat sales enclosures, pottery showrooms, a bottle and crate yard, and a few industrial plants. The aforementioned presages the outbreak of canal-based tourist enterprises. These encompass, for instance, *Jax Donuts*, a Chinese pagoda-like motel (yes, a Chinese...), Greek art showrooms, a hamburger/toast snackbar, a massive supermarket, a large Bus station, as well as any number of snackbars, souvenir stalls, foreign language newspaper and book shops. The location gets very busy and postcards are outrageously expensive.!

Both Old and New Highways narrow down and combine to cross over the canal on a bailey bridge style dual carriageway. The railway has its own bridge, to the north-west of the road crossing.

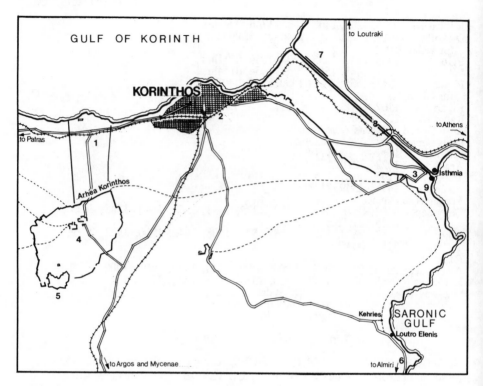

GULF OF KORINTH

to Loutraki

KORINTHOS

to Patras

Arhea Korinthos

to Athens

Isthmia

Kehries

SARONIC
GULF

Loutro Elenis

to Argos and Mycenae

to Almiri

Key

1   Lechaeum (Lechaion) Port
2   New Korinthos
3   Isthmia
4   Ancient Corinth
5   Acrocorinth

6   Hellen's Bath
7   The Diolkos
8   The Korinth Canal
9   Ancient Kenchreia Port

Illustration 6 The Ancient Surrounds of Korinthos

There is a certain fascination about the arrow straight, deep sided, rough hewn, rock face cutting, at the bottom of which lies the Canal. Any yachts on passage look tiny, but tug drawn passenger liners almost fill the channel, literally.

The history of the site has been sketched in the historical introduction to Korinthos City. In its planning, the affair is rather reminiscent of a United Kingdom motorway, for the initial 'gleam in the eye' was as early as the Corinthians supremacy, between the 8th and 5thC BC! In AD40 Emperor Caligula commissioned engineers to survey the site, but Egyptian constructors persuaded them that there was a difference in the water levels of the Gulf of Korinth and the Saronic Gulf. They argued that, as the western waters were (supposedly) higher, if the canal were dug, the Argo-Saronic island of Aegina would be submerged! In AD67 Emperor Nero caused work to start, from both ends, an effort that ceased with his death. It is interesting that he, and the earlier Corinthians, chose very much the same line of construction as the actual digging, which took place some 1800 years later, between 1881-1893. The Canal is 6½km long, the height of the cutting is 90m, the width is 30m, the depth of water is 7½m, and a path tracks the western edge.

On the north side of the west bank is a caravan Post Office, where currency exchange can be transacted, and which is open daily, between 0800-2000hrs, except Sundays, when the hours are 0900-1800hrs.

In conclusion it is to be hoped that no visitor, who simply stops off here, judges the rest of Greece by this almost uncontrolled hurdy-gurdy. It would be similar to landing at Heathrow, driving around the M25, stopping off at the Reigate motorway cafe, and then summing up one's impression of England, prior to returning to Heathrow!

Excursion to Isthmia village (Circa 7½km) **& on to Loutro Elenis and Kato Almiri** (circa 13km). Take the road to the Canal. Close to the same, and alongside the aforementioned *Jax Donuts*, turn right. The countryside is 'standard', and a slip road leads to the unimpressive looking:

Isthmia Museum Located close by the ancient site where are the remains of a sanctuary and stadium, with the starting line still visible. This stadium was the venue for bi-annual, pan-hellenic games, first staged in 582BC, and which continued on during Roman rule.

A branch road to the right descends to the modern-day village of:
ISTHMIA (circa 8½km from Korinthos) This straddles the south-east end of the canal cutting, at sea level, with the majority of the settlement on the eastern bank. To solve the problem of access, the canal is bridged, and to solve the problem of lack of height, the bridge has a mechanism by which it is lowered to the bed of the canal - clever! This explains the fact that even on a very dry day, it often appears to have been raining, but only on the sopping-wet steelwork of the bridge.

The tree shaded streets of the spacious, tourist absent, pretty little village are laid out on a grid formation, with, on the east bank a not very wide but sandy sweep of beach.

Apart from a Post Office, there are two splendidly situated refreshment establishments on either side of the canal mouth. The aptly named *Cafe Isthmia Bridge* is on the west bank, whilst a taverna is close to the eastern 'mouth of the cutting'. The tugs used to guide shipping through the canal are berthed at the village quayside. For those travellers who wish to escape the depredations of other tourists, this is a haven of peace and serenity.

From the turning down to Isthmia village, the main coastal road continues southwards, allowing views out over the pretty looking main bay on which lie Loutro Elenis and Kato Almiri. There are any number of filling stations. Immediately beyond the first glimpse, the route rumbles past a Korinth city rubbish dump! Next along is a side-turning down to the swish *Kalamaki Beach Hotel*.

KEHRIES (approx 10km from Korinthos) The hamlet strings along the roadside, edging a pleasant, small pebble and shingle beach cove, on which are drawn up a few fishing boats, but entirely unsuitable for swimming. This is followed by a longer, wider sweep of similar but rubbish bestrewn beach, with a sandy foreshore, and bordered by a tree shaded, 'local' campsite. The road rises up from Kehries, prior to dropping down to:

LOUTRO ELENIS (approx 11km from Korinthos) Tel 0741. The first of two very Hellenic, similar, rather scrappy resorts, straggling along the main road, with a scattering of shops, restaurants and reasonably smart, modern hotels.

A long stretch of pebble beach is accessed along a slip road, which incidentally tracks through to Kato Almiri.

The main road businesses include: *Villa Stella Apartments; Hotel Politis* (Class B, tel 33249), where en suite single rooms cost 7000drs & doubles 10000drs; and the *Hotel Kakanakos* (Class C, tel 33211), with en suite bathrooms, a single charged at 2600/3820drs & a double 3820/4875drs.

The highway tavernas tend to be of the open-air, country and western, lamb or chicken shack type, are not inexpensive and belt out ear-splitting live music of a questionable quality. A sample meal, for two, of lamb with kidneys (500gm & 900drs each), a plate of chips (cold, sparse & 150drs), a Greek salad (450drs), 2 cans of Amstel (200drs each), a bottle of drinking water (120drs), bread & service (50drs a head), totals 3020drs.

A few smarter restaurants and hotels edge the backshore and slip road, the latter including the *Hotel Belle Helene* (Class B, tel 33470), where the en suite single rooms, cost 4000/5500drs and 4500/6200drs for a double.

KATO ALMIRI (about 13km from Korinthos) Smaller than Loutro Elenis, a branch road tracks down to the waterfront Esplanade, mainly edged by scrubbly cafe-bars, set in scrubbly surroundings. The *Hotel Almiri Beach* (Class B, tel 33301), is supplemented by two campsites *Camping Poseidon* (Tel 33302) and *Camping Niarritz* (Tel 33441).

Perhaps the most interesting area is at the far, south end of Almiri. Here the track passes by a couple of out-of-place, smart, music hall style restaurant/cocktail bars, to an area of wire fence enclosed, small, now derelict salt flats. On these has been laid out a basket ball pitch. On the far right-hand side (*Fsw*) a freshwater stream courses into a walled, large

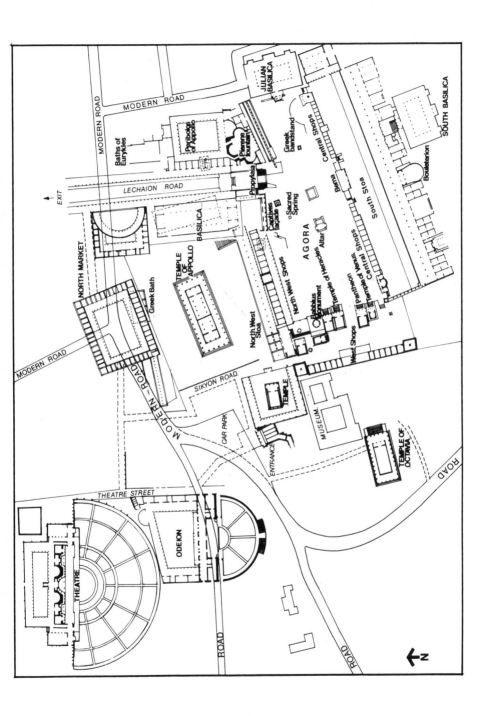

Illustration 7 Ancient Corinth

rectangular pond, set in a ruin of brick walls, and stone dwellings. In amongst these is bivouacked one Nikos, an elderly fisherman. The river disgorges into a narrow lagoon, crowded out with masses of sea rosemary.

Excursion to Arhea Korinthos for Ancient Corinth & Acrocorinth (circa 7km). (Illus. 7 & 8)
ARHEA KORINTHOS The village has sprung up to exploit the visitors to the two archaeological sites. Thus the main street and square, that edge the northern wall of the remains of Ancient Corinth, are crowded with a jostle of memorabilia shops and peripteros.

Perhaps the best direction of approach, if most unlikely, is from the south-east. This route allows splendid views out over the main body of the **Ancient Corinth archaeological site** (as the road drops down to the village proper). In the distance is the, towering, boulderous outcrop, around and on which are draped castellated walls and medieval remains, which dominates the whole surrounding area.

The main square of Arhea Korinthos, at the east end of the High St, is bordered by, amongst other businesses, cafe-bars/tavernas, a grocery, butcher, and, to one side, a signed, modern WC block. The latter is assiduously cleaned and presided over by a small, black-clothed lady. My choice of the establishments, at which to seek refreshment, is the *Zacharoplasteion Gretzino Sophios*. This is run by a smiley lady, with good English, where the excellent Nes meh ghala is served in pottery cups, with pottery saucers, but does cost 200drs. Next door is an establishment offering '...breakfast, coffee, bacon & eggs and orange juice'.

To the north-east of the main square, from alongside the glitzy *Marinos Car-bar Restaurant*, on the left of the Korinthos road 'out of town', is the Post Office, where were available, as recently as 1990, a range of what must be the cheapest postcards, in all of Greece. Despite, or perhaps because they were nothing to do with the local area's delights, they were priced at 8drs!

Continuing on beyond the Post Office, opposite a BP filling station, is *Tasso Rooms/Taverna*, presided over by its owner, the delightful, slight of build, silver-haired old character. Close by is a small, ruined, but under repair, mosque-like building, with a Turkish inscription over one of the door lintels, and the bus turn-round. Further on, at a road junction, is a notice proclaiming the delights of *Furnished Rooms Dimo Gerontas*, but they are 3km distant, on the road to the coast. Only about 1km away, along the same road, and adjacent to a ruined chapel, with a white wall enclosed, large graveyard, is *Rooms Restaurant Shadow*.

Turning right, at the aforementioned junction, leads up a hillside to a baker. More accurately, after the right, a left along a narrow side-street is necessary for the bread. Whilst hereabouts, and not turning off to the left (for the baker), but continuing straight on, advances towards probably the most interesting accommodation in town, namely:
Rooms Marinos, Argous St   Tel 31209
Directions: As above, on top of the low hill, to the east side of ArheaKorinthos village. Also accessible, to those approaching from the south-east, by turning right, prior to the village and ruins.

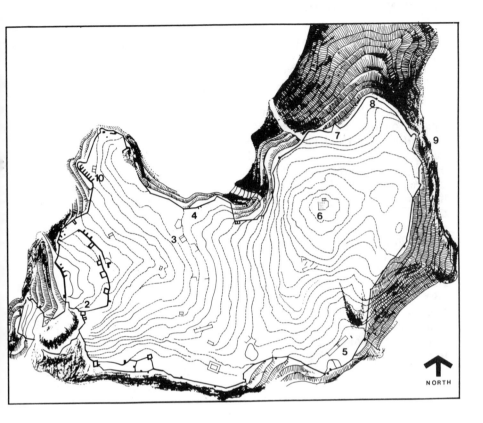

Key

1   Moat & Outer Gate
2   Inner Gate
3   Mosque
4   Little Gate
5   Upper Peirene

6   Eastern Summit
7   North East Gate
8   Outer Gate
9   Eastern Approach
10 House Remains

Illustration 8 Acrocorinthos Archaeological Site

The middle-aged husband and wife team of this swept-up, if home-from-home pension, set in a spacious garden, are really very pleasant. He speaks the most English, she is 'mumsy', and doesn't miss an opportunity to appraise enquirers of this fact. The nice, airy, double rooms have spacious bathrooms en suite, which cost 3500drs a night, including breakfast.

The village police station is between Rooms Marinos and the village main square, on the left of the south-east approach. Apart from a number of fascinating, little old stores hidden away, there is a dry-cleaners, some public telephones, a taxi rank (Tel 31464), with an empty-of-prices black-board, and, on Sundays, a street market that ranges along the High St. At the west end of the High St is a spacious excursion coach and car park. To the north and adjacent of the latter is a now abandoned *Xenia Hotel* - most of the windows are broken and the reception rooms are in ruins.

The tour buses start to arrive at about 0930hrs and are in 'real' earnest by 1030hrs, so best to plan any visit to the site, prior to that time. Once the evening 'dusks', the village almost empties out - until the next day dawns.

Ancient Corinth Archaeological Site (& Museum) (Illus. 7) Open weekdays 0800-1800hrs, Sat, Sun & hols 0830-1500hrs. Closed Jan-March, Easter Sun, & Dec 25th. Entrance 1000drs. To gain admission it is necessary to climb the High St, to the west, and proceed around to the left. The exit is smack in the middle of the village. The entrance displays the usual caveats in respect of dressing decently, as well as forbidding video cameras.

The museum has a dedication, 'This building was erected in 1931 by Ada Small Moore, in memory of Edward Elonso Small, a Greek scholar'.

Mythological associations have Oedipus growing up here as an infant, with his foster parents. Due to being rebuilt by Julius Ceasar, in 44BC, after being laid waste in 146BC, most of the remains are Roman. During the Roman suzerainty, when Ancient Corinth had a 15km long perimeter wall, the inhabitants gained a reputation for excesses of the flesh.

Any introduction to Ancient Corinth must advise that it is one of the most amazing, most fantastic of all Greece's site's. The museum is superb, even if the adjacent toilets are grotty. A criticism is that most of the layout is unlabelled, thus it is advisable to purchase one of the excellent English language guide books, costing about 650drs, prior to gaining admission.

The everyday spirit of Greece is not lost though, as the lovely fountain might well be empty of water, despite a plentiful supply in the vicinity, but is usually full of empty crisp packets and Coke tins!

Ancient Acrocorinth (Illus. 8). Open daily between 0830-1800hrs, with entrance costing 400drs. The hilltop site can be reached by taxi (at around-trip cost of about 2000drs) along an initially surfaced road. This sets out from the west side of Arhea Korinthos village, beyond the entrance to the Archaeological site, but becomes no more than a bulldozed swathe. Otherwise it is a one & half/two hour, 4km hike, so walkers must bear in mind the usual rejoinders to wear sensible clothing, including a hat, and to pack some drinking water. There is a cafe-bar taverna, prior to the citadel's entrance, which is open usually between 0900-2100hrs.

Although this sixty acre site cum mountain top Acropolis (575m high), was settled in ancient times, the main fortifications are attributable to the Byzantines, Franks, Venetian and Turks, in that order. The importance of the location, and its occupation, can be realised if it is appreciated that supposedly, prior to modern-day air pollution, it was possible to see, and be seen from the Athens Acropolis.

The libertine behaviour of the Corinthians, under Roman rule, which resulted in St Paul's pulpit-thumping Epistles, can be appreciated by the fact that the Temple to Aphrodite was in the charge of some thousand sacred ladies - of the night! Where's that religion gone?

ROUTE TWO (Illus. 9)
To Nafplio via Sanctuary of Epidavros, Galatas, Ermioni, Portoheli & Tolo (circa 206km). From Kato Almiri (Excursion from Korinthos), the main road climbs into the low, lovely, pine tree forest-clad, mountainside. The route gently chicanes from side to side, allowing glimpses out over the Saronic Gulf, even if the distant, mainland coastline, to the north-east, is rather spoilt by a huge refinery at Megara.

At about 29km, a left-hand track makes off to **Monastery Ag Marinis,** with the mountain plain village of **Sofiko** to the right. There are several filling stations scattered along the roadside. At 30km, a pleasant, ten kilometre long metalled side road makes off to the left. Proceeding along this, allows magnificent views over the offshore islands of **Diaporii, Ag Ioannis, Ag Thomas** and **Ipsili,** with **Aegina island** in the distance, as well as the small coastal plain on which lies:

KORFOS (40km from Korinthos) Tel 0741. To the nearside is a marshy area, followed by a pretty spit of land which projects into the sea. Some tree cover encourages a few camper-vans and tents to corral there. Beyond this, in the crook of a wide, 'U' shaped, pebble edged bay, that continues on round to a headland, is the main body of the settlement. A few of the olive trees are very old.

Korfos is a languid find and still, in essence, a fishing boat village... , but is in the very early stages of exploitation.

At the outset of the settlement is the two storey, low-key *Hotel/Taverna Mirto* (Class D, tel 95231), followed by *Rooms*. At this near end, the beach is rather scrubbly, with the *Hotel Argo* (Class C, tel 95258) on the left, which only offers furnished suites at a cost of 12500/16500drs. Hereabouts the shoreline is broken up by an outcrop of rocks. The *Hotel Korfos* (Class B, tel 95217), with en suite singles costing 3500drs & doubles 4500drs, is another two storey, 1930s style building.

A sweep of shore heralds the village proper, whereat a small supermarket, and several quayside tavernas. Across the road are a number of *Rooms*, a 'Navy Club' bar, beyond which is the oldest part of Korfos, which runs out as the bay sweeps on to the east. There is a rather well organised childrens' playground and buses make the journey here.

My favourite, central taverna (next door to an 'extended' periptero), with accommodation and an awning sheltered patio on the water's edge, is *George's Rooms/Taverna* (Tel 95220). George Ntaskas is a very nice man,

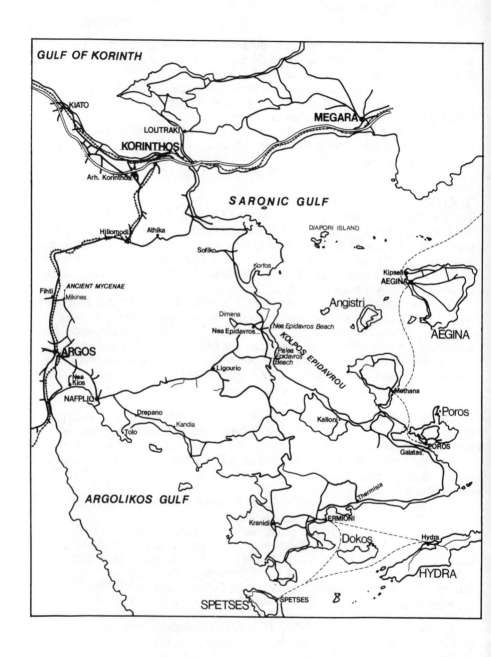

Illustration 9 Routes Two & Three

with good English, and a rather crone-like mother, who 'lurks'. Most of the guests are German, who usually know a good thing when they can grab it, in addition to a few cognoscenti English yachties. A double room costs 3000drs a night, and apartments are available at a price of 5000drs.

Both George's and Korfos are excellent locations - be sure to visit before the inevitable 1990s development spoils the place.

Returning to the main route, the mountain countryside is as before, with similar views. The road falls sharply towards a chisel-shaped cove, which 'houses' a fish farming enterprise. A small windmill has been attractively converted to a private dwelling, and at about 41km the **Monastery Agnoundos** is on a rise, to the left. Some of the distant, granite mountaintops are so white that they appear to be snow-covered, whilst others support trees, all the way to their summit.

At 45km, a side road is indicated to New Epidavros Beach, almost immediately followed by the sign for:
NEA EPIDAVROS & Nea Epidavros Beach (46km from Korinthos) Tel 0753. Selecting the beach first, the broad road immediately narrows down to a tarmac covered, if donkey wide path, bordered by massed orange groves. The access road passes by a *Rooms*, a motel of sorts, a snackbar/restaurant, the occasional, single storey, wooden, family shack, then the fairly modern *Camping Nea Epidavros* (Tel 31296), on the right, and on the left *Camping Diamantis* (Tel 31239), which boasts a 'queen laundry' and mini-market. Set back from the shore, on the left-hand (*Fsw*), is the fairly modern, two storey *Hotel Avra* (Class E, tel 31294), where en suite singles cost 4100drs & doubles 5500drs. The Avra is followed by the *Hotel/Restaurant Marilena* (Class E, tel 31279), where a single room sharing is priced at 2000drs, and an en suite double 4000drs.

To the right, edging the somewhat scrubbly, narrow beach, of grey, fine & broad pebble, with some grey foreshore sand, is a small, simple taverna, beyond which the beach continues to sweep on. About centre is a fishing boat quay, the far side of which are some fishing boats and pedaloes pulled up on the shore. Even further on is a disco.

Up against the low, left-hand hillside is a bulrush lined inlet, in which small boats are moored. To the rear of this side is a football pitch, a messy area, on which are piled old lorry tyres. Despite the disjointed, drabness of this fairly large cove, the two hotels appear quite acceptable.

The town doesn't seem to me to be so new, more under total reconstruction. One of the only reasons to pop-in is to climb the steep, narrow street to the baker's, on the left, which sells puddingy bread, as well as pies, and where the lady serving speaks excellent American.

South of Nea Epidavros, off the main road, is a turning down to:
PALEA EPIDAVROS (circa 50km from Korinthos) Tel prefix 0753. This is a tree shaded, pretty, busy, 'swept-up' and prosperous seaside village, much of its wealth founded on oranges. The comparatively adjacent, world famous archaeological site of **Epidavros**, (some 16km distant), and the resultant 'drench' of tourists, from all over the world, might well have something to do with the overlay of well-being.

The access road 'bottoms-out' on the left-hand (*Fsw*) one, of two relatively small bays, which are divided by a massive headland. On the way down passes: the swish, two storey, classical building housing *Marialena Apartments/Restaurant* (despite which smartness, there are goats and sheep in the backyard); a supermarket; several *Rooms*, including one owned by Mr Epidgolfo; a terrace of shops; the nice looking *Hotel Epidavria* (Class D, tel 41222), where a double sharing the bathroom cost 2700drs; another *Rooms* (Tel 41207); a baker; a shop selling fruit (and ice cubes); and the *Hotel Maik* (Class C, tel 41213), where en suite single rooms cost 3500drs & doubles 6000drs, after which the street spills on to the spacious, landscaped Esplanade. The latter is bordered by a number of smart establishments, which include the: *Hotel/Restaurant Possidon* (Class C, tel 41211), with en suite doubles charged at 5500/6000drs; *Restaurant Zorba's*; *Hotel Maronika* (Class C, tel 41391), where en suite single rooms cost 4400drs & doubles 5500drs; *Hotel Christina* (Class C, tel 41451), who charge 3000/3500drs for an en suite single room & 3500/5500drs for a double room; and the *Hotel Aktis* (Class C, tel 41407), where en suite doubles cost 5520drs per night. There are a number of smart cocktail bar style establishments, with an attractive church and clock tower on the left.

Apart from the tourist aspects, Palea is a busy little fishing boat port. It is strange to reflect that, whereas nowadays the left-hand bay is the prime, major development, in the days of antiquity, the right-hand Gialassi Bay was predominant.

The seaward entrance to the left-hand bay harbour is marked by two, singular, solid looking beacons, starkly poking up out of the water. To the right, on the left-hand flank of the referred to peninsula (that blocks off that side and separates north and south waterfronts), is a pleasant, sandy spit of beach.

South from the Esplanade, along the road that skirts the bottom of the peninsula and links with the southern bay, wends by: the town and port Police, in side-by-side offices; *Rooms Elena*; *Rooms* (Tel 41207); a butcher; Post Office; another baker; and the *Hotel Rena/Taverna Kardia* (Class C, tel 41311), where all rooms have their own bathroom, singles costing 3500drs & doubles 4500drs. The 'en-suite' *Taverna Kardia* advertises that it is 'the taverna to the walnut wood (with) special Greek kitchen & grill. Salad of the season, ice coffee, long drinks, beer, wine from the village, good music, beautiful view'. Taverna to the...?

Incidentally, Travel Tours is set into the *Hotel Maik* building, as is the real estate business 'Mike's Apartments, Houses and Building Land for Sale'. Other 'did you know' information is that a taxi from Palea to Ancient Epidavros costs about 3500drs and one to Athens 22000drs.

The peninsula headland is archaeologically extremely interesting. It canbe accessed either from the Esplanade, which track passes by a football pitch and *Rooms*, or along an initially metalled route that angles off to the left of the Nafplio road, and connects Palea to the southern Gialassi Bay. Selecting the latter choice, alongside a simple farmstead on the right, and up against the gates of which are casually piled various amphora and bits and pieces, is a most unexpected, amazing, ancient Odeion. This was lost to sight over the centuries, due to the presence of an olive grove, some of the old trees of which, still incongruously, appear to sprout from the marble seats. I bet a few forks were bent when the grove was planted! The **Odeion Dionysos** dates from the 4thC BC, and many of the seats were fascinatingly inscribed with the names of those who endowed them.

A nearby chapel is very early Christian. On top of the peninsula, in amongst the olive groves, are various chunks of ancient masonry, whilst the southern flank has remains of a Cyclopean wall, best observed from the southern bay.

The previously referred-to **Gialassi Bay** is little developed, although it was the site of the harbour of Ancient Epidavros. The tarmacadamed road passes: through orange groves; by a taverna, as well as a surrealist concrete building, in which is located *Disco Kaparki*; the entrances to two hotels; *Camping Verdelis* (Tel 41425); and *Camping Nicholas II* (Tel 41218), which boasts a swimming pool. The hotels are the *Hellas* (Class C, tel 41226), charging 5420drs for an en suite single room & 6320drs for a double, and the *Apollon* (Class C, tel 41295), where en suite singles cost 4500/5000drs & doubles 5500/6700drs. The road slips down between the two campsites, both of which are well shaded, to a small pebble, 400m long, 5-7m wide beach which stretches away to either hand. This shore has been awarded a 'Golden Starfish'. No, this is not a spoof GROC accolade, but the proper Government job. Mmmh!

At the far, south end of the shore is supposedly the fabulous holiday home of the classical musician Askanarsi, or was, as he has sold it.

To wrap-up the description, I cannot resist reporting that, on my last visit, tied to a sign demanding 'No Camping', was the awning of a Greek camper van. Ho, hum!

From Palea Epidavros, there is only one route to follow to the ancient Sanctuary of Epidavros, the last 'staging post' for this site being:
LIGOURIO (64km from Korinthos) Tel prefix 0753. A rather grey, unattractive location, the outskirts of which are dominated by skeletal building frames popping up from the barren farmland. They are probably to house even more ceramic, souvenir and pottery shops!

The village core is more traditional, despite the restaurants. There is a baker, a barber's, a Post Office, several filling stations, a chemist and a taxi rank. I believe the *Oasis Restaurant* is to be recommended, and of the four or five hotels, the *Koronis* (Class D, tel 22267) is easily located. At the latter, bedrooms are available sharing bathrooms or with en suite facilities, singles priced at 2500/ 3000drs, and doubles 3000/3500drs.

One highlight, in this rather shabby village, is a small, eye-catching, Byzantine church, opposite which is a souvlaki-hut, set alongside a restaurant. The inhabitants strictly observe the siesta.

The 2km stretch to the Sanctuary passes by a Health Centre, prior to the pine tree shaded, almost tastefully landscaped, dual carriageway branching off to the left, to the:
Sanctuary of Epidavros (Illus. 10) Entrance costs 1000drs. The site is open between 0800-1900hrs weekdays, 0830-1500hrs Sun & hols, and closed

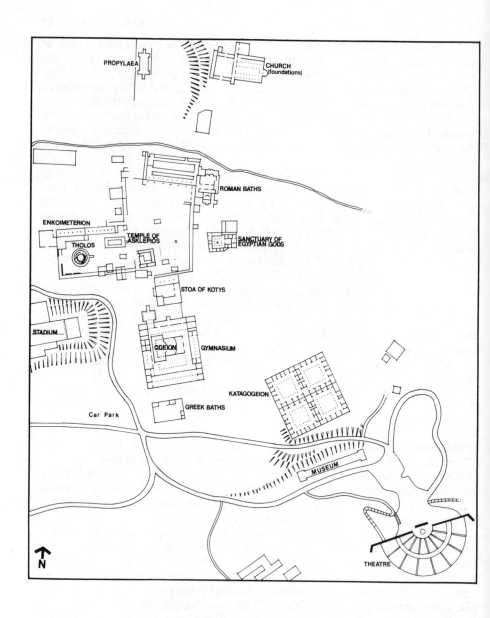

Illustration 10 Sanctuary of Epidavros

traditional days ie 1st Jan, 25th March, Easter Sunday & 25th December. The entrance fee includes admission to the museum, as long as visitors retain their ticket stub. The average guide book costs 800drs.

Epidavros was founded in the 6thC BC, as a religious and healing centre, rather than a fortified state. It was dedicated to the god Asklepios and although once as large as say Delphi or Olympia, the ruins are, in the main, visited because of the truly magnificent, exceptionally well-preserved, pine tree surrounded Theatre.

Construction of the latter probably started in the 3rdC BC, and was finally extended to 55 rows of steepling seats, to accommodate an audience of some 12000. Famed for its acoustics, the Odeion hosts a summer season of classical Greek plays and performances, presented by the National Theatre. The annual festival takes place between the end of June and the beginning of September, with performances starting at 2100hrs. Details can be obtained from the Athens Festival office (4 Stadiou St, Athens, tel 3221459), whilst the Epidavros box office telephone number is 21008. Rosemary, my constant companion on these research trips, ostensibly to save me falling over from the staggers, or other ailments, but who really comes along to contradict me, is of the opinion that the Epheseus Odeion, Turkey, has a prettier setting, but (mercifully) agrees there is no doubt that Epidavros is the more impressive.

Coaches arrive and depart, seemingly on an endless conveyor belt, parking in the spacious area provided. There is an *Xenia Hotel* (Class B, tel 22003), where double rooms sharing cost 3100/4700drs & en suite 5000/6600drs, per night. Signposts point to the public toilets, there is a Post Office caravan, telephones, a drinking water fountain, a stamp collectors' booth, and an oft shut Tourist information booth. Incidentally, water taps are thoughtfully spaced-out around the excavations. The museum, the entrance to which can be rather difficult to locate, is rather small, with the majority of the exhibits being friezes.

Buses depart from the entrance to the site, to: Nafplio at 0740, 1100, 1200, 1300, 1600 & 1800hrs; and Galatas at 1430hrs.

From the Sanctuary, the route crosses a dry, rolling, hummocky plateau, dotted about which are olive groves and plots of agricultural land. **Adami** village has a garage, filling station, a baker, kafeneion and a little chapel, decked with external bells. Marble working appears to be a local industry.

Continuing to aim for Methana, the route at first traverses a cultivated, rolling countryside, lacking much tree cover, prior to the road winding through rather boulderous scenery. From **Ano Fanari**, where the mountain plateau's edge is breasted, and there is a pretty little Byzantine church, there are magnificent views out to sea. These perspectives encompass the headland on which stands Methana, as well as the islands of **Angistri** and Aegina, with attractive panoramas along the coastline, as far as Kalloni.

Where the road descends steeply in the area of **Kalloni** (67km), it passes through orange and lemon groves, fig trees, orchards of apples and olives, as well as fields of carnations, for this is a renowned centre for the flowers. The spaced-out village has three or more filling stations, a kafeneion or two, and a general store.

The road parallels a narrow strip of grey shingle, polluted shoreline. The swathe of land between them is a bamboo swamp of now unworked salt pans. At about 114km, whereat a kafeneion, filling station and a shop, is the winding, 13km long turning off to the left that heads towards:

METHANA (127km from Korinthos) Tel prefix 0298. The seaside town is built on the south-east side of a tear-drop shaped, peninsula of land. The road circles round to the right, to approach along an attractive, if rocky section of coastline. This is edged by clear blue seas, where it is possible to have a dip, prior to swinging round and dropping down to cross over a causeway. A harbour is to the right, and a startlingly azure, sulphurous smelling, thermal lagoon to the left, the latter bordered by the long, low *Hotel Aiphai*, where all rooms have to share the bathrooms, and a single costs 2000drs & a double 3500drs. It must be noted that this hotel and the thermal baths are absolutely jam-packed with old people, taking the cure. To use the full thermal treatment it is necessary to have a doctor's certificate and attendance costs 300drs, whilst those in good heart (literally) can have a dip for 200drs. That is if any space can be found in the water.

Yes, Methana is a 'Kosta Geriatric' resort, peopled by extremely friendly and helpful inhabitants. The very wide, tree lined Esplanade, which runs north-south, is bordered by a massive sea wall, on the right, and the town on the left. From the outset, and proceeding from south to north along the Esplanade, almost immediately to the right is a car park and wide quay wall. To the south of this is the harbour, in which are berthed a noticeable number of private yachts. Strung along the north side of the quay is a seemingly failed, if substantial project bordering the town beach. There are abandoned changing rooms and a lido building. Even the beach showers no longer function. The pebble beach is rather kelpy, but it is pleasant to advise that after a few metres, the sea-bed becomes sandy.

On the town side of the Esplanade, interspaced by various streets and alleys, which climb to the parallel High St, are: the first floor offices of Methana Saronic Travel & Tourist Bureau; a Sosco filling station, alongside which the buses park; *Mr Lazaro's Taverna*, with external murals, and on which is fixed the bus timetable chalk board; a baker; a scooter & bicycle hire firm; several butchers; souvenir shops; tavernas; a cinema, close to the *Hotel Methanion* (Class C, tel 92227), where singles sharing cost 3000drs, a double sharing 3500drs & en suite 4000drs; and the 'dead' *Hotel Ghionis*.

Almost opposite the large Ferry-boat Quay, is a substantial lateral side-street, flanking a summer-dry river-bed, that also links with Odhos Konstantinou, the High St. A sign indicates the Police station and a taxi rank. Continuing along the Esplanade passes by: more shops; stores; and coffee bars, flanking two or three substantial buildings, that appear to be convalescent homes; and the *Hotel Avra* (Class B, tel 92382), where all rooms have en suite bathrooms, with a single charged at 4130/4540drs & a double 5740/6315drs. Beyond the *Avra*, the Esplanade goes on and on...

Many of the entrepreneurial shopkeepers bridge the large gap between the front of their building, and the roadside gutter, with awnings, so increasing their shop-floor space by the width of the pavement.

Ascending the aforementioned side-street, across the Esplanade from the Ferry-boat Quay, leads, as described, to the High St. Proceeding south passes by: an OTE, open weekdays 0800-2200hrs, Sun & hols 0900-1400hrs & 1700-2200hrs; the *Hotel Dima* (Class C, tel 92253), with an entrance in the adjoining street of Ag Triados, and where singles sharing the bathrooms are priced at 2900drs & doubles 3600drs, and doubles with an en suite bathroom 4700drs; souvenir stalls; a fruit & vegetable shop; Post Office; a zacharoplasteion; several stores; an old-fashioned dress shop; a pharmacy; mini-market; butcher; laundry; souvlaki snackbar; a yoghurterie; ironmongers; and a kafeneion.

Probably due to the overwhelming presence of the aged, meals are comparatively inexpensive, and eateries are denuded of dishes very early in the evening hours. For example, at the previously identified *Lazaro's Taverna*, a tasty, plentiful meal, for two, of a plate of stuffed tomatoes, a plate of spinach, two plates of super-fresh meatballs, with chips, ½kilo of retsina, bread & service, cost some 2000drs. All the family are involved, service is exceptional, and water was automatically placed on the table.

There is a clinic in a back street, behind the OTE, and the one and only rock/cocktail bar, the *Pub Every Day*, is a bit pushed for custom, not surprisingly in amongst all these 'crumblies'.

Bus timetable - the 'bus station' has already been located.
Methana to Nafplio & Argos
Daily   0915hrs

Ferry-boat & Hydrofoils This is a busy port of call, and craft arrive and depart from the main quay. Apart from excursion craft and scheduled ferries, there are hydrofoil services, the tickets for which are sold from desks close to the docking point.

Ferry-boat timetable
Outward (from Piraeus)

Day	Departure time	Islands/Ports of Call
Daily	1050, 1105, 1235hrs.	Poros
	1150, 1620, 1820, 2020hrs.	Poros, Hydra, Ermioni.
	1120hrs	Spetses.
	1130hrs	Poros, Hydra, Spetses, Portoheli.
Inward (to Piraeus)		
Daily	9 boats	Aegina, Piraeus.

Hydrofoil timetable
Outward (from Zea Port, Piraeus)

Daily, exc. Sun.	1710hrs	Poros, Hydra, Ermioni, Spetses, Potoheli.
Wed	0925hrs	Poros, Ermioni, Spetses, Leonidio, Kiparissi, Gerakas, Monemvassia, Kithira, Neapoli.
Inward (to Zea Port, Piraeus)		
Daily	1010hrs	Aegina, Zea Port.
Wed	2000hrs	Aegina, Zea Port.

In conclusion, Methana must be rated a most interesting, island-like location, even if the beach is not outstanding, added to which the average age of the residents, and visitors appears to be in excess of sixty years.

To the west of Methana is a road that routes along in a clockwise semi-circle to **Kaimeni Hora**. The Cyclades white village is set down in an encircling grove of olives, high up on a volcano blackened rock face. By following the signs 'Pros Ifestos' from the village, it is about a ¾hr hard labour clamber to the edge of the ancient volcano crater. Quite a sight.

Returning to the main road, the route courses along a plain, with mountains on the inland side, and the flow of agricultural fields broken up by the occasional dwelling. A spattering of industry and filling stations heralds the rather messy outskirts of:
GALATAS (124km from Korinthos) Tel 0298. From west to east, on the left is *Camping Cairo Angelo*, opposite *Pub Diogenis*, either of which might be inactive. Beyond a couple of side-by-side garages, on the left-hand side, is a *Rooms*, in a 'Colonels' style, 3 storey pension (Tel 25356).
    The epicentre of Galatas is the waterfront, from whence small Ro-ro ferries shuttle back and forward to nearby **Poros Island**. The formally laid out Esplanade is under total reconstruction, yet again. A taxi rank (Tel 22888) is close to the Ro-ro Quay, as are the bus stop and ticket office.
    Buses depart for Trizin, Epidavros and Nafplio (for an Athens bus connection), along the High St/Esplanade Odhos 25th March, in a north-westerly direction. Buses leave for Lemonodassos and Ermioni, in a south-easterly direction.
    Apart from a number of travel offices and cafe-bar tavernas, the *Hotel Papassotiriou* (Class C, tel 22841), borders Odhos 25th March, across from the Ro-ro Quay, with en suite singles costing 3500drs & doubles 6000drs. Also on Odhos 25th March is the *Hotel Saronis* (Class D, tel 22356), only offering en suite double rooms at a cost of 4765/5500drs.
    Continuing south-east along the Esplanade passes by a pension-like *Rooms* (Tel 24657), as well as more accommodation at the *Pensions Arimitis* and *Irini*. At the far end of the village, a landfill site is utilised for car parking and is, literally, a 'bit of a tip'.

The coastal road allows super views of Poros Island, separated from the Peloponnese by a narrow sound, almost giving the impression of being a river estuary.
    The route swings away from the shore, alongside a spit of grey pebble, rather messy beach, edging a weedy sea-bed. In the corner of the beach and road is an apparently 'dead' taverna.

A few kilometres on is:
Lemonodassos A large, well-irrigated area over which are planted some 180 acres of lemon tree groves. The wise stick to the road, whilst the hardy, who wish to make the final assault on foot, can select the signed track, to the right of the main road. This angles off on the apex of a left-hand curve, alongside a small chapel, immediately prior to the village (of Lemonodassos). Signposts pointing along the track indicate No Parking & To Kadassi Inn. It takes about twenty minutes to walk the dusty footpath, edged by concrete water conduits, now dry, but once used to irrigate the groves. A rather ramshackle taverna marks the end of the trail.

Here the friendly owner serves glasses of pressed lemon juice. The sound of running water fills the air and round the corner, beyond the taverna, is a 'real live' if stunted waterfall. Certainly the views are pleasant.

The main road winds back towards the coastline, briefly bordering a quite high concrete sea wall. Below this is a very narrow, pebble beach, with some sand, which is subject to kelp and a scattering of rubbish. The cove is at the bottom of a rather wide, shadeless, 'U' shaped bay. From here, the narrow main road winds and climbs steeply into the hills, curving round through all points of the compass, prior to finally striking out - due west. About where the route commences to descend, into view hoves the islands of **Hydra** and **Dokos**.

Close to an outcrop of carnation fields are a succession of sandy coves and headlands, in the area of the hamlet of **Vlaheika** - and not a taverna in sight. The observant will spot a well-preserved, roadside, donkey-driven, water well mechanism. As if to make up for all this excitement, the approach to the scattered hamlet of **Metohi** is uninteresting and scrubbly. A solitary boat quay probably allows shipment of the local agricultural produce, mainly tomatoes. Beyond an extensive sea lagoon is a grove of fruit trees, the *Rooms/Taverna Koulis*, and a sign to the *Taverna Adonis*.

At about **Pigadia** (circa 150km) is an estate of angular holiday blancmanges - sorry, holiday apartments, and the *Porto Hydra* village development, alongside which is the enormous *Hydra Hotel*, all on the left of the road. Across the highway, is the *Ranch Hydra* - the what? The latter is followed by the 'town' rubbish dump, and then a sign to the *Helio Club*. Pigadia imperceptibly runs into:

THERMISIA (156km from Korinthos) Tel prefix 0754. Through some 'oversight', the location continues to display evidence of a core village! As the occasional sign is in French, Thermisia must be on that nationality's list of locations to visit. The church is pink, and there is a *Taverna Jardin* (Gallic again), as well as a baker, filling station, fruit & vegetable store, a taverna or two, a couple of supermarkets, and a Police station.

Beyond a junction, the main road continues to track the coastline, passing by *Camping Hydrawave* (Tel 41095), and then a large, almost land enclosed lagoon-like bay. To the inland side are a range of Nevada style mountains. The route cuts across the base of a broad peninsular and then a deeply inset bay, along which are scattered a few bits of pebble beach, and scrubbly backshore. Over a causeway is a still unattractive, 8m widespread of shadeless, grey pebble beach, supporting a small 'shack of a taverna'. The coast becomes rocky, about adjacent to a tiny offshore islet. After climbing inland, past rather messy gorse supporting countryside, a bottle factory, warehouse, and filling station, there is a junction. To the right cuts back to **Iliokastro**, whilst to the left is:

ERMIONI (166km from Korinthos) Tel prefix 0754. This well-heeled, low-rise seaside resort and port pleasantly serpentines along a sea wall.
The access road joins the extensive Esplanade from the north. Facilities

and services include: a down-at-the-heel car hire firm; a Post Office; travel offices; a chemist; a Tourist Information office (which is really a tour office), next door to the two storey 1960s *Hotel Olympion* (Class D, tel 31214), where all rooms share the bathrooms, singles costing 2000drs & doubles 3500drs; a Bank of Greece; shops; kafeneions; a number of hotels, including the *Nadia* (Class D, tel 31102), the *Ermioni* (Class E, tel 31219), which only offers double bedrooms, sharing, at a cost of 2600drs, and the *Mantia*. The excursion coaches line up hereabouts. Beneath the *Hotel Ermioni* is the *Taverna Spirandrias*, and approximately across the Esplanade is the Ferry-boat Quay. Close to the latter is the excellent *Kafeneion Staikmos*, where a Nes meh ghala costs 150drs, and they offer a good dish of mezes. Also hereabouts is a taxi rank and an Agricultural Bank, which changes Eurocheques. About centre of the waterfront is a War Memorial, near which is a side-street leading past a small souvlaki snackbar, a fruit shop, grocer and a baker. As the side-street curves on round into the old section of the settlement, there is a Police station.

Along the next side-street, south of the War Memorial, is an OTE open the old weekday hours of 0730-1510hrs. The international nature of Ermioni is emphasised by the notices in the OTE, which explain how to dial Paris, Greater Paris, as well as the regions of France. Mmmh! Interestingly, a barrel-maker is hidden away up here, sometimes the barrels appearing to be much too large to get out of his workshop doors.

Back on the Esplanade, typical of the luxury restaurants accepting credit cards, is the *Restaurant Genosis*. On offer here are at least three speciality menus varying between 2500-5500drs, with prices also listed in French francs. The a la carte dishes include: spinach/cheese pie 450drs; spaghetti 500drs; Greek salad 500drs; moussaka 650drs; stuffed tomatoes 500drs; chicken 650drs; pork kebab/pork steak 900drs; and a pizza for two 1000drs.

More accommodation is available at a *Pension* (Tel 31387). Almost at the far, south end of the waterfront is a bread shop, followed by a two storey, old building housing the *Hotel Akti* (Class E, tel 31241), where all bedrooms share the bathrooms, singles cost 700drs & doubles 3800drs.

Continuing on south, beyond the formal Esplanade, passes by *Apartments to Let*, across the street from a pebbly little cove into which project a couple of 'twiggy' wooden piers, on which are drawn up a number of small fishing boats. Progress finally runs out on the edge of an extensive park.

Buses. Local services connect with Kranidi.

Ferry-boat & Hydrofoils
Ferry-boat timetables
Outward from Piraeus
Daily   1200hrs   Spetses
Inward to Piraeus
Daily   1850hrs   Hydra, Poros, Methana, Aegina

Hydrofoil timetables
Outward (from Zea Port, Piraeus).
Daily   1825hrs   Spetses, Portoheli.
Sun   1740hrs   Spetses, Portoheli.
Wed   1025hrs   Spetses, Leonidio, Kiparissi, Gerakas, Monemvassia,
                     Kithira, Neapoli.
Inward (to Zea Port, Piraeus).
Daily   0835hrs   Hydra, Poros, Methana, Aegina, Zea Port.
Wed   1855hrs   Poros, Methana, Zea Port.

From Ermioni, a coastal road approximately follows the bumps and lumps
of the knobbly coastline. En route, at the junction of a Kranidi turning, is
a baker and filling station (as well as a peculiar sign 'Barking'), in the
middle of nowhere.

About 3km out of Ermioni, the road joins a small, flat, exposed bay
with a pebble and rock shore, in which is set a narrow swathe of clean
shingly sand. This is shaded by a mature grove of gum trees, towards the
far end. The first turning off the route is to the rather isolated, modernish,
four storey building of *Lena Mary Beach Hotel Nudist Centre*, protected by
a gated entrance and a guard hut. Is this to keep voyeurs out, or to keep
the inhabitants in?

Also from the main road, a sign indicates 'Watersport', along a side
road, which advances to a shadeless, broad stretch of pebble beach,
popular with locals. Over a hump is another 'helping of the same', but
with brown sand in which is mixed pebbles. Between the two is a closed
hotel, with yet another, at the far side of the second beach.

At Kineta, set in comparatively unattractive, if not grotty, pongy
countryside, is a large hotel complex, the *Club Aquarius*.

The approaches to Kosta and Portoheli have a Canvey Island
appearance, with semi-permanent caravans dotted about, but very few
bungalows. In the middle of this wilderness is an outcrop of street names.
Yes..., street names, close to an alligator swamp' of an old alikes (salt
pans). The build-up becomes more noticeable, in the vicinity of the *Club
Galaxy*, a six storey hotel, the architecture of which irresistibly reminds
one of a concentration camp. Maybe it will be useful, if war is declared!

From about the signed turning (14km from Ermioni) to the
southernmost point of this lump of Peloponnese, that is to Kosta, there are
a fair number of taverna/restaurants, as well as a bakery/pizzeria, sprawled
along the roadside, set in an 'Aldershot gunnery range' countryside. The
latter gives way to marine pines, and, with the island of Spetses looming
large, this choice of route arrives at the seaside way station of:

KOSTA (circa 186km from Korinthos) Tel prefix 0754. The road passes
by: a *Rooms*; Disco Romantic Hill; *Camping Kosta* (Tel 51571); Disco
Stardust; a restaurant/snackbar and car park; only to skid to a halt
alongside a self-service snackbar, on the right, and a very snazzy, three
storey hotel, to the left. These last mentioned establishments edge a
shovel-shaped bay, with beaches to left and to the right, the left-hand (*Fsw*)
one being no more than a narrow smidgin of sand, almost covered in beach
umbrellas and sun-beds. The right-hand one is more shingly pebble, than

sand, with plenty of sun umbrellas. A minus point is that there aren't any beach showers.

Over to the left is even more car parking and the quay at which the glossy, distinctive, Italian style cabin speedboats wing their speedy way to and from Spetses island.

The *Lido Hotel* (Class B, tel 51393) charges 2400/5700drs for single bedrooms & 4240/9110drs for doubles, both with en suite bathrooms. A sign requests guests and visitors to 'Keep off the Grass'.

The *Self-service Snackbar* is not particularly inexpensive, but is very efficient and popular. A plate of moussaka costs 500drs, a briam 420drs, a plate of tasty octopus 600drs, and bottle of beer 150drs. A plus point is that it possesses drinking water and toilets.

Conveniently the 'Society of Restaurateurs and Cafeteria Owners of Portoheli' have erected a street plan of both Kosta and Portoheli.

Local Buses

Daily	0530, 1045hrs	Kranidi, Epidavros, Athens
	0530, 1045, 1415, 1715hrs	(Kranidi, Epidavros), Nafplio
	0745, 1015, 1115, 1215, 1315, 1645, 1915hrs	Portoheli

From Kosta, a minor, if metalled branch road runs along the western coastline. Opposite a little chapel is a disco. A succession of small coves follow each other, some pebble, some sandy, known only to the locals, who have made a determined effort to restrict the number of wild campers and the great unwashed. Signs abound forbidding this and that.

The smart, if large cubic *Cillas Emilion*, is set in lovely verdant valley, as is the *Thelassa Studios*. Beyond a small, deeply indented pebbly cove, and opposite a lighthouse, or channel light buoy, about where the road becomes unsurfaced, is the *Happy Mag Complex* - what is the Happy Mag? The far side of the latter is a pebble cove, rather marred by rubbish, and a scattering of rich men's villas.

From the Ermioni/Kosta junction, the road skirts a rippling, hard-packed shingle and sand shoreline, edging the bay on which stands:
PORTOHELI (192km from Korinthos) Tel prefix 0754. On the way to the centre of things is a sign *Family Houses for Rent*, and opposite more rippling beach, is the *Hotel La Citie* (Class B, tel 51265), also known as *Thermissia*. Small boats are pulled up on the nicely tree lined shore, which is broken up by little concrete quays. Beyond a boulderous stretch, is a spit-and-cove of sand, off which operate water sports activities, including jet ski, and windsurfers, whilst across the waterfront is the *Hotel Porto Heli* (Class A, tel 51490).

The bay, packed with moored yachts and motorboats, is skirted by an Esplanade besides which are, amongst other delights, the: *Disco Playboy*; *Anchor Restaurant Bar*; a Pension; a Pub; fish taverna; the *Cactus Pub*; a filling station; a number of low-rise buildings, interspaced with villas; a five storey hotel; Portoheli Tours; *Candy & Pizza Panorama*; an OTE, only open for the strange weekday hours of 1420-2200hrs; a scooter hire firm; several Rent A Car firms; and a Post Office caravan. The latter's

opening hours are Mon-Sat, between 0800-2000hrs & Sun 0900-1800hrs. The Esplanade is paralleled by a quay wall edging slip road with, in between the two, a landscaped park and car parking, and there seems to be lots of rinky-dinky roundabouts. In amongst the awning shaded cocktail bars, close to a War Memorial, is a local kafeneion beyond which, continuing from east to west, is: the Ferry-boat Quay; the local-popular *Taverna O Kostas*; a newsagents; and a rather lovely, Skopeliot-like chapel; after which, and another chapel, the road curves away inland.
     Yiannis operates a taxi service, and in the streets back from the waterfront are vestiges of the old Portoheli.

Bus Service

Daily	0530, 1045hrs	Kranidi, Epidavros, Athens.
	0530, 1045, 1415, 1715hrs	(Kranidi, Epidavros), Nafplio.
	0730, 1000, 1100, 1200hrs	Kranidi, & back to Portoheli).
	1300, 1630, 1900hrs	Kosta.

Ferry-boat & Hydrofoil Services
Ferry-boat timetables
Inward (to Piraeus)

Daily	1410hrs	Spetses, Hydra, Poros, Methana, Aegina, Piraeus.

Hydrofoil timetables
Outward (from Zea Port, Piraeus)

Thurs, Sun	1130hrs	Tiros (Trikeri), Leonidio, Kiparissi, Gerakas, Monemvassia.
Sat	1100hrs	Leonidio, Kiparissi, Monemvassia, Kithira, Neapoli.

Inward (to Zea Port, Piraeus)

Daily	0815hrs	Spetses, Ermioni, Hydra, Poros, Methana, Aegina, Zea Port.
Daily exc Fri	1245hrs	Spetses, Ermioni, Hydra, Poros.
Daily exc Fri & Sun.	1700hrs	Spetses, Hydra, Poros.
Mon & Wed	1500hrs	Spetses, Hydra, Poros.
Sat	1530hrs	Spetses, Ermioni, Hydra, Poros.
Sun	1530hrs	Spetses, Hydra, Poros.

In conclusion I preferred Ermioni to the more souless Portoheli, despite, or perhaps because the latter has two agents selling land and houses!

KRANIDI (circa 199km Korinthos) Tel prefix 0754. The old village is bypassed. From the south, almost opposite the Health Centre, is the modernish *Hotel Hermionida* (Class C, tel 21750), where all bedrooms have en suite bathrooms, with singles priced at 3810/4430drs & doubles 5140/6025drs. Other 'delights' include a filling station, chemist, dentist, bank, and a bus station, on which a notice in English advises 'Here tickets'. At the centre, the narrowest point in the High St, are traffic lights. A sign to the left indicates *New Camping Relax 2km.*
The northern outskirts of Kranidi are rather industrial and the countryside of gentle hills and painfully dry mountainsides, supports spaced out olive groves, on the lower slopes, but only gorse bushes higher up.

Fourni is a whitewashed, spaced out hamlet, beyond which the route starts to climb and cross the saddle of the low mountainsides, to reveal a plateau, on the far side of which is the town of **Didima**.

The route zig-zags up and down the granity mountain range and, proceeding westwards, finally allows dramatic views of the coastal plain, some offshore islands, and the far Peloponnese coastline, across the Argolikos Gulf.

Immediately prior to the **Iria** turning, is a ruined tower on the   right. Following the Iria road, once over a summer dry river-bed, the   route tracks across a rather soulless, flat plain. Where the road turns sharp right is a caique harbour, alongside which is a taverna, *Rooms* and a mini-market. A surfaced track drops down to the narrow, large pebble, tree lined shore, which stretches away to the north-west, backed by the same concrete track, both paralleled by the main road. Where the foreshore is not large pebble, they are medium   sized, and a bit messy. Accommodation is available at a *Rooms* (Tel 91283), beyond which the shore contains some grey sand. The remarkably straight road is lined by oleanders and a hodge-podge of single storey buildings. Further on is a campsite, *Iria Beach* (Tel 0753 - 91253).

Once having completed this large loop, and returned to the main road, on the left is the agreeable looking *Poseidon Camping*, edging a not overly attractive 10m wide, brown sand beach, with fine pebble at the sea's edge, some kelp and a general scattering of pebble. In fact, the shore, in places quite substantial, continues on along the bay's edge.

KANDIA (circa 263km from Korinthos) Tel prefix 0753. At the outskirts is a disco and some evidence of an embryonic holiday apartments development. The main road is between 100-150m away from the bay. Beyond nice looking *Kandia Beach Camping* (Tel 91353), a turning makes off through some swampy, salt-flat scenery, to end up in a bit-of-a-scrapyard-of-a-settlement, bordering a 100m long, up to 20m wide, sandy beach, with a taverna at each end.

The main road climbs sufficiently to allow views along the coastline and the lagoon-like inlet edged by the settlements of Vivari and Drepano. A conical hill juts up out of the plain and is probably the last remnant of a long extinct, long disappeared volcano.

VIVARI (circa 270km from Korinthos) Tel prefix 0752. There is a small, very fine pebble beach, but most of the waterfront is edged by a sea wall. There are two hotels. The most agreeable looking is *Areti* (Class C, tel 92391), with doubles, sharing, costing 4000drs, & en suite 4200drs, and the *Marina* (Class C, tel 92248), where en suite single rooms are priced at 3200drs, and double rooms sharing the bathrooms at 4600drs & en suite 5300drs. There are several tavernas, as well as at least five *Rooms*, variously with 'kitchen' and 'bathroom'.

Next along is the sizeable town of Drepano (Tel prefix 0752), which boasts a tour office, alongside the Post Office, and a Main Square, off from which is a baker.

From Drepano, right is for Nafplio, whilst to the left is the Kosta 'cul de sac' road for Tolo. Selecting the latter, almost immediately is a fork to the left for **Plaka Beach**, alongside which are a multitude of signs for apartments and camp sites. These include the *Plaka Beach Camping* (Tel 92294) and *Triton Camping* (Tel 92228), whilst hotels include the *Danti* (Class B, tel 92294), where all rooms are en suite, with singles charged at 5500/6500drs & doubles 6500/8000drs, and the *Plaka* (Class C, tel 92020). Another sign indicates the *Bungalows Maronic* - I'm sure they are! The beach is mainly a gorgeous sweep of sand, even if the sea-bed is rather difficult biscuit rock. This is a popular water sports venue, with windsurfers, pedaloes and ski-boats on offer.

From the Plaka Beach road, which forms a triangle, heads towards Tolo, past a number of *Rooms*, apartments and bungalows for rent, with many signs in German. Alongside the junction of the other road of the triangle is *Camping Zenith Beach*, close to the hamlet of **Old Asini**, now really no more than a pebble cove, which has been awarded the Golden Starfish, and whereat is a tiny kafeneion cafe-bar and *Kastraki Camping* (Tel 59386). Nearby is the site of **Ancient Asine**, occupied as early as 2000 BC, and a fortified town in the 2ndC BC.

From hereabouts the vantage points allow views along the coastline all the way to Tolo, some offshore islands, one of which is small with a pretty chapel, and the strait between them.

TOLO (circa 270km from Korinthos) (Illus. 11). Tel prefix 0752. The location irresistibly reminds me of certain locations on the Spanish Costa Brava, and apart from the language, could well be! Tolo certainly owes little to authentic, ethnic Greek culture.

The town resort stretches out approximately north-south, along the eastern side of a bulge of land projecting into the Argolikos Gulf. The main, very sandy beach is close to the north, or top end of Tolo and is, more often than not, absolutely packed. The sand-duned backshore 'climbs' steeply towards the main road, across sea-grass and some gorse. To add to the delights of sand castles and burying father and or the family car, there are at least two firms competing for the water sport business. These activities encompass windsurfers, canoes, pedaloes, as well as a ski-run. Sample charges are: use of a private enterprise beach shower 20drs; pedaloes 600drs per hour; canoes 300drs; and windsurfers 800drs. There is a beach bar.

En route to the south end of town, proceeding along the High St, Odhos Bouboulinas, passes by the: *Hotel Barbouna* (Class D, tel 59162), on the right, where en suite bedrooms cost 4900drs for a single & 5000/5800drs; *Rooms*; *Tolo Lido II Camping* (Tel 59396); *Hotel Zeus* (Class C, tel 59089), with all bedrooms en suite, singles priced at 4500drs & doubles 6000drs; the two storey, Spanish style *Hotel Soleil* (Tmr 1), all following hard on each others heels. The *Hotel Esperia* (Tmr 2) (Class C, tel 59339), where en suite bedroomsarecharged at 4700/5600drs for a single & 6000/7000drs for a double, is proceeded by a row of tavernas and restaurants, a baker, still with the dune-hidden seashore to the left, apartments, a hotel, and a *Rooms*, about where the beach trickles to an end, temporarily. Incidentally, the foreshore continues on as a hard-packed, busy, sandy, 4m wide swathe, with the occasional interruption, all the way

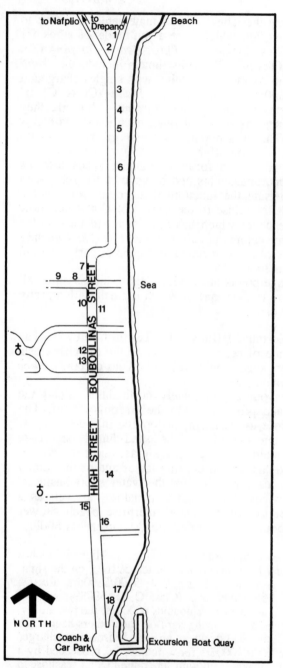

Key
1   Hotel Soleil
2   Hotel Esperia
3   Hotel Solon
4   Hotel Artemis
5   Hotel Flisvos
6   Pegasus Cruises
7   Commercial Bank
8   Post Office
9   Laundry
10 Pegasus Tours
11 OTE
12 Baker
13 Credit Bank
14 Hotel Aris
15 Police
16 Hotel Koronis
17 Hotel Minoa
18 Hotel Acteon

(Tmr) = Town map reference
(Fsw) = Facing seawards
(Sbo) = Sea behind one
(Fbqbo) = Ferry-boat Quay behind one

Illustration 11 Tolo (schematic plan)

down to the bus/car/coach turn-round, at the very southern end of town. The profusion of signs resembles a form of unsightly graffiti. *Rooms* are followed by: the *Hotel Solon* (*Tmr* 3) (Class B, tel 59204), where en suite bedrooms are charged at 3400/3800drs for a single & 5000/7300drs for a double; *Hotel Elena's* (Class C, tel 59158), with en suite bedrooms priced at 4100/5000drs for a single & 5100/6100drs for a double; a money exchange; the air conditioned *Hotel Artemis* (*Tmr* 4) (Class C, tel 59458), with en suite single bedrooms charged at 3695/4435drs & a double 4435/5320drs; *Marine Area* - 'the best taverna'; the Beach Ball Souvenir Shop; *Peter's Restaurant* - 'on the beach'; *Hotel Assini Beach* (Class C, tel 59347), only offering doubles, sharing at a cost of 4000/5000drs & en suite 4500/6000drs; *Restaurant Mouragio*; a foreign language book & newspaper shop; *Swiss Camping* - 'the best camping'; *Hotel Flisvos* (*Tmr* 5) (Class C, tel 59223), with en suite singles costing 4200/5040drs & doubles 5200/6240drs; *Hotel Tolo* (Class C, tel 59248), with en suite singles charged at 3600/4380drs & doubles 4600/5550drs; a fruit & vegetable shop - 'English, German & Scandinavian spoken'; Pegasus Cruises (*Tmr* 6) - owned by the firm that dominates the tour and travel market in Tolo; *Lido Village Tolo*; and *Apartments Possidon*. Hereabouts the High St at last starts to spread out a little, with, in an older building, *Hotel Santa Maria* (Class B, tel 59525), then Rent A Car, *Rooms* - 'with kitchen & toilet', *Rooms Arcadia*, the *Cafeteria on the Beach* - 'breakfast omelettes', *Nellies Hotel Apartments* - 'fully air conditioned', and the *Restaurant Je Revien*.

Beyond a double bend in the road, the High St sprawl continues on past: stores; a supermarket; the Post Office (*Tmr* 8); *Manolis Grill House; Hotel Epidavria* (Class C, tel 59219), with en suite bedrooms costing 4000/4500drs for a single & 5200/5700drs for a double; the *Hotel Aris* (*Tmr* 14) (Class C, tel 59231), with en suite singles costing 3960/4560drs & doubles 3825/5760drs; *Villa Irini* (Class C, tel 59188), with en suite singles priced at 3145/3770drs & doubles 4165/5055drs; *Hotel Koronis* (Class C, tel 59292); Rent A Car; a Clinic; and *Rooms*, beyond which the street at last runs out on a damn large coach and car park, alongside a small harbour, edging the sound between the town and an offshore island.

A rough track continues on, and not to be forgotten are the *Hotels Acteon* (*Tmr* 18) (Class C, tel 59084), with en suite singles costing 4500/5000drs & doubles 5700/6500drs, and the *Minoa* (*Tmr* 17) (Class C, tel 59207), with en suite single bedrooms costing 4200/5400drs & doubles 5400/6600drs.

Sample taxi prices for a 'load-full', return trip, are as follows: Olympia 2000drs; Adrinsena/Agapolis/Vases 17000drs; Athens and the Acropolis 16000drs; Mycenae 5000drs; Epidavros/Isthmia/Korinthos/Mycenae 15000drs; Epidavros 5000drs; Athens airport 12000drs; Sparta/Mistra 16000drs; and Delphi 23000drs.

Opposite a High St Bank, is a private telephone set-up. The 'Mr Big' of the tours & travel business is Pegasus Cruises/Tours (Tel 59430) (*Tmr* 10). Typical excursions are: Athens 7000drs; Mycenae, Epidavros 4000drs; Olympia 6000drs; Mistras 5000drs; Epidoria 1300drs; and Delphi 8500drs. A sample on offer from Pegasus Cruises are: Hydra & Spetses 3500drs; Monemvassia or Poros & Hydra 3500drs; Hydra or Spetses 2300drs; Nafplio by night 1500drs; and Escape to Astros 3200drs.

Apart from the clinic, there are a doctor and dentist.

From Tolo to Nafplio, the road cuts off the corner, leaving Drepano to the east, passing through the modern-day village of:

ASINI (circa 280km from Korinthos). The settlement is dominated by the previously referred to, cone-like upstand of volcanic rock, which is topped off by a tiny chapel. There are quite a few accommodation opportunities here, including *Rooms Antrogini*, *Lefkas* and *Maria*, as well as *George's Taverna & Rooms*. Other facilities include a filling station.

The main road passes through an avenue of gum trees, and by several more filling stations, to the extremely wide, main street of **Aria** village. This is almost a suburb of Nafplio, and the far end is dominated by a hump of rock topped off with an enormous fortress. This is understandable as it is the feature that towers over Nafplio City.

A Nafplio street

The glory that was Mistras

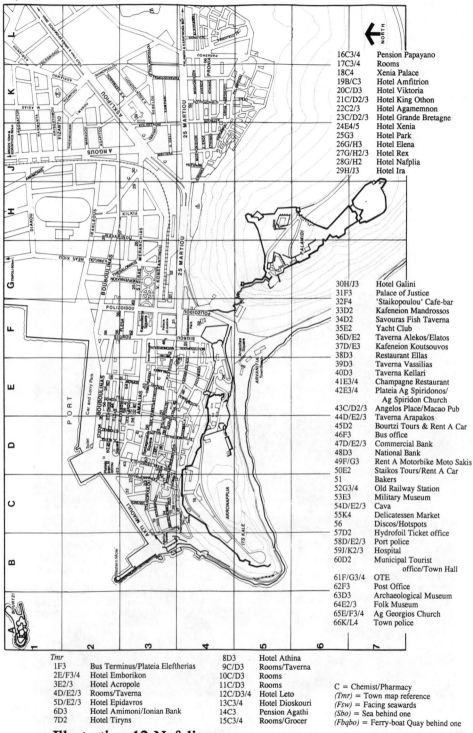

16C3/4	Pension Papayano
17C3/4	Rooms
18C4	Xenia Palace
19B/C3	Hotel Amfitrion
20C/D3	Hotel Viktoria
21C/D2/3	Hotel King Othon
22C2/3	Hotel Agamemnon
23C/D2/3	Hotel Grande Bretagne
24E4/5	Hotel Xenia
25G3	Hotel Park
26G/H3	Hotel Elena
27G/H2/3	Hotel Rex
28G/H2	Hotel Nafplia
29H/J3	Hotel Ira

30H/J3	Hotel Galini
31F3	Palace of Justice
32F4	'Staikopoulou' Cafe-bar
33D2	Kafeneion Mandrossos
34D2	Savouras Fish Taverna
35E2	Yacht Club
36D/E2	Taverna Alekos/Elatos
37D/E3	Kafeneion Koutsouvos
38D3	Restaurant Ellas
39D3	Taverna Vassilias
40D3	Taverna Kellari
41E3/4	Champagne Restaurant
42E3/4	Plateia Ag Spiridonos/ Ag Spiridon Church
43C/D2/3	Angelos Place/Macao Pub
44D/E2/3	Taverna Arapakos
45D2	Bourtzi Tours & Rent A Car
46F3	Bus office
47D/E2/3	Commercial Bank
48D3	National Bank
49F/G3	Rent A Motorbike Moto Sakis
50E2	Staikos Tours/Rent A Car
51	Bakers
52G3/4	Old Railway Station
53E3	Military Museum
54D/E2/3	Cava
55K4	Delicatessen Market
56	Discos/Hotspots
57D2	Hydrofoil Ticket office
58D/E2/3	Port police
59J/K2/3	Hospital
60D2	Municipal Tourist office/Town Hall
61F/G3/4	OTE
62F3	Post Office
63D3	Archaeological Museum
64E2/3	Folk Museum
65E/F3/4	Ag Georgios Church
66K/L4	Town police

Tmr	
1F3	Bus Terminus/Plateia Eleftherias
2E/F3/4	Hotel Emborikon
3E2/3	Hotel Acropole
4D/E2/3	Rooms/Taverna
5D/E2/3	Hotel Epidavros
6D3	Hotel Amimoni/Ionian Bank
7D2	Hotel Tiryns

8D3	Hotel Athina
9C/D3	Rooms/Taverna
10C/D3	Rooms
11C/D3	Rooms
12C/D3/4	Hotel Leto
13C3/4	Hotel Dioskouri
14C3	Pension Agathi
15C3/4	Rooms/Grocer

C = Chemist/Pharmacy
(Tmr) = Town map reference
(Fsw) = Facing seawards
(Sbo) = Sea behind one
(Fbqbo) = Ferry-boat Quay behind one

Illustration 12 Nafplio

5 NAFPLIO (Nauplion)

Illustration 12

FIRST IMPRESSIONS: Magnificent fortress; smelly harbour; tall, lovely old Dickensian buildings; Malta-like backstreets.

VITAL STATISTICS: Tel prefix 0752. Population 10,500.

HISTORY Despite rich, early chronicles, between the 7th & 3rdC BC, when the promontory Akronafplia was fortified as an acropolis, strangely the location was deserted in the Roman era.
  It was the Byzantines, in the 12thC AD, who started the restoration of Nafplio's fortunes. They were succeeded, in fairly quick succession, by the battling Franks (in 1210), the Venetians, who purchased it (in 1389), the Turks, who captured the town (in 1540), to be followed by General Morosini, he of Crete, who took back Nafplio, for Venice, in 1686. During this latter occupation, the Venetians caused to be erected the precipitous Palamidi outcrop topped fortress. In 1715, the Turks recaptured Nafplio, only for the Russians to register a temporary hold, before yet another return of the Turks.
  At the outset of the Greek War of Independence (1821-22), the Hellenic forces besieged the town and ousted their centuries-long overlords. Subsequently, and unfortunately for the inhabitants, two local chieftains then engaged in a running battle for supremacy - so what's new? That is, until the British Navy stuck their oar into this local skirmish. At the end of the War of Independence, the first Greek president, Ioannis Kapodistrias, took up residence and established the seat of government (1829) at Nafplio. Unfortunately, Mr Kapodistrias was assassinated by two brothers from Mani. In 1833 Prince Otto of Bavaria, recently elected first King of Greece, by the Great Powers, disembarked at Nafplio to establish his reign. To reward the worthy citizens for their welcome, in 1834 he relocated the centre of government to Athens!
  It is a little known fact that Crete was not the only location for a 'supreme' Second World War British forces excavation bog-up. Oh, no! In April 1941, three Royal Naval transport ships fouled up the harbour, and two destroyers were lost, under evening fire.

GENERAL Perhaps it would be considered too facile to simply write that if I had to visit one, only one Greek city, or port or town, anywhere in the land, it would be here. I accept this is a sweeping statement, essaying a broad number of options, but, for all that, Nafplio remains my choice, even after mature consideration. The somewhat medieval Old Quarter, gathered around the very large harbour, is ideally complemented by an island-quaint, upper town, and if that were not enough, the whole settlement is overlooked by a splendidly majestic castle. Even the barely adequate town beach is more than satisfactorily compensated for by a magnificent expanse of sandy beach, round at the adjacent Karathona Bay. In addition, the picturesque setting, with the offshore islet of Bourtzi, is pleasantly adorned by the faded elegance of some nicely preserved Hellenic 'Georgian and Victorian' buildings.

Apart from Palamidi Castle, probably the most arresting, eye-catching feature of Nafplio, is the treatment meted out to the, now abandoned railway station, associated buildings, trackways and sidings. Instead of allowing them to fall into disrepair and disintegrate, to become yet another municipal car park or, worse still, cause them to be razed to the ground, the powers-that-be have acted with most unusual enterprise. They have had the 'whole shebang' imaginatively enparked, with the buildings put to alternative uses (*See* Places of...). In addition, Nafplio is fortunate to have a glut of parks and squares, one of the loveliest of which is the small, marble paved, Plateia Syntagmatos, which is bordered by some magnificent buildings.

If there is an obvious drawback, it has to be admitted that the port only enjoys a very limited, height-of-summer months hydrofoil schedule. On the other hand, the Peloponnese-wide bus service is excellent, allowing a number of judicious connections.

ARRIVAL BY TRANSPORT Really the only feasible option are Buses, as the hydrofoil services only include Nafplio, during July, August and September. Furthermore, in spite of railway lines being drawn in on some maps, the branch line from Argos has not been in operation for many years. However, the bus service well makes up for these deficiencies, and the terminus (*Tmr* 1F3) is conveniently central.

THE ACCOMMODATION & EATING OUT
The Accommodation A wide choice, including not one, but two Xenia's and a Youth Hostel. To the west of the Bus terminus Sq (or Plateia Eleftherias) is the Old Quarter, bounded by the Port Esplanade (Akti Bouboulinas) to the north, the Harbour Esplanade (Akti Miaouli) to the north-west, whilst the south is 'fenced' in by the hill Akronafplia and the cliff-face.

Starting out from Bus terminus Sq, heading west along Odhos Plapouta, and on the right, in the second block is the:
Hotel Emborikon (*Tmr* 2E/F3/4) (Class D) 31 Plapouta St   Tel 27339
Directions: As above.

An old style outfit, which might well have been rated E Class. All rooms share the bathrooms, with a single charged at 2000drs & a double 3000drs.

Closer to the harbour are the:
Hotel Acropole (*Tmr* 3E2/3) (Class D) 7 Olgas St   Tel 27796
Directions: From the Bus terminus (*Tmr* 1F3) proceed north (towards the port) along Leoforos Sigrou, as far as the junction with Amalias St. Here turn left (*Palace of Justice behind one*) across the recently 'piazza'd' Plateia Iroon, on the left of which are a number of pleasing old buildings. From Amalias St, turn right along the narrow side-street of Siokou and the hotel is the far side of the third block on the right (*Facing the Port*).

An en suite single costs 2600/2900drs, whilst doubles sharing bathrooms cost 3300/3550drs, & doubles en suite are 4000/4250drs.

Incidentally, en route to the *Acropole*, bordering Odhos Alexandrou, the previous east-west street, and to the left, is a *Rooms/Taverna* (*Tmr* 4D/E2/3).

Back at Amalias St, and continuing west to the next side-street, turn right towards the Port to Ipsilandou St, whereon, to the left, is the:
Hotel Epidavros (*Tmr* 5D/E3) (Class D) Ipsilandou St   Tel 27541
Directions: As above, and on the left.
   Single bedrooms, sharing the bathrooms, are charged at 3500drs, whilst doubles sharing cost 3500/4000drs & en suite doubles 3800/4400drs.

Also in the area, edging Othonos St, which is parallel to and one back from Akti Bouboulinas, the Port Esplanade, and close to the junction with Riga Fereou St, is the:
Hotel Tiryns (*Tmr* 7D2) (Class D) 41 Othonos St   Tel 28104
Directions: As above.
   All bedrooms have en suite bathrooms, with a single priced at 3500drs & a double 5000drs.

Back at Odhos Amalias, and at a jink in the line of the street, next door to a branch of the Ionian Bank, is the:
Hotel Amimoni (*Tmr* 6D3) (Class C) 6 Diogenous/Koleti St   Tel 27219
Directions: As above, and on the left.
   An old-fashioned hotel, in which bedrooms share the bathrooms, with singles charged at 2000/2300drs & doubles 2500/2800drs.

South of Amalias St, along Koleti St, with the marble paved Plateia Syntagmatos to the right (*Port behind one*), leads to the:
Hotel Athina (*Tmr* 8D3) (Class C) Syntagmatos Sq   Tel 27695
Directions: As above, and on the left (*Port behind one*).
   All bedrooms have en suite bathrooms, with singles costing 3500drs & doubles 5000drs.

Climbing south-west off Syntagmatos Sq into the upper, Old Quarter, ascends to an area rich in accommodation. For instance, on the right (*Port behind one*) of Odhos V. Georgiou 'A', in a very nice looking three storey building, is a **Rooms/Taverna** (*Tmr* 9C/D3). A little higher up, along Spetson St, the next lateral street off Odhos V. Georgiou A, and on the left, at No 3, is a *Rooms* (*Tmr* 10C/D3), of rather strange appearance. The accommodation is owned by Christina (Erika Alexis) Papos, and is more than noticeable by, not only the profusion of flowers, but an old-fashioned taxi driver's seat and trick-cycle, all prominent. Mmmh! Just around the corner from the last establishment is another **Rooms** (*Tmr* 11C/D3), on the left (*Port behind one*) of the stepped, upper end of Farmakopoulou St.

Continuing up Odhos Farmakopoulou, across Konstantinoupoleos St, advances to Zigomala St, along which, to the left (*Port behind one*), and on the right is:

Hotel Leto (*Tmr* 12C/D3/4) (Class D) 28 Zigomala St   Tel 28093
Directions: As above.
   Single rooms sharing the bathrooms are charged at 3000/3500drs & with an en suite bathroom 4500/5000drs, whilst doubles sharing cost 3500/3800drs & with en suite bathrooms 5500/6000drs.

To the right (*Port behind one*) of Odhos Farmakopoulou, west along Zigomala

St and to the right, down a few steps at the top end of Vironos St, and on the right is the:
Hotel Dioskouri (*Tmr* 13C3/4) (Class C) Zigomala/Vironos Sts   Tel 28550
Directions: As above, and rather hidden away behind the 'front garden' vegetation.
All rooms have en suite bathrooms, with singles costing 4920/5310drs & doubles 5980/6250drs.

Back on Odhos Zigomala, and facing west almost immediately to the fore is:
Pension Papayano (*Tmr* 16C3/4) 6 Zigomala St   Tel 27036
Directions: As above and stretching from the front to back of the block.
The very swept-up accommodation is in an agreeable, three storey house, gentle, quiet area, and is run by a nice lady. The double rooms, which are but have their own bathroom, cost 3500/4000drs.

Further west from the last mentioned pension leads to Plateia Psaromahala. To the left (*Facing west*), and on the left is a *Rooms* (*Tmr* 17C3/4). To the right, at the far, north-east corner of the square, is a *Rooms* above a Grocer (*Tmr* 15C3/4), whilst on the north side of Nosokomiou St, bordering that side of the square, is the agreeable looking **Pension Agathi** (*Tmr* 14C3, tel 23058).

To the south side of Plateia Psaromahala is a James Bond style tunnel leading to the:
Xenia Palace (*Tmr* 18C) (Class L) Akronafplia   Tel 28981
Directions: As above.
I rarely, if ever, list a luxury hotel, but I think there is every excuse here, as this is a not bad location!
En suite doubles cost either 11500drs or 13100drs, per night. Oh well!

From the heights of Plateia Psaromahala, falling in a northerly direction, towards Akti Miaouli, descends to Staikopoulou St, towards the west end of which is the:
Hotel Amfitrion (*Tmr* 19B/C3) (Class A)   Tel 27366
Directions: As above.
All rooms have en suite bathrooms, with a single costing 5600/8250drs & a double 7800/11300drs.

Further (east) along Staikopoulou St is the four storey building of the:
Hotel Viktoria (*Tmr* 20C/D3) (Class C) 3 Spiliadou   Tel 27420
Directions: As above.
Despite the category, awfully smart. All bedrooms have en suite bathrooms, with singles charged at 5870/7900drs & doubles 6935/8700drs.

Close to, if not actually bordering Akti Miaouli, are the:
Hotel Agamemnon (*Tmr* 22C2/3) (Class B) 3 A. Miaouli   Tel 28021
Directions: As above
The rooms, with en suite bathroom, cost 4955drs for a single & 6825drs for a double.

And the:
Hotel King Othon (*Tmr* 21C/D2/3) (Class D) 3 Farmakopoulou   Tel 27585
Directions: Between the diverging streets of Akti Miaouli and Staikopoulou.
All the bedrooms share the bathrooms, with singles charged at 3000/3500drs & doubles 3500/3800drs.

By the junction of Farmakopoulou St and the Esplanade, at Ioan N. Iatrou Sq, is the *Grande Bretagne* (*Tmr* 23C/D2/3) (Class D, tel 27375).

Returning to the Bus terminus (*Tmr* 1F3), proceeding east along Leoforos 25th Martiou, and turning south along Polizoidou St, or by crossing the park, Plateia Staikopoulou, descends to the other side of the headland, to Arvanitas Sq and the other Xenia, the:

Hotel Xenia (*Tmr* 24E4/5) (Class L) Arvanitas Sq   Tel 28981
Directions: As above, and to the right (*Facing South*).
   Rooms for two cost either 11500drs or 13100drs. Well they would, wouldn't they?

Back at the centre of things, proceeding east along Leoforos Sidiras Merarchias passes by or near, various en suite bathroom hotels, including the: *Hotel Park* (*Tmr* 25G3) (Class C, tel 27428), with singles costing 4555/5280drs & doubles 5690/6630drs; *Hotel Elena* (*Tmr* 26G/H3) (Class C, tel 23888), with singles priced at 3450/4140drs & doubles 5695/6830drs; *Hotel Rex* (*Tmr* 27G/H2/3) (Class C, tel 28094), where singles cost 5300drs & doubles 7500drs; *Hotel Nafplia* (*Tmr* 28G/H2) (Class C, tel 28167), with singles priced at 4430/4965drs & doubles 5495/6115drs,; *Hotel Ira* (*Tmr* 29H/J3) (Class E, tel 28184), with singles sharing costing 2000drs & en suite 2500drs, whilst doubles sharing priced at 3500drs & en suite 4000drs; and the *Hotel Galini* (*Tmr* 30 H/J3) (Class C, tel 28103), with singles at 3190drs and sharing/en suite doubles at 4875/5630drs.

YHA 15 Argonafton St   Tel 27754
Directions: East of the Bus terminus (*Tmr* 1F3) along 25th Martiou, forking left and left again on to Argous St. The seventh side-steet off to the right is Argonafton St (*Tmr* J/K1). It is about a 20min trudge.
   A 'family friendly' establishment, with a night-time curfew, also offering breakfast and snacks, and charging 650drs per head per night, plus meals.

Camping Despite the surrounding countryside being swamped with campsites, the city doesn't possess even one within its suburbs.

THE EATING OUT The majority of restaurants and tavernas are spread along the waterfront Esplanade, Akti Bouboulinas, around Plateia Ioan N. Iatrou, beside one or two of the Old Quarter streets, and in and around Plateia Syntagmatos.

Close to the Bus terminus is the very useful:
'Staikopoulou' Cafe-bar (*Tmr* 32F4).
Directions: South of the bus terminus, about centre of Plateia Staikopoulou.
   Apart from the usual cafe-bar offerings - the old but clean, pleasant smelling, separate male and female toilets, have running water and are large enough for 'participants' to enjoy a 'stand-up wash down' (Irish isn't it?). Very opportune for bus-sticky travellers, requiring to 'empty sump', 'drain rad', and freshen-up. This fact is not lost on the proprietors, who have a strategically positioned gratuities box.
   Also fairly close-by, the north side of Plateia Kapodistria (*Tmr* F3) is edged by restaurant/fast-food cafe-bars, and there is a souvlaki-pita snackbar on the corner with Odhos Polizoidou.

One of the best Esplanade establishments is:
Kafeneion Mandrossos (*Tmr* 33D2).
Directions: Towards the far, west end of Akti Bouboulinas, alongside the side-street Riga Fereou.

Pleasant, unhurried but attentive service. For the sake of the owner, and clients alike, it is to be hoped that Dimitri, a pleasant, likeable young man, continues in his present employment as a waiter. A bonus is that, having been born in Canada, he speaks excellent 'pigeon' 'Grelish' (or Greek English). A couple of Nes meh ghala and an ouzo cost 350drs, whilst a bottle of Amstel costs 170drs. Unusually, Dimitri is reasonably willing to make dining out recommendations.

One of his commendations was the:
Savouras Fish Taverna (*Tmr* 34D2).
Directions: Just across the side-street.

This is a 'dedicated psarataverna'. Sample prices per kilo are: 4500drs mullet; 6750 'another' mullet; 625drs squid; 1600drs shrimps; 3750drs for coley; & 5000drs karides.

To the other side of the *Mandrossos* is *Kolios Taverna*, whilst proceeding east along Akti Bouboulinas passes by *Taverna Psara*, two side-by-side restaurants, and the:
Taverna Alekos/Elatos (*Tmr* 36D/E2).
Directions: As above.

A very friendly owner who is quite likely to drag a prospect into the kitchen. It strikes me as an excellent lunch-time stop, but some dishes might become tired, by the 'reaches' of the night. Whilst the owner schleps, the young waiters are encouraged to get a move on - thus the service is fast, and efficient. Drinking water is placed on the table, as a matter of course. An enjoyable meal, for two, of tzatziki (200drs, tasty but not overlarge), gigantes (500drs - super), a moussaka (500drs - good, very good), keftedes (500drs - nice), carafe retsina (250drs), bread & service (50drs each), cost a total of 2050drs. Other dishes available include: spaghetti bolognese 500drs; roast veal 700drs; roast chicken 500drs; lamb chops 900drs; pork chops/or a souvlaki 700drs; squid 600drs; shrimps 1200drs; a tomato & cucumber salad 250drs; Greek salad 450drs; lemonade/Seven-Up 100drs; & an Amstel beer 150drs.

Continuing east along the Esplanade, past the side-street of Kotsopoulou, is a *Pizzeria Restaurant*, and a glitzy soda-pop bar, following by the side-street Odhos A. Siokou and, in the next block, a sign *Yacht Club* (*Tmr* 35E2). This, it goes without saying, is not a yellow-wellie, grotty yachty set up, more a sort of taverna bar, serving simple meals in the evening.

In the next block along (6th east), which is set back, behind the small Plateia Bouboulinas, is or was *Boite Sirena* (*Tmr* 56E2/3), a traditional Greek music nightspot, but on my last visit it appeared to be closed.

As advised, there are three or four fairly traditional, main square taverna/restaurants bordering the south side of Plateia Ioan N. Iatrou (*Tmr* C/D2/3). Whilst hereabouts, on the right of Odhos V. Georgiou 'A' (aka Ethniki Antistasis), which runs south of the aforementioned square, is the incredibly smart, glitzy cocktail bar, *Angelos Place*, next door to which is the *Macao Pub* (*Tmr* 43C/D2/3).

Leaving the waterfront, and on Amalias St is the:

Kafeneion Koutsouvos (*Tmr* 37D/E3).
Directions: Towards the west end of Odhos Amalias, and on the right (*Bus terminus behind one*), in the same block as the *Hotel Epidavros*.
The owner's signs are eye-catching - 'Breakfast special every day, 06.30(am)-11.30(pm). Home-made rice pud, milk, tea, Nescafe, assorted soft drinks...', and so on. Many of them are in English. Despite this, the place is not overly garish, even if the blue wicker seats and pink topped metal tables are not the usual, old-fashioned, mainstream kafeneion style. Prices are, if anything, more costly than some of the Esplanade competitors.

Fairly close-by is the lovely Plateia Syntagmatos, which becomes very animated and busy with families, in the evening hours, even if the local kids take over a section as a football ground. On the east side of the square is the:
Restaurant Ellas (*Tmr* 38D3).
Directions: As above.
A traditional, tiled floor restaurant, with black waistcoated waiters, and a high ceiling, suspended from which is a very slowly rotating fan stirring the upper air - and flies. As befits such an establishment, a routine menu, but I found the 'Gestler-like' head waiter rather off-putting.
South of Plateia Syntagmatos is the Old Quarter, east-west, narrow street of Staikopoulou, edged by high, 18thC buildings and some unimaginable pieces of architecture. Hereabouts are a couple of 'worthy of a mention' eateries, namely the *Taverna Vassilias* (*Tmr* 39D3), Staikopoulou St, alongside the junction with the side-lane of Odhos Efthimopoulou, marking the outset of an eastward row of tavernas and cafes. The next one to the *Vassilias* is the *Taverna Mesidopolion*, with a nicely painted, little sign over the door. Almost opposite is a rather hidden-away Turkish fountain, whilst other Staikopoulou establishments include the *Gelateria Cafe* (also known as the *Pink Panther Cocktail Bar*), *Zorba's Taverna*, and the *Pelican Cafe*. Hereabouts is a taverna that stretches along Odhos Soutsou, a narrow alley connecting Staikopoulou and Konstantinou Sts.

Taverna Vassilias (*Tmr* 39D3) Staikopoulou St.
Directions: As above.
This was the other establishment recommended by Dimitri, our 'friend' at *Kafeneion Mandrossos*. The accolade was well deserved and the taverna is extremely popular. A most enjoyable meal, for two, of a Greek salad (500drs), veal in sauce with chips (750drs), lamb with rice and chips (680drs), an 'open' retsina (250drs), 3 ouzos (yes, three for 270drs), bread & cover (60drs each), cost a total of 2570drs.

To the west of *Vassilias*, along Odhos Staikopoulou, passes by the *Route 66 Pub*, *en route* to the *Taverna Kellari* (*Tmr* 40D3). The latter also has its advocates, with a meal of the day, a 'representative' menu, and the food on display looking good. Next door, at No 14, is yet another eaterie of 'beckoning' appearance.
Odhos Kapodistria, which is parallel and south of Staikopoulou, runs into Plateia Ag Spiridonos (*Tmr* 42E3/4), overshadowed by more enchanting, lovely buildings - a fascination almost equalled by the bewildering state of the town drains - and adjacent to which is a Turkish fountain. Kapodistia St hosts the:
Champagne Restaurant (*Tmr* 41E3/4).
Directions: As above, to the east of Plateia Ag Spiridonos, and on the south side of the street.
I'm listing this 'genuine' French restaurant, despite its unhellenic ambiance,

and that the menu is on the 'pricey side' of genuine, French prices! As I have boringly written, on other occasions, when considering this type of establishment, why not stay in France? A sample of prices are: smoked ham 1100drs; cocktail of moules 650drs; 12 escargot 1100drs; fish soup 1000drs; omelette with champignons 700drs; canarde a la orange 1300drs; poulet and olives 1000drs; beef bourbignon 1200drs; rochette de beouf 1300drs; gratin de courgettes 750drs; mousseline de carrotts 750drs; a pate of fromages 1100drs; a ½ litre of Sangria (a Spanish drink, surely?) 750drs; Chateau D'Avre wine 2200drs (my God, that's almost more than I would spend on a meal, although I have to admit that I am salivating as I pen these words); a Beaujolais village (wine) '89 1400drs; and a Cote du Rhone 2200drs.

There is one other vein of eateries to be mined. This is in amongst the area of the three picturesque streets parallel to, and south of Akti Bouboulinas, namely Odhos Othonos, Olgas and Alexandrou. Apart from the *Taverna/Rooms* (*Tmr* 4D/E2/3), Alexandrou St, there is the very 'local popular' *Taverna Arapakos* (*Tmr* 44D/E2/3), on Odhos Othonos. Another possibility, hereabouts, is the *Taverna Palio Archontika* (*Tmr* E3), beside Odhos Siokou, fairly close to the junction with Amalias St.

THE A TO Z OF USEFUL INFORMATION
AIRLINE OFFICE Despite there being no airfield in the vicinity, Olympic Airways is represented by **Bourtzi Tours (& Rent A Car)** which has two offices. One is beside the Bus office (*Tmr* 46F3) and the other (*Tmr* 45D2) is behind the Town Hall.

BANKS There is not an over-abundance, but Amalias St has two, the **Ionian** (*Tmr* 6D3) and the **Commercial** (*Tmr* 47D/E3), whilst the **National Bank** (*Tmr* 48D3) stretches from the south edge of Plateia Syntagmatos, through to Odhos Staikopoulou.

BEACHES Arvanitia, the 'town beach' (*Tmr* E5) is no more than a 50m long strip of round pebble. From the large car park and square, alongside the *Hotel Xenia* (*Tmr* 24E4/5), a concrete path and steps descend through a pine tree planted, steeply shelving strip of land. The sea is crystal clear. Concrete sun bathing and diving platforms have been let into the rocks that border the shore. There are four working showers, as well as spotless toilets, all overseen by an attendant. One of the toilets is thoughtfully set aside for the disabled. Mind you, if you were not disabled before using the nominated unit, you might well be, after the event as, 'to arrive', it is necessary to negotiate a series of steep steps. There isn't a cafe bar or Cantina. The children's playground becomes crowded, early in the day.

Well, the town beach will suffice for a quick dip, but the 'sand in the crown' is:

Karathona Bay & Beach (4km from Nafplio). Either an hour's uphill walk, along Leoforos 25th Martiou, in the direction of **Palamidi** fortress, from which road keep to the left, or a ten minute taxi ride.
    A lovely, wide sweep of fine grit and sand that extends 'beneath the waves'. At the outset to the bay are some extensive, possibly abandoned building foundations, and a skeleton of roads. It is to be fervently hoped that these are a relic of the rule of the Colonel's, as were so many other similar

pipe-dreams. The backshore of the up to 10m wide beach is bordered by a surfaced beach road, edged at the nearside by groves of mature gum trees, and inland of which is a swathe of hard-packed gravel, grit and sand. More young trees have been planted and despite signs to the contrary, a few camp beneath their boughs. A lonely Cantina, with a throbbing generator, looks after the daylight hour visitors.A notice indicates the presence of organised sailing and surfing, but these are probably 'off and on' water sport activities. In fact, it is quite possible that the only tangible evidence of the latter will be a few pedaloes, with which to break into a sweat.

Despite the permanence of the beach road, it only leads round to the far, east side of the bay, where are a couple of small tavernas. Beyond them, on the horn of the promontory, is a fisherman's cottage and a few outbuildings. Offshore is an attractive, little, rocky islet, and some fishing boats are anchored. It has to be pointed out that cliff-steps are signed 'Ag Pikolaos'.

In conclusion, Karathona is a simply glorious place to sunbathe, swim and laze the day away.

BICYCLE, SCOOTER & CAR HIRE Scooters and motorbikes are available from **Rent A Motorbike Moto Sakis** (*Tmr* 49F/G3), close to the junction of Odhos Polizoidou with Sidiras Merarchias.

There are quite a few car hire companies and my choice would be **Staikos Tours/Rent A Car** (*Tmr* 50E2, tel 27950). Eleni, who looks after the office, is extremely helpful and speaks excellent English. Incidentally, they have outlets in Portoheli and Athens. Other car hire businesses are: **Bourtzi Tours** (*Tmr* 45D2); **Albion Travel**, across Amalias St from the *Kafeneion Koutsouvos* (*Tmr* 37D/E3); and **Champ Rent A Car**, on Odhos Staikopoulou, opposite the *Hotel Viktoria* (*Tmr* 20C/D3).

BOOKSELLERS There are a number of foreign language newspaper and paperback bookshops, in and around the streets that climb up to the *Xenia Palace* (*Tmr* 18C4).

BREAD SHOPS Perhaps the city's best **Baker** (*Tmr* 51E2/3) is on Odhos Sofroni, close to Akti Bouboulinas. There is another **Baker** (*Tmr* 51E/F3/4), south of the Bus terminus, on the right (*Facing west*) of Odhos Papanikolaou. The latter sells some fairly evil-looking pies, as well as croissants and a 'feta job' of solid appearance. Yet another **Baker** (*Tmr* 51D/E3), hides away on the north side of Staikopoulou St, east of the junction with Odhos Kokinou.

BUSES The buses 'terminus' (*Tmr* 1F3) along the streets of Sigrou and the outset of 25th Martiou. The well organised **Bus office** (*Tmr* 46F3) borders Sigrou St, and is flanked by a pair of cafe-bars.

Bus timetables
Nafplio to Athens (100 Kifissou St)
Daily   0500, & every hour until 1930hrs.
Return journey
Daily   0600, 0730, & every hour until 2030hrs.
One-way fare 1700drs; duration 2½hrs.
Nafplio to Mikenes (for Mycenae)
Daily   1000, 1200, 1330, 1700, 1900hrs.
Return journey
Daily   1300, 1500, 1800, 2000hrs.
P.S. I know - 5 out & 4 back!
One-way fare 1000drs (tickets on the bus); duration 1hr.

Nafplio to Argos
Daily   0600, & every ½hr until 2130, 2230hrs
Return journey
Daily   0630, & every ½hr until 2200, 2300hrs
One-way fare 170drs; duration ½hr.
Nafplio to Argos, via Nea Kios
Daily   0815, & every hour until 1815, 1900hrs.
Nafplio to Galatas (for Poros Island)
Daily   0500, 1245, 1400hrs
Return journey
Daily   0600, 0930, 1645hrs
One-way fare 1000drs; duration 2hrs.
Nafplio to Tolo
Daily   0700, & every hour until 2130hrs.
One-way fare 170drs; duration ½hr.
Nafplio to Drepano
Daily   0800, 0930, 1030, 1130, 1300, 1400, 1615, 1830, 1930hrs.
Nafplio to Midea (north-east of Nafplio)
Daily   0800, 1000, 1200, 1400, 1930hrs
Nafplio to N. Roino (north-east of Nafplio)
Daily   0730, 1000, 1400, 1700, 1930hrs.
Nafplio to B. Ilia
Daily   0720, 1400, 1930hrs.
Nafplio to Kranidi, Ermioni, Kosta & Portoheli
Daily   1015, 1400, 1700hrs
Return journey
Daily   0530, 1015, 1415, 1700hrs Mmh!
One-way fare 1000drs.
Nafplio to Ag Dimitrio
Daily   0600, 1400, 1930hrs
Nafplio to Arahneo (north-east of Nafplio)
Daily   0600, 1400hrs.
Nafplio to Ligourio (& Palea Epidavros & Ancient Epidavros)
Daily   0530, 1015, (P. Epidavros & A. Epidavros), 1430 (P.Epidavros &
               A. Epidavros), 1700 (A. Epidavros), 1930hrs (A. Epidavros).
Return journey (from Ancient Epidavros)
Daily   1200, 1300, 1600, 1800hrs
One-way fare 350drs (tickets on the bus).
Nafplio to Nea Epidavros
Daily   1045, 1430hrs
Nafplio to Iria (south-east of Nafplio)
Daily   0610, 1400hrs
Nafplio to Kranidi
Daily   1045, 1400, 1700(Sundays), 1845hrs.
Nafplio to Storopoti
Daily   0520, 1400hrs.
Nafplio to Asklipio
Daily   1015, 1200, 1400, 1430, 1700hrs
Return journey
Daily   1200, 1300, 1600, 1800hrs.

CHILD CARE There is a children's playground at the Town (Arvanitia) Beach, whilst the pleasantly planted park of Plateia Kopodistra (*Tmr* F3) has childrens' swings. A most unusual opportunity is the 'Childhood Memories' Museum, sponsored by the Peloponnese Folklore Foundation, located in one of the old disused railway station engine sheds (*Tmr* 52G3/4). Admittedly the exhibit is only open weekends, between 1000-1300hrs.

CINEMA I'm not sure that any now survive, their old premises nowadays, more often than not, being taken over by disco outfits.

COMMERCIAL SHOPPING AREA It is rather strange, considering the size, age and history of Nafplio, that it does not sport a central market, somewhere

in the Old Town. In fact, it is necessary to winkle-out food and basic supplies.
Close to the Bus office (*Tmr* 46F3) is a grocer. If there is a focal area, it might be considered to be the far, west end of Amalias St, where there are quite a number of small shops, stores and butchers. To the west of the Military Museum (*Tmr* 53E3) is a supermarket, whilst further on (to the west), and the other side of the street, is a very smart **Kava** (*Tmr* 54D/E2/3) - very smart, not one of 'your' more usual, ouzo reeking warehouses, or holes in the wall.

To the south and around Plateia Syntagmatos (*Tmr* D3) are some quite swept-up fruit & vegetable shops.

A most worthwhile shop is the **Delicatessen Market** (*Tmr* 55K4), almost in the eastern suburbs, set amongst some interesting older buildings. This very clean, well-run store is a joy to behold, selling some diverting cheeses, as well as yoghurts, a range of delicatessen, tinned foods, and drinks. Just outside is a working drinking fountain, whilst diagonally across 25th Martiou is a fruit shop.

DISCOS The 'hot quarter' is in and around the north/south streets, on the port side of Plateia Kopodistria (*Tmr* F3), namely alongside Sigrou and Polizoidou Sts. In the 'spotlight joints', from Akti Bouboulinas, proceeding in an anticlockwise direction, are the **Music Club** (*Tmr* 56F2/3), the **Disco Idol** (*Tmr* 56F2) and the **Disco Memory** (*Tmr* 56F2/3), the latter close to the junction of Polizoidou and Flesa Sts.

The **Boite Sirena** (*Tmr* 56E2/3) is more a Hellenic nightclub but, as mentioned in The Eating Out, may now be closed. Another popular rock bar is the **Koukou** (*Tmr* 56D/E2), alongside the *Pizzeria Restaurant*.

A 1km distant, uphill-all-the-way, alternative is **Disco Kerki**, which borders the Palamidi/Karathona Beach road.

FERRY-BOAT & HYDROFOILS Ferries do not call, but a height of summer months hydrofoil makes weekly scheduled visits. Mind you, a bus to, for instance, Galatas (for Poros island), Kosta (for Spetses island), or Tolo, for excursion boats to one or two islands, allows a traveller plenty of opportunity to 'plug into' the busier hydrofoil possibilities.

Nafplio is the end of the line for this particular hydrofoil service, so it is necessary to stop off at the islands of Spetses or Poros, to be able to run-on, south down the east side of the Peloponnese to, for instance, Leonidio, Kiparissia, Gerakas, Monemvassia, Kithira island or Neopoli.

Hydrofoil timetable (July, August & early September).
Daily   0715hrs   Tolo, Portoheli, Spetses island, Ermioni, Hydra island,
exc Mon   Poros island, Methana, Aegina island, Zea Port(Piraeus).

One-way fares to			
Tolo	360drs;	duration	20mins
Portoheli	1015drs;	"	50mins
Spetses	1232drs;	"	1hr
Ermioni	1330drs;	"	1½hrs
Hydra	360drs;	"	2hrs
Poros	1949drs;	"	2½hrs
Methana	2480drs;	"	2¾hrs
Aegina	2580drs;	"	3hrs
Zea Port	2922drs;	"	4hrs

FERRY-BOAT & HYDROFOIL TICKET OFFICES The **Ceres office** (*Tmr* 57D2, tel 27456/28054) is almost at the very west end of Akti Bouboulinas and doubles as the *Yannopoulos Travel Agency*. Opening hours are: Mon-Fri 0830-1300hrs & 1800-2000hrs; Sat 0830-1430hrs; and closed Sundays.

HAIRDRESSERS There is a Ladies hairdresser next door to the   Commercial Bank (*Tmr* 47D/E2/3), one beside the Port police (*Tmr* 58D/E2/3) on Odhos Kotsopoulou, another (*Tmr* D/E2/3) on the north side of Odhos Ipsilandou, on the block between the lateral side-streets of Kotsopoulou and Siokou, and yet another close to the Staikopoulou St baker (*Tmr* 51D/E3).

LAUNDRY There is a Dry Cleaners to the west of the **Kava** (*Tmr* 54D/E2/3), on Amalias St, and a **Dry Cleaners & Washing Shop**, beside Odhos Staiko-poulou, diagonally (south-west) across the street from a baker (*Tmr* 51D/E3).

LUGGAGE STORE None, it being necessary to rely on the goodwill of a convenient business.

MAPS The best of the tourist town maps is the one produced by Stam. Bozinakis, with the flags of various nations along the bottom of the cover.

MEDICAL CARE
Chemists & Pharmacies (*Tmr* C). There is one, a block south of the Bus terminus, adjacent to the Papanikolaou St Baker (*Tmr* 51E/F3/4), and yet another on the north side of Plateia Syntagmatos (*Tmr* D3).
Dentist Above the supermarket, to the west of the Military Museum (*Tmr* 53E3) on Amalias St.
Hospital (*Tmr* 59J/K2/3) From the Bus terminus (*Tmr* 1F3) proceed east along 25th Martiou and fork half-left on to Leoforos Asklipiou - on the Tolo road.

MUNICIPAL TOURIST OFFICE (*Tmr* 60D2) It is a pleasant surprise to find city authorities enlightened enough to run an office. This one is located in the ground floor of the Town Hall. Despite the confusion in respect of opening hours (Daily 0900-2100hrs, or 0900-1400hrs & 1700-2200hrs - take your choice), and the reluctance of the large girl who runs the office to hand over information - like drawing dragon's teeth - the facility is most welcome.

OTE (*Tmr* 61F/G3/4) To the west of the old Railway station. The doors are open weekdays & Saturdays, between 0700-2400hrs; Sundays & holidays, between 0730-2400hrs.

PARKING In rebuilding the quay to the north of Akti Bouboulinas, the authorities have created a massive car and lorry park. The expansion of the area can be appreciated by the huge width between the kerb of Akti Bouboulinas, the adjacent disused port railway line, and the present quay wall.

PETROL There are any number of suburban filling stations.

PLACES & EVENTS OF INTEREST
Akronafplia or **Its Kale** An ancient acropolis which was fortified by successive conquerors. Its Kale is the Turkish nomenclature. When the fortress on Palamidi was constructed, so was a staircase between the two. Now the ruined fortifications guard the *Xenia Palace*!
Bourtzi islet On this was constructed a small castle, by the Venetians, in 1471, to help protect the harbour entrance. At one time, I believe, a chain was suspended in the water from the Bourtzi to the Pentadelphia bastion of the town fortifications (now less prosaically the Western mole). Certainly the Turks filled the 450m wide channel with rocks. In the 19th century the Nafplion public

executioner hid away here, and in the 20th century there was a hotel. Trip boats shuttle back and forwards daily from the quay, charging some 350/400drs, for the ½hr round trip.

Churches
Ag Spiridon Church (*Tmr* 42E3/4). This was where the first president of the newly united Greek nation, Ioannis Kapodistrias, was assassinated, in 1831. Close by are the steps of Odhos Potamianou that climb southwards towards: *Ag Sofia* The Catholic church.
Ag Georgios (*Tmr* 65E/F3/4). This Byzantine church is of interest as an Italian artist, whilst painting the murals, sought inspiration from the Last Supper by Leonardo da Vinci - okay, he copied it!

Mosques On the east side of Plateia Syntagmatos (*Tmr* D3) is a now boarded-up Turkish mosque, which enjoyed (or didn't) a spell as a cinema. This observation leads me to point out that the Turkish Serai (or Governors residence), which forms part of the south-west side of Syntagmatos Sq, and once a mosque, was used for some of the early Greek Parliamentary assemblies, during and after the War of Independence.

Galleries There are a number of art galleries (picture showrooms?) dotted about the place.

Museums
Archaeological (*Tmr* 63D3). Once a Venetian barracks, with a colonnaded facade, edging the western side of Plateia Syntagmatos, and built between 1686-1715. The exhibits, which include a suit of armour dating from the Mycenaen period, are very interesting - and would be so much more so if Athens had not 'purloined' the 'pick of the dig'. Open weekdays, Sundays & holidays between 0830-1500hrs, but closed Mondays. Entrance is free.
Childhood Memories See Child Care.
Folk Art Museum (*Tmr* 64E2/3) Located at the eastern end of the lovely back street, Odhos Ipsilandou. (Incidentally, the parallel Odhos Alexandrou is equally attractive.) The shady, almost sunless entrance opens out into an arboured courtyard whereon is a discreet, classy cafe. A highly rated exhibition with entrance costing 200drs. The doors are open daily, between 0900-1430hrs, but are closed Tuesday & public holidays.
Military Museum (*Tmr* 53E3) Housed in the original building of the first Military Academy of (modern-day) Greece, opened in 1820. Entrance is free, it is open daily between 0900-1430hrs, but closed Tuesdays.

Parks & Squares The city abounds with both parks and squares, some very attractive, but the most praiseworthy example must be the treatment of the discontinued railway terminus (*Tmr* 52G3/4). The whole layout of buildings and railway lines have been given the treatment, and combined with the pedestrian only, Odhos Vas Kontantinou, present a lovely riot of palm and pine trees, as well as plants, flowers and bushes. The buildings have been put to a variety of uses which include a music rehearsal room, a cafe, public toilets and a Childrens' Museum. Splendid. The park has the to-be-expected aviary, the wired off birds appearing pretty bored with life.

Palamidi Fortress (*Tmr* G/H5/6) To the south-east of, and dominating the Old Quarter, from the 215m craggy heights. Originally only (just) accessible by a 1000 step (or so), steep ascent, the castellated heights can now be reached along a 2km long, metalled road that forks off that heading for Karathona Bay. A taxi costs about 500drs one-way. For those who choose to walk, it is about a 45min trudge. The direction is more than adequately signposted, initially along Leoforos 25th Martiou.

The entrance to the fortress, constructed between 1711-1714, is open weekdays, between 0800-1845hrs, Sat & Sun between 0830-1445hrs, and entrance costs 250drs. The layout is rather unusual and the views are outstanding. On a pragmatic note, the loos are shared, there is often a total lack of toilet paper, and the little cafe-bar is expensive, with 2 frappe coffees costing 350drs, perhaps they charge for the donkey to porter the ingredients!

POLICE
Port (*Tmr* 58D/E2/3) As is often the case, their office is sited with a total disregard for the officers being able to see the port!
Town (*Tmr* 66K/L4) Rather a long way from the centre of town. On the way there, from Leoforos 25th Martiou, passes by a Turkish drinking water fountain dated 1871.

POST OFFICE (*Tmr* 62F3) Fairly conveniently situated, close to the junction of Sigrou & Sidiras Merarchias Sts.

SPORTS FACILITIES There is a football stadium!

TAXIS The main rank ranges along Sigrou St, in the environs of the Bus terminus (*Tmr* 1F3).

TELEPHONE NUMBERS & ADDRESSES
Hospital (*Tmr* 59J/K2/3)	Tel 27309
Hydrofoil (Ceres) representative (*Tmr* 57D2)	Tel 27456/28054
Olympic representative (*Tmr* 45D2)	Tel 27456/28054
Police (Town) (*Tmr* 66K/L4)	Tel 27776
Taxis	Tel 24120
Town Hall (Information Office) (*Tmr* 60D2)	Tel 24444

TOILETS There are public facilities at the Old Railway Station (*Tmr* 52G3/4). They are squatties, there is often toilet paper but they are not always cleaned. *See Staikopoulou Cafe-Bar* (*Tmr* 32F4), The Eating Out.

TRAINS Sadly no, but the station and associated workings are well worth a visit. I wonder what skulduggery, what political chicanery resulted in Nafplio loosing its branch line from Argos?

TRAVEL AGENTS & TOUR OFFICES *See* Airline Office, Bicycle, Scooter & Car Hire, and Ferry-boats & Hydrofoils.

YHA *See* The Accommodation

EXCURSIONS TO NAFPLIO CITY SURROUNDS
Excursion to Tiryns Archaeological Site (5km) Follow the Argos road through the suburbs of Nafplio. The latter are littered with car and lorry associated businesses - repairs, mechanics, spray shops, filling stations and breakers. In amongst this semi-industrial squalor, excavation and demolition, are smacked down one or two smart hotels!

To the right of the route is:
Tiryns (5km from Nafplio) (Illus. 13) Open Mon-Fri, between 0800-1900hrs; and Sat & Sun 0830-1500hrs. Entrance costs 400drs per head and visitors must be decently dressed.

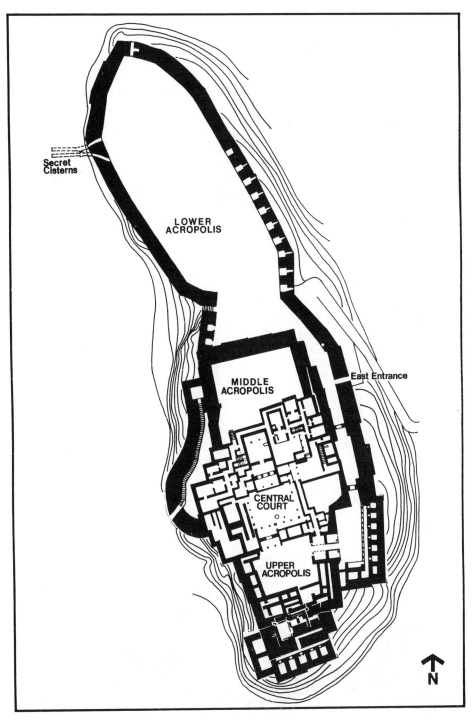

Illustration 13 Tiryns Archaeological Site

There are two major problems with this site. Firstly, and unusually, it is raised above ground level, and well-hidden away behind an outer wall, which is in a remarkable state of preservation, so there is no chance of having a quick glance down over the site. Oh, no! Secondly, one coach party is a crowd - and they turn up in droves, so for those who wish to visit, arrive as early as possible.

Some of the stones weigh up to 14 tons, and despite losing about half their height, as long ago as the 4thC BC, their width remarkably remains in excess of 8m. This Mycenaen acropolis citadel, mainly fashioned as it is observed today, was reconstructed in the 13thC BC, on a low knoll, standing some 25m above sea-level, and beside the sea! Yes, alongside the Mediterranean. In the intervening years the waters have receded up to 1½ kilometres.

ROUTE THREE (*See* Illus. 9)
NAFPLIO TO ARGOS (12km) The countryside bordering the route is rather squalid and the disused Nafplio branch railway line parallels the road, for much of the distance, on the left-hand side. As it is overgrown and in need of attention, it looks very similar to the 'in use' railway lines. Just to the north of **Dalamanara** (8km from Nafplio) is a really enormous out-of-town supermarket.

The route appears to be pointing directly towards a hilltop, crested by the remains of a castle, before passing over a slimy mud river-bed, the railway track, and the Athens 'ring road', prior to the outskirts of Argos.

Elafonisi harbour

Thinking about a drink? Gerolimenas

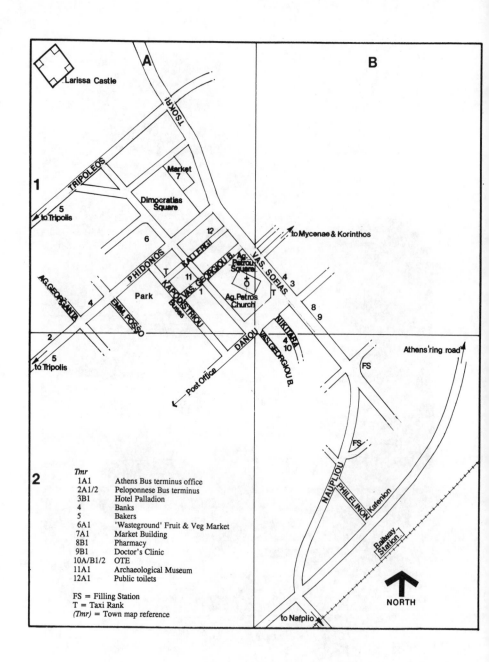

Illustration 14 Argos

6 ARGOS (Argo)

Illustration 14

FIRST IMPRESSIONS Dusty & unattractive.

SPECIALITIES Farming, cattle breeding & tobacco growing.

VITAL STATISTICS Tel prefix 0751. Population 21,000.

HISTORY The modern-day town is built on and over the greater part of an ancient city. This ancient city state held sway in the region for four hundred years, from about 668BC to 229BC, after Mycenae had been overcome by invading Dorians. Much of this period was spent locked in combat with the fearsome Spartans.
     In the 5thC AD Argos became a bishopric, and succumbed to the Franks, in 1212. After their arrival, the Byzantine fort was greatly enlarged, much of its history paralleling that of Nafplio.
     During the War of Independence, in 1825, the Turks, 'in the shape' of Ibrahim Pasha, destroyed the city.

GENERAL The first impressions of a dusty, disorganised, unattractive town, are more than amply borne out by any in-depth investigation! For some reason many of the streets appear to be unmade, whilst any number are under 'disrepair'. Furthermore, it is a rather difficult location in which to orientate, and is very thinly spaced out. Apart from the importance of Argos to the Argolid community, its proximity to the archaeological site of Mycenae has ensured the city remains in the public eye.

ARRIVAL BY BUS A pivotal location for passenger re-routing, allowing the Athens connection to link up with the extensive Peloponnese network.

ARRIVAL BY TRAIN The city is a major halt on the clockwise Peloponnese circuit.

THE ACCOMMODATION & EATING OUT
The Accommodation Only 'C' & 'D' class, if expensive hotels. These include the:
Hotel Palladion (*Tmr* 3B1) (Class D) 5 Vas Sofias   Tel 27346
Directions: Close to the Main Square, Ag Petrou, and a modern hotel.
     A single room, sharing the bathrooms, cost 4000drs, a single room with en suite bathroom costs 5700drs, & an en suite double 8500drs.
     Also on the square is the:
Hotel Mycenae (Class C) 12 Ag Petrou Sq   Tel 28569
Directions: As above.
     Similar prices to the *Palladion*.

Hotel Telessila (Class C) 2 Danou/Vas Olgas Sts   Tel 28351
Directions: South of the Main Sq. ´

Hotel Apollon (Class E) 13 Gr Papaflessa   Tel 28102
Directions: From Danou St, bordering the south flank of the Main Sq, select
and follow Nikitara St to the BP filling station, at which turn left, and
immediately right, whereon the hotel, on the left.
   Singles sharing the bathrooms are priced at 2500drs & ensuite 2789drs,
whilst a double sharing is 4000drs & en suite 4560drs.

Hotel Theoxenia (Class D) 31 Tsokri St   Tel 27370
Directions: Proceed north-west along Vas Sofias, from the Main Sq, in the
direction of the hilltop castle, on to Tsokri St. The hotel is close to the market
(*Tmr* 7A1).
   The bedrooms all share bathrooms, with a single charged at 2250drs &
a double 3500drs.

Camping None in the town.

THE EATING OUT
None of the eateries rates a mention. The
kafeneion across the 'ring-road' from the Railway station is particularly
sleazy.

THE A TO Z OF USEFUL INFORMATION
BANKS (*Tmr* 4B1) There is a **Commercial Bank** on the east side of Plateia Ag
Petrou, a **National Bank** (*Tmr* 4A/B1/2) on Odhos Nikitara, to the south-east
of the Main Sq, and an **Agricultural Bank** (*Tmr* 4A1) on Phidonos St.

BREAD SHOPS One Baker (*Tmr* 5A2) is diagonally across Phidonos St from
the Peloponnese Bus terminus, and another (*Tmr* 5A1) is beside Odhos Tripo-
leos, west of Plateia Dimocratias, the upper of the city's two main squares.

BUSES There are two termini, the Athens Bus office (*Tmr* 1A1) is west of
Plateia Ag Petrou, whilst the Peloponnese Bus office (*Tmr* 2A1/2) is beside
Odhos Phidonos. Note that due to Vas Georgio 'B' St being a pedestrian
way, the buses pile-up on nearby Odhos Kapodistriou.
   The offices are beside the relevant terminus.

Bus timetables
(1) **Athens Terminus** (*Tmr* A1)
Argos to Athens (100 Kifissou St) via Korinthos
Daily   0530, 0730 & every hour to 2030hrs
Return journey
Daily   0600, 0730 & every hour to 2030hrs
One-way fare 1500drs; duration 2¾ hrs
Argos to Limnes, via Ira & Honikas (for Inahos)
Daily   0620, 1230, 1420, 1930hrs
Argos to Nafplio
Daily   0430, 0630, 0700, 0800, & every ½hr to 2100hrs
One-way fare 150drs.
Argos to Nafplio, via Nea Kios
Daily   0700, 0820, 0915, 1015, 1115, 1215, 1315, 1400, 1515, 1615, 1715hrs
       (& Nea Kios only) 1830, 1930, 2030hrs
Argos to Nafplio via Anifi & Ag Triada
Daily   1000, 1200, 1600hrs.

Argos to Nemea
Daily   0630, 1315hrs
One-way fare 350drs.
Argos to Mycenae
Daily   0700, 1030, 1230, 1415, 1830, 1930hrs
One-way fare 200drs; duration 25min.
Argos to Elliniko via Kefelari
Daily   0730, 1315hrs.
Argos to Koutsopodi
Daily   0700, 0900, 1000, 1100, 1200, 1315, 1415, 1600, 1830, 1930hrs.
Argos to Kiveri via Mili
Daily   630, 0730, 0900, 1000, 1100, 1200, 1300, 1415, 1700, 1830, 1930hrs.
Argos to Kefalari
Daily   0730, 1415, 1930hrs.
Argos to Ag Triada & Panaritis
Daily   0730, 0830, 0930, 1100, 1215, 1300, 1415, 1520, 1630, 1930hrs.
Argos to Vrousti via Galati
Daily   0645, 1230hrs.
Argos to the Sanctuary of Epidavros
Daily   1015, 1200, 1430hrs.

2. Peloponnese Terminus (*Tmr* 2A1/2)
Argos to Tripoli
Daily   0830, 0915, 1000, 1130, 1315, 1530, 1730, 1930, 2230hrs
One-way fare 600drs; duration 1¼hrs.
Argos to Sparti
Daily   0915, 0930, 1030, 1230, 1545, 1645, 1900, 2030, 2215hrs
One-way fare 1000drs; duration 2½hrs.
Argos to Olympia
Daily   0800, 1215, 1800hrs
One-way fare 1750drs; duration 4½hrs.
Argos to Astos
Daily   1030, 1315, 1800hrs

COMMERCIAL SHOPPING AREA The Market (*Tmr* 7A1), located at the north corner of Plateia Dimocratias, is an eye-catching, large building, which is being restored. The central aisles are bordered by colonnaded walls, into which arches are recessed.
    To the south-west of the formal market building is a 'waste ground' Fruit & Vegetable market (*Tmr* 6A1). Wednesday is the official city market day.

MEDICAL CARE A Pharmacy (*Tmr* 8B1) is beside Vas Sofias, south-east of the Main Sq, and a few metres further south, beside the same street, is a Doctor's Clinic (*Tmr* 9B1).
The Hospital is to the left of the main Korinthos road.

OTE (*Tmr* 10A/B1/2) Beside Odhos Nikitara. Open weekdays only, between 0700-2400hrs.

PETROL (*Tmr* FS) There are several filling stations to the south-east of the city centre.

PLACES & EVENTS OF INTEREST Some quite interesting Greek and Roman ruins are to be found by proceeding along Danou St, past the Post Office, and right along Theatrou St, for about 1km.

The Roman Agora is to the south-east side of the Tripolis road, whilst to the north-west are Roman baths, a Roman Odeion and a Greek theatre. The latter theatre, once seating some 20,000 people, was thus one of the 'big' one's of ancient times. The site opens Mon-Sat 0830-1500hrs; Sun & hols 0900-1430hrs. Entrance is free.

The ruins of Larissa Castle are a ¾/1hr walk from either the Greek theatre or Odhos Tsokri.

Archaeological Museum (*Tmr* 11A1) Open daily, except Mon, between 0830-1500hrs. Entrance 400drs. A praiseworthy, well organised museum.

POLICE The town police are located to the right of the Korinthos road.

POST OFFICE Beside Danou St.

TAXIS (*Tmr* T) Rank on the south-east corner of the Main Sq.

TOILETS (*Tmr* 12A1) Beside Odhos Kallergi, between the squares of Dimocratias and Ag Petrou.

TRAINS The Railway station is 1km distant from the Main Sq, at the edge of the south-eastern outskirts. It is an uninspiring 'little' location. A cold water machine does, taxis don't, and an 'interesting' little kafeneion, across the ring road from the station, is a rather dirty, greasy spoon.

Train timetable
Daily dept 1022, 1210, 1726hrs.
Tripolis   1147, 1327, 1855hrs
Kalamata   1438, 1549, 2148hrs
Return journey
Daily dept 0302, 1045, 1450, 1936hrs
Mykine   0312, 1059, 1501,   - hrs
(for Mycenae)
Korinthos   0402, 1159, 1552, 2035hrs
Athens   0543, 1355, 1742, 0543hrs
One-way fares   to   Athens   800drs
                       Korinthos 300drs
                       Tripolis 400drs
                       Kalamata 950drs
                       Mykine   80drs

EXCURSIONS TO ARGOS CITY SURROUNDS
Excursion to Mycenae (14km) (Illus. 15). Select the Korinthos road east from Argos. This advances through the usual 'outskirts slum', past the hospital and across a fairly flat plain, supporting groves of fruit trees. The railway line is close by.

At the crossroads settlement of **Fihti** (10km from Argos) is the Railway station for Mikines, and the archaeological site of Mycenae.

At Fihti turn right for the village of:-
MIKINES (12km from Argos Tel prefix 0751. En route passes by the well shaded *Camping Atreus* (Tel 66221).

The village has plenty of *Rooms*, as well as the: *Hotel Agamemnon* (Class C, tel 66232), where en suite double rooms cost 7000drs per night; and a small *Youth Hostel* (tel 66224), at 20 Ifigenias St, where the

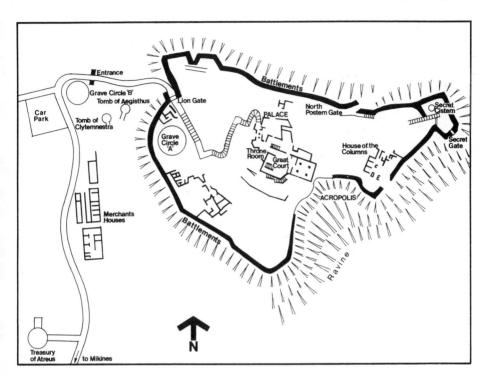

Illustration 15 Mycenae Archaeological Site

sexes are (nominally) divided, and the per head charge is 650drs.
Rumour, only rumour suggests that this Youth Hostel does not quite live
up to the 'old' United Kingdom standards.   In fact, it is hinted that
this stablishment is an absolute jungle, with the Greek management

allowing French and German inspired, all-night parties. I suppose it all depends upon your stand-point!

Other Mikines 'delights' take in restaurants, tavernas, souvenir shops (measured by the metric shard), thousands of tour buses, the *Hotel/Restaurant Belle Helleni* (Tel 66255), established in 1862, probably with bits and pieces from the archaeological site, and where a double bedroom costs 4000drs, *Camping Mycenae* (Tel 66247), *Dassis Rooms*, and the *Restaurant Bar Electra*.

The road gently climbs through and beyond the village, also passing by *Homers Restaurant Bar* (well, he would have had to have been here, wouldn't he?), as well as the *Hotel Restaurant Petit Planete* (Class B, tel 66240), where the bedrooms with en suite bathrooms cost 6000drs for a single and 8000drs for a double.

After 2km, the road decants on to the car and coach park of the archaeological site, beside which a Post Office caravan opens weekdays 0800-2000hrs, and Sundays & holidays 0900-1800hrs.

Ancient Mycenae (24km from Argos) (Illus. 15) The site is open weekdays 0800-1700hrs, weekends & holidays 0830-1500hrs. Entrance costs 1000drs, and the ticket must be kept in order to see the Treasury Tomb of Atreus.

The large, shadeless site sprawls over an extremely exposed mountainside, so come armed with a hat and water.

Although inhabited from around the 6000BC, the period that resulted in the fame of the great city commenced about 2000BC, reaching its peak in the flowering of the Mycenaen civilisation, between 1650-1100BC. The 'mythological first division' have strong associations with the location, as faithfully detailed in Homers *Iliad* and *Odyssey*. It is said, by those far more likely to be able to support the supposition than me, that mythology and historical mesh rather neatly, which makes reading the various exploits of the gods just that little more interesting.

The enclosing walls of the citadel are Cyclopean, so referred to as the ancients considered that only giant gods, such as the one-eyed Cyclops, would have had the strength to place the massive stones in position. As the walls were originally up to some 10m thick and 17m high, maybe they had a point.

Star exhibits of this archaeological 'super spot' include: the Grave Circles, Royal Tombs, the Treasury of Atreus, supposedly the burial place of the legendary Agememnon, the Lions Gate, and the Palace.

ROUTE FOUR (Illus. 16)
ARGOS TO TRIPOLI via **Nea Kios** (65km) From Argos the Nafplio road leads to **Dalamanara** village (4km), where a right-hand turning leads to a T-junction, on a low, 'Essex' marshland of a coastal plain. The right-hand choice parallels the very broad sweep of sandy, if shadeless and shallowly shelving beach.

As the route proceeds westward, there are signs of some biscuit and sea-bed rocks, in addition to a low-key but persuasive pong, none of which has stopped a disco being banged down in this rather unlovely, windswept area.

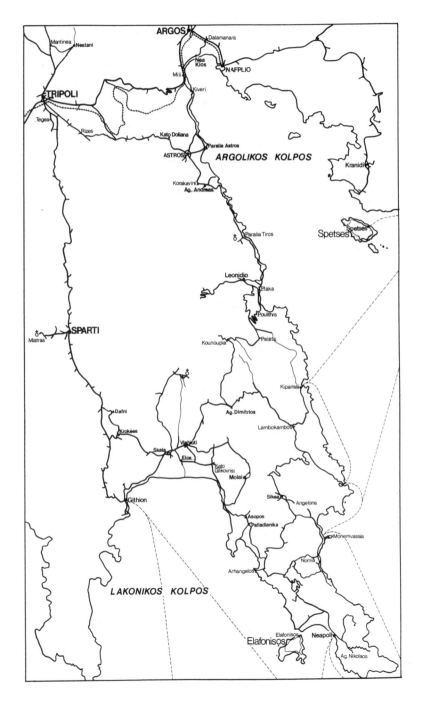

Illustration 16 Routes, Four, Five & Six

NEA KIOS (10km from Argos) Tel prefix 0751. The gum tree shaded 'High St' borders a quay wall, passing by: a Post Office; a sports ground stadium; and the two storey *Hotel Ignatia* (Class C, tel 51062), where a double bedroom, sharing the bathrooms costs 4600drs & an en suite double 5600drs. Beyond a children's playground, is a river-mouth, small harbour packed with boats and small caiques. There is more accommodation at the *Hotel Aktaeon* (Class D, tel 51477), where double bedrooms, sharing the bathrooms, cost 3600drs.

The main centre of the town is to the right, whilst the rather dirty coloured sea here edges a long stretch of pebbly, kelpy beach. The shore is spotted with canvas shelters and beach showers, whilst the windswept, inland side of the road is rather scrubbly and inflicted with a sprinkling of villa development, interspersed by groves of bamboo. As the road proceeds westwards, the 'not ever so' tempting shoreline gradually narrows down, and the sea-bed becomes shallower, with marshland to the right. The far end waterfront is rather rocky, with young palm trees newly planted and an outcrop of pleasant looking, 'mature' villas.

The coastline-hugging road is bordered by a sea wall on the outskirts of: **MILI (Myli, Moloi)** (16km from Argos) Tel prefix 0751. The main road rushes by this railway station, whilst a slip road angles down to a very pleasant length of waterfront.

At the outset to the inland side of the village is the abundantly tree shaded, rather doo-hickey *Camping Lerna* (Tel 47520). Alongside the campsite is the widespread garden of *Taverna Lerna*, where a meal for two of chicken & chips, fried zucchini, Boutari retsina (no kortaki available), bread & service, cost 2250drs. Across the road from the campsite is a small quay and a pleasant curve of pebble beach - okay for a swim.

The short, rural main road 'High St' is crammed with chicken-shack chippies, & souvlaki huts (which smoke, or belch into life in the evenings), as well as a restaurant and taverna. Shops include a baker, pharmacy, small supermarket, fruit shop and a periptero. The attractions of the High St are rather negated by the constant roar of traffic.

On the other hand, to escape the noxious effects of the motor car, it is only necessary to cross over the railway tracks and drop down to the very nicely landscaped waterfront. This is an oasis of shady, neat, calm, bordering a clear sea, and a clean stretch of pebble beach, towards the south end of which is a quite substantial pier. Some 3m into the water, and the sea-bed is slowly shelving, and sandy. There are a couple of apparently prosperous and expensive taverna/restaurants, the *To Mouragio* and, almost opposite the pier, the *Faros Fish Taverna*.

To sum up, Mili is a most interesting, off the tourist-beaten-track location, beyond which the main road curves inland, although a coastal road continues on 'due' south, in the direction of Astros (*See* Route Five, Chapt. 7). The far side of an Italian inspired filling station, the route winds and climbs steeply up the mountainside. Close to the summit are a pair of Spanish style, wayside, single storey restaurants.

It must have been quite a pad.   Acrocorinthos

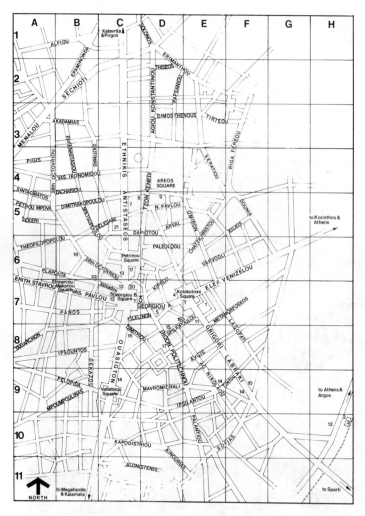

Tmr

1E7	Main Bus terminus
2H9/10	Railway Bus terminus
3H9/10	Railway Station
4D7	Hotel Arcadia
5D7	Hotel Alex
6C7	Hotel Galaxy
7C5	Hotel Anaktorikon
8C/D4/5	Hotel Artemis
9D4/5	Hotel Menalon
10F9	Hotel Kynouria
11E7/8	Rizes Village Bus stop
12H10	Cafe-bar Restaurant
13	Banks

14	Bakers
15D7/8	Kava
16C7/8	Supermarket
17	Dry Cleaners
18B6	OTE
19D/E7/8	Archaeological Museum
20C6/7	Police
21C5/6	Town Hall/Tourist Office
22B/C6/7	Post Office

P = Periptero
T = Taxi rank
(Tmr) = Town map reference

Illustration 17 Tripoli

7 TRIPOLI

Illustration 17

FIRST IMPRESSIONS Modern, spacious layout.

SPECIALITIES Manufacturing & wine production; fruit & vegetables.

VITAL STATISTICS Tel prefix 071. Population circa 22000.

HISTORY In ancient times, the plain settlements of Tegea, to the south, and Mantinea, to the north, were the local centres of civilisation. Only after their destruction did Tripoli take shape.

The Franks fortified the town, which the Venetians captured in 1688, only for the Turks to take over, in 1770. During the Greek War of Independence, the Hellenic forces, led by Kolokotronis, laid siege to Tripoli for three months, in 1821. Once they succeeded, the defenders and Turkish inhabitants were massacred. The Pasha retook the city in 1824, only to cause it to be razed to the ground as his forces subsequently retreated. Rebuilding commenced in 1834.

GENERAL Labelled as a major Peloponnese hub, or crossroads. Considering the history, it is not entirely surprising that Tripoli is a rather modern city and, in contrast to Argos, a joy to behold - if that is a fair comparison. Furthermore, Tripoli is fortunate to retain some attractive, old side-streets, leading off the main squares, bordered by buildings which seem to press in on their very pavements.

In fact, Tripoli could be labelled the 'tale of three squares' as the Plateias Kolokotroni (*Tmr* D/E7), Georgiou 'B' (*Tmr* C7) and Ethnarcou Makariou (*Tmr* A/B6/7) are pivotal to all visitors. Kolokotroni is modern and bustling, with a small, beflowered circular garden; larger Georgiou 'B' has an old-fashioned ambiance, with peripteros and Victorian buildings edging alleys and lanes that scurry hither and thither; whilst small, E. Makariou is almost suburbanly pretty, with trees, shrubs, and roses planted in the central garden.

ARRIVAL BY BUS It will very much depend from whence a traveller arrives, as there are two major bus termini. The main one (*Tmr* 1E7) is beside Plateia Kolokotroni, and the other (*Tmr* 2H9/10) is close to the Railway station. Fortunately, it is only a 10min walk from one to the other.

ARRIVAL BY TRAIN A main halt on the clockwise Peloponnese railway line linking Athens to Kalamata, via Korinthos.

THE ACCOMMODATION & EATING OUT

The Accommodation Despite an over-abundance, there are a few reasonable and convenient possibilities.

Hotel Arcadia (*Tmr* 4D7) (Class B) Kolokotroni Sq   Tel 225551
Directions: A modern, seven storey building beside the principal square.
    All bedrooms have en suite bathrooms, with a single priced at 4180/4800drs & a double 6680/7560drs.

Hotel Alex (*Tmr* 5D7) (Class C) 26 Vas Georgiou 'A'   Tel 223465
Directions: On the left (*Kolokotroni Sq behind one*) of the street linking the two main squares, Plateia Kolokotroni and Plateia Georgiou 'B'.
    Single bedrooms sharing the bathrooms, are charged at 2485/2750drs, whilst doubles sharing cost 3725/4080drs, & doubles en suite 4610/5055drs.

Hotel Galaxy (*Tmr* 6C7) (Class C) Georgiou B Sq   Tel 225195
Directions: Edging one of the other main squares.
    All bedrooms have en suite bathrooms, with a single room costing 3990drs & a double room 5320drs.

In the direction of Plateia Areos, proceeding north along Odhos Ethnikis Antistaseos, are the:
Hotel Anaktorikon (*Tmr* 7C5) (Class C) 48 E. Antistaseos   Tel 222545
Directions: On the right (*Georgiou B Sq behind one*) of the avenue.
    A single room, sharing the bathrooms, is priced at 2500drs, singles en suite cost 4580drs, a double sharing 3650drs & a double en suite 5500drs.

Hotel Artemis (*Tmr* 8C/D4/5) (Class C) 1 Dimitrakopoulou St   Tel 225221
Directions: On the right of the street (*Facing Areos Sq*).
    All the bedrooms have en suite bathrooms, a single costing 4065drs & a double 5870drs.
And the
Hotel Menalon (*Tmr* 9D4/5) (Class C) Areos Sq   Tel 222450
Directions: On the south side of Areos Sq.
    All bedrooms have en suite bathrooms, with a single priced at 2600drs & a double 3800drs.

Returning to Plateia Kolokotroni, and proceeding in the direction of the Railway station, south-east along Odhos Grigori Labraki leads to the:
Hotel Kynouria (*Tmr* 10F9) (Class E) 79 G. Labraki   Tel 222463
Directions: As above, and on the left.
    An old-fashioned establishment, only offering double bedrooms, sharing the bathrooms, at a cost of 2400drs.

Camping None in or around the immediate vicinity of the city.

THE EATING OUT It has to be stressed that there is an overall lack of souvlaki pita, although the underground, Main Bus terminus cafe is worth a try. There is a convenient cafe-bar on the south-east side of Plateia Kolokotroni (*Tmr* D/E7) - even if the service is lackadaisical to non-existent. It is one of those places where a punter can sit around, seemingly for hours, patiently, oh so patiently waiting. Then, lo and behold, a chum of the waiter plonks himself down and, even before his backside is securely positioned on the seat, this interlopper's order is being taken and fulfilled!
    The environs of Plateia Georgiou 'B' (*Tmr* C7) are more fertile 'grazing' grounds. Apart from a zacharoplasteion and cafe-bars, on the south-west side

is the *Restaurant Ethnikon*, whilst on D. Athiadou St, is a very old *Kafeneion*. Beside the Rizes village Bus stop (*Tmr* 11E7/8), on Grigori Labraki St, is *Lakis Zacharoplasteion* and a slightly greasy *Restaurant/Taverna*.

Across the main road from the Railway station (*Tmr* 3H9/10) is a 'sleazo' *Cafe-bar Restaurant* (*Tmr* 12H10), where tickets are purchased for the Railway station buses.

There are several old-fashioned tavernas beside Odhos Ouasigton (*Tmr* C8).

THE A TO Z OF USEFUL INFORMATION

BANKS A number are gathered about Plateia Georgiou 'B' and include the **Bank of Crete** (*Tmr* 13C7) at the square's junction with Vas Pavlou, the **Commercial Bank** (*Tmr* 13C6/7), adjacent to the junction of Odhos Athiadou with E. Anstistaseos St, and the **National Bank** (*Tmr* 13C6) beside E. Antistaseos St. The new **Ionian Bank** is beside Odhos Ouasigton, *en route* to the Market Sq, Plateia Valtetsiou (*Tmr* C9), opposite a Fish shop. Incidentally, the old Ionian Bank on Odhos 28th Octovriou has been turned into a coffee bar, but there are other banks still in business lining this street.

BOOKSELLER Bordering the north-east side of Plateia Georgiou 'B' (*Tmr* C7) is an English language newspaper and bookshop.

BREAD SHOPS One **Baker** (*Tmr* 14F9) edges Grigori Labraki St, and he sells a tasty sausage roll. A **Baker** (*Tmr* 14E/F9) is to the west of G. Labraki St, tucked in the angle of the junction of Odhos Tilefou and Odhos Ag Nikolaou, and yet another (*Tmr* 14C9) is on the left of Odhos Ouasigton (*Plateia Georgiou 'B' behind one*).

BUSES Tripoli has a more than usually jumbled Bus station arrangement. All looks well at first, with a mega, part-underground main facility (*Tmr* 1E7), off the south-east corner of Plateia Kolokotroni. Supplementing this is a local service, from the west side of Plateia Kolokotroni (*Tmr* D/E7). An informal terminus (*Tmr* 2H9/10) borders the main ring road, serving the Railway station connections. If that were not sufficient 'to the route thereof', yet another street-side Bus Station (*Tmr* 11E7/8) lurks beside Grigori Labraki St, close to Plateia Kolokotroni - the Rizes/Tegea connection. Mmmh!

Bus timetables
1. **Main terminus** (*Tmr* 1E7).
Tripoli to Athens (100 Kifissou St), via Argos & Korinthos.
Daily   0500, 0645, 0830, 0930, 1045, 1230, 1345, 1500, 1630, 1730, 1930hrs
  Return journey
Daily   0630, 0800, 0930, 1045, 1215, 1345, 1515, 1700, 1800, 2030, 2300hrs
One-way fare 2000drs; duration 3hrs.
Tripoli to Patras
Daily   Two a day.
Tripoli to Pirgos
Daily   0800, 1200, 1800hrs.
One-way fare 1500drs; 3½hrs.
Tripoli to Astros
Daily   0530, 1315hrs.
Tripoli to Leonidio
Daily   1315hrs
Tripoli to Megalopoli
Daily   0445, 0630, 0900, 1100, 1245, 1500, 1700, 1915hrs
One-way fare 400drs; duration ½hr.

Tripoli to Dimitsana (west of Tripoli)
Daily   1345, 1800hrs
One-way fare 750drs; duration 1½hrs.
Tripoli to Ag Petros (south-east of Tripoli)
Daily   0600, 1300hrs
Tripoli to Vourvoura (south-east of Tripoli)
Daily   0615, 1300hrs
Tripoli to Tropea (north-west of Tripoli)
Daily   0800, 1200, 1330, 1800, 2115hrs
Tripoli to Andritsena (west of Tripoli)
Daily   0445, 1130hrs.
One-way fare 850drs; duration 1hr.
Tripoli to Dards (north of Tripoli)
Daily   1330hrs

2. Kolokotroni Sq Local buses (*Tmr* D/E7).
Destinations include: Steno, Neohori, Partheni, Pallandio, Vouno, & Tzivas.

3. Grigori Labraki St Local buses (*Tmr* 11E7/8).
Buses to Rizes & Tegea archaeological site (south-east of Tripoli).
Daily   0700-2100hrs, every hour.
One-way fare 150drs; duration 15min.

4. Railway station terminus (*Tmr* 2H9/10).
Tripoli to Sparti
Daily   At least four buses a day.
One-way fare 550drs; duration 1 1/3hrs.

Other southern Peloponnese bus route itineraries include
Kalamata & Pilos.

Bus Offices The main bus office (*Tmr* 1E7) is in the underground section of
the terminus, as are several small coffee/snack bars, a luggage store, toilets, a
drinks store, general shop and a post box. Phew! The Railway terminus bus
office is tucked into the *Cafe-bar* (*Tmr* 12H10), across the ring-road from the
railway lines. The Rizes bus office (*Tmr* 11E7/8) is in the adjacent
'sticky-cake' *Zacharoplasteion*.

COMMERCIAL SHOPPING AREA There can be no doubt that Odhos
Ouasigton is the old commercial street and shopping mall of the city. In
amongst the to-be-expected shops are an ironmonger's, a tin plate store, and
fish shops, prior to the full flowering of the Market. The latter radiates out
from Plateia Valtetsiou (*Tmr* C9), from which epicentre stalls, stores and
shops edge the adjoining streets, lanes and alleys. Of these, Odhos Ipsilantou
is 'rich' in rabbit & chicken butchers, egg shops and fruit & vegetable stores.
    Other possibilities include: the area in and around Plateia Georgiou 'B',
more especially in the north-west vector; a worthwhile **Kava** (drink shop - *Tmr*
15D7/8), on Odhos Spiliopoulou; and a noteworthy **Supermarket** (*Tmr*
16C7/8), on Odhos Dimitriou. Beside Odhos Gregori Labraki is a workshop,
wherein the proprietor specialises in canvas and leather work - a reminder of a
trade that was once a pillar of Tripoli's manufacturing thrust.

ELPA Their office (*Tmr* C5/6) is to the right (*Plateia Georgiou 'B' behind
one*) of Ethnikis Antistaeos St.

LAUNDRY There at least two Dry Cleaners. One (*Tmr* 17C6), south of

Plateia Petrinou, is off to the right (*Plateia Georgiou 'B' behind one*) of Ethnikis Antistaseos St, the other (*Tmr* 17D8) is beside Iroon Politechnou St.

LUGGAGE STORE There are facilities at the Main Bus terminus (*Tmr* 1E7) and at the Railway Station (*Tmr* 3H9/10).

MEDICAL CARE
Chemists & Pharmacies Some towns lack them, some have a superfluity. Tripoli possesses a rich vein, with at least three pharmacies spaced around Plateia Kolokotroni (*Tmr* D/E7), and more on 28th Octovriou St (*Tmr* B/C6). **Dentists** Once again, there are a number, with one beside Odhos Iroon Politechnou (*Tmr* D8/9).
Hospital Yes, off the map. Own up Geoffrey, you're not sure!!!

MUNICIPAL TOURIST OFFICE (*Tmr* 21C5/6) To the left (*Plateia Georgiou 'B' behind one*) of Ethnikis Antistaseos St, and in the ground floor of the Town Hall. Open daily between 0830-1430hrs.

OTE (*Tmr* 18B6) Alongside 28th Octovriou St, and open daily 0600-2400hrs.

PETROL There are two filling stations beside Kolokotroni Sq(*Tmr* D/E7).

PLACES & EVENTS OF INTEREST The main church is the twin-towered Ag Vasilios (*Tmr* C/D7), alongside Odhos Georgiou 'A', close to Plateia Georgiou 'B'.
  The squares and parks help make the city attractive, especially the three-in-line Kolokotroni (*Tmr* D/E7), Georgiou 'B' (*Tmr* C7) and Ethnarcou Makariou (*Tmr* A/B6/7) plateias, each one with an entirely different character.

Museum, Archaeological (*Tmr* 19D/E7/8) Open weekdays 0830-1500hrs, Sundays & holidays 0930-1430hrs, but closed Mondays. Entrance is free. The Museum is located close to the junction of Evagelistrias and Spiliopoulou Sts, and is housed in a pleasant, yellow, neo-classical, two storey building. To gain access, visitors must walk through a lovely, if small garden. Worth a visit, especially as it costs no more than the walk!

POLICE
Town (*Tmr* 20C6/7) Close to the junction of Ethnikis Antistaseos and the north-east corner of Plateia Georgiou 'B'.
Tourist *See* Municipal Tourist Office.

POST OFFICE (*Tmr* 22B/C6/7) Beside Odhos Plapouta.

TAXIS There are ranks at Plateia Kolokotroni (*Tmr* D/E7), Plateia Georgiou 'B' (*Tmr* C7), and at the Railway Station (*Tmr* 3H9/10).

TELEPHONE NUMBERS & ADDRESSES

Hospital	Tel 238542
Police (*Tmr* 20C6/7)	Tel 222411
Town Hall (*Tmr* 21C5/6)	Tel 239392

TOILETS There are public conveniences located in the Main Bus station underground concourse (*Tmr* 1E7), alongside Plateia Petrinou (*Tmr* C6), and at the Railway station (*Tmr* 3H9/10).

TRAINS The pleasantly gum tree shaded Railway station (*Tmr* 3H9/10) is in the south-east outskirts of Tripoli, a not inconvenient 10mins walk from Plateia Kolokotroni.

Train timetables
Tripoli to Athens
Daily Dep. 0140, 0932, 1328, 1817hrs
Argos	0302, 1045, 1450, 1936hrs
Mikines	0312, 1059, 1501, - hrs
Korinthos	0402, 1159, 1552, 2035hrs
Athens	0543, 1355, 1742, 2219hrs

Tripoli to Kalamata
| Daily Dep. | 1147, 1327, 1855hrs |
| Kalamata | 1438, 1549, 2148hrs |

One-way fare to Athens 1200drs; duration 5hrs.

EXCURSIONS TO TRIPOLI SURROUNDS

Excursion to Tegea (8km) *See* Illus. 16. To the south of Tripoli. An ancient city state, and the most important in the area until 550BC, when the Spartans finally overcame the inhabitants. At the outset is a museum, open daily 0830-1500hrs, entrance costing 200drs, and from which signs indicate the direction of the remains of The Temple of Athena Alea.

Excursion to Mantinea (14km) *See* Illus.16. To the north of Tripoli. In ancient times Mantinea was a long-time protagonist of Tegea, but little now remains. On the other hand, visitors cannot but help be drawn, as is a rabbit to a venomous snake, by the intriguing, unsettling Byzantine church style building, with Chinese overtones! Unsettling? Well, further inspection reveals that the construction is an amalgam, a hodgepodge, a jigsaw of disparate building materials and styles. All becomes clear when it is realised that the 'church' is a folly, designed and built by a Greek-American architect, during the 1970s.

ROUTE FIVE TRIPOLI TO NEAPOLI via Leonidio, Kiparissi, Gerakas & Monemvassia (229km).

From Tripoli, the 'country lane' road to the coast adjacent to Astros, passes close by the archaeological site of **Tegea**, through **Stadio** (8km) and **Rizes** (11km). The summer-dry River Tanos is Loire-sized and heralds the approaches to:

ASTROS (44km from Tripoli) Tel prefix 0755. Much of the clean, inland town is a one-way street layout.

There is a baker, a restaurant, a filling station, the latter by the junction with the High St, a National Bank, and the *Hotel Anthini* (Class D, tel 22498), where a single sharing the bathrooms costs 2150drs, a single with an en suite bathroom 2350drs & a double sharing 3350drs. The Main Square, close to the High St junction, boasts a taxi rank, and nearby is a Health Centre. There is one other hotel, the *Paralia* (Class C, tel 51412), where all rooms have en suite bathrooms, with a single priced at 4000drs & a double 5200drs.

Alongside the route out of Astros is a 'Kung Fu' body building outfit(!), a Post Office, an Agricultural Bank and an extensive store.

From Astros, *en route* to Paralia Astros, passes by a couple of discos, which seem rather a fair hike out of town, for a night's ecstasy. (Think about it, or preferably don't!)

Reverting to **Route Four**. In choosing to leave the shore road, south of Mili, a chunk of coastline description was omitted, so..., prior to describing Paralia Astros (and continuing south), the narrative returns to the 'parting of the ways', back at the fork, about 1km south of Mili.

The main road swings inland towards Tripoli, whilst the coastal road heads for Astros through:

KIVERI (circa 15km from Argos) A very pleasant seaside village which benefits, vis-a-vis Mili, from being off the main Argos-Tripoli highway. At the outset is a *Rooms* and a filling station. About centre of the village is a drinking water fountain and a general store. The pleasant, pebble beach has been awarded the Golden Starfish. The paved waterfront is nicely planted with oleanders, the pierhead is to the left (*Fsw*), a river flows into the sea, and a few fishing boats are drawn up on the foreshore. The 'mandatory' fish taverna is kept company by a number of restaurants, and there is yet another *Rooms*.

At the southern end, the route climbs up on to a low mountain. Close to a dirt track down to a shadeless pebble/sand stretch of beach, is accommodation, in a house surrounded by olive trees, and adjacent to an extensive church (or monastery?). For a time, the road hugs the mountainside, about 200m above sea-level, paralleling a 'standard', indented, snaking coastline down below.

After dropping towards sea-level, passing by a 'scramble' down to a tiny cove of pebble, and another to a larger cove, the outskirts are reached of:
XIROPIGADO (circa 20km from Argos) Once a tiny fishing hamlet, this is now a small, restrained resort, with any number of *Rooms*.   These include *Zavitsa* (Tel 71251), the four storey *Edelweiss* (Tel 71207), the facade of which is probably, regularly scaled by storm troops of yodelling Germans, and the *Restaurant/Rooms Blue Sky* (Tel 71209). Other accommodation telephone numbers are: 26829; 22095; 71259; & 21334.

At the north end of the settlement is a steep path down to a beach. The latter is mainly pebble, but with gritty sand at the sea's edge, and a hint of pure sand, here and there. Towards the south is a direct access to the shore, where bathers benefit from the provision of beach showers, as they do water sports activities. Visitors may avail themselves of the services of a travel office. At the far end is a rather incomplete quay, from alongside which a concrete track allows a steep climb back up to the main road.

Further south, and tucked into the sea-level cliff edge, are a number of rather tempting, if difficult to attain, little beaches. One is signposted *Summery Snackbar Time Out*, which leads to a long stretch of grey sand and gritty beach, with a bush-bordered backshore.

The main route progresses to the Tanos river valley, and a graffiti of road signs, at a 'junction of the ways'. To the right leads to Astros. To the left crosses an area of marshy land, to a hard-standing-bordered, 4m wide strip of gently shelving, grey sand beach, the backshore of which is rather grittier, more pebbly. The shore undulates to the south, all the way round to a castle topped headland. The surroundings are low-lying and swampy, with a profusion of bamboo, and areas of salt-beds. The road cuts through about 15m distant from the backshore, occasionally revealing messy bits of still grey sand beach. Prior to the mouth of the River Tanos, is a grove of fig trees followed by the new'ish, tree shaded *stros Camping* (Tel 51500). Close to the campsite, and to the left *(Facing south)* is a *Rooms*. The marshy surrounds do not bode well for mosquito-free nights!

Now back to **Route Five.**

PARALIA ASTROS (48km from Tripoli) This approach is to the north of the referred-to castle headland. The beach is bordered by a sea wall with a few villas inland. The *Paradissos Inn* (Class C, tel 51186) only offers apartments, costing between 5050-12000drs per night, and is opposite a pebbly, kelpy section of beach, backed by a duney marsh. There are one or three other buildings scattered about.

The headland marks the outset of a more developed Paralia Astros, an embryonic Kosta resort. *Rooms*, apartments, and the *Motel Villa Park* are followed by a pleasant row of gum trees lining the inland side of the road. On the southern side of the headland is a large harbour and a pretty waterfront. The houses attractively stretch up the hillside, and, if one was asked, it would have to be stated that the result is a quintessentially Greek location, melded with a smooth Italian sophistication. There are several tour offices, and the pebble beach continues on in a nice, if unshaded sweep. Near where the original village 'breaks through', the backshore is separated from the road by one row of buildings, in which are several *Rooms*, and a doctor's clinic, all quite close to a smart hotel.

Even beyond the point at which the tarmacadam surface of the Esplanade runs out, the now reasonably wide coastal strip runs on, anything up to 20m wide, and along the edge of which has been planted tamarisk trees. A typical 'grid of streets', marking out an intended development, but set in amongst the 'bundy', is a tribute to Hellenic optimism. The 'parish' boundary is indicated by a tall factory chimney, probably of some long forgotten olive or tomato canning works.

To sum up, despite Paralia Astros being far from undiscovered, it is a nicely developed, low-key resort, based on a once tiny fishing hamlet.

Back at the Paralia Astros/Astros road junction are the pair of discos, to which reference has already been made (*See* Astros). Continuing in a southerly, inland direction, the route passes through olive groves and what appears to be a marshy, inland lake. The spaced-out village of **Korakovouni** (52km) is followed by the more compact **Ag Andreas**(53km), which is set at the foot of a mountain range and surrounded by groves of olives growing in a distinctive red soil. On the other side of a summer dry river-bed are two filling stations and a small sign to:

PARALIA AG ANDREAS (56km from Tripoli) Part of the lovely drive to the coast is edged by gum trees, close to a small cemetery. In the bed of the River Vrasiotis is an old, stone bridge, prior to the road running out at the river inlet. Here are moored some small fishing boats. An outer wall forms a harbour with, to the left (*Fsw*), a line of rocks and a spit of shingle beach enclosing a tiny lagoon. The very attractive scene is completed by a taverna and a chapel.

From Ag Andreas, the route climbs on to the mountainside to 'corniche' and undulate along the coast (here and there). Shady *Camping Arcadia* (Tel 31190) is very popular with the Germans, and lies around a pebble beach of a sea inlet, about which the road horseshoe's.
    The route reveals coastal views of various coves and bays. One 300m length of pebble shore boasts a rustic fish taverna, as well as some smart, single storey accommodation. Other 'beach-lines' are shorter, if much of the same, some favoured by camper-vans and wild campers, one having a chapel, a refreshment type taverna, and *Camping Zaritsi* (Tel 0757 41429). Some of the interior views are dramatic, with fairly massive mountains piled up.
    The route cuts inland to circumnavigate a mountain gulch, whereat a motor track makes off down to a pebble beach. This supports a few pedaloes and windsurfers, and is serviced by a hotel and restaurant.

PARALIA TIROS (76km from Tripoli) Tel prefix 0757. This large village is set on the edge of a pleasant bay overlooked, on the far side, by a trio of distinctive, Cycladian windmills.
    At the outskirts are *Rooms*, the *Hotel Tyros* (Class D, tel 41235), where all rooms have en suite bathrooms, with a single costing 3200/3700drs & a double 3250/4200drs, and a filling station, all on the left (*Facing south*).
    At a crossroads, a sign, to the left, indicates the *Tiros Beach*, and the waterfront. The access road passes by fairly low-key development, with only a few buildings over two storeys high. In amongst these are a: *Rooms*; travel agency; *Rooms* (Tel 1261); apartments; Real Estate office; *Rooms*; more *Rooms*; a doo-hickey supermarket; and *Rooms*. Beyond these is a concrete Esplanade held back by a wall, against which the sea laps. The sea bed is pebble. To the right (*Fsw*) sweeps past an 'overdressed' *Karnagio Taverna*, kitted out with enough marine bits to build a boat. It is supposed to be a pub, and is togged out as a ship's deck. Whatever ghastly image this description conjures up, it has been quite eye-catchingly executed. Paralia Tiros was a fishing community that has worked at becoming a holiday resort, a 1950s holiday resort. Most of the Esplanade is lined by restaurants, tavernas and *Rooms*. A great boost to the citizens aspirations must be the thrice-weekly hydrofoil service.
    Towards the far right-hand end is a baker, as well as some private houses, a mini-market, and a few hotels. These include: the three storey *Kambissis* (Class C, tel 41424), with en suite singles priced at 4500drs & doubles 6000drs; the Apollon (Class C, tel 41393), with en suite singles at 4000drs & doubles 5600drs; and opposite a chunk of pebble beach, the *Hotel Blue Sea* (Class C, tel 41369), where en suite singles are charged at 4000drs &

doubles 5000drs. Continuing on, beyond a small chapel, with an enormous, separate bell tower, is the *Restaurant Arcadia*, **Rooms**, 'Chambre a Lour', and, at the far end, a part subsidence-submerged quay.

To the left (*Fsw*) along the concrete Esplanade, passes by 'more of the same', as well as some small shops, **Rooms**, a section of sea wall enclosing a narrow stretch of pebble, with a fleet of fishing boats anchored in the bay. There is a pharmacy, Dapia Tours tourist office, the *Hotel Tsakonia* (Class D, tel 41322), where all bedrooms share the bathrooms, a single costing 3000drs & a double 3200drs. The foreshore beach continues on, before finally coming to an end, up against the *Hotel Anessis* (Class D, tel 41398), with en suite singles priced at 3700drs & doubles 4950drs.

Hydrofoil timetables

Tues/Sat	1205hrs	Leonidio, Kiparissia, Gerakas, Monemvassia.
Thurs/Sun	1205hrs	Leonidio, Kiparissia, Gerakas.
Tues/Sat/	1610hrs	Portoheli, Spetses(island), Hydra,
Thurs/Sun		Zea Port(Piraeus).

One-way fare to Zea Port 3230drs; duration 3hrs.

Returning to the main route, several filling stations and more **Rooms** herald the end of the parish of Tiros. The road climbs back on to the mountains for a repeat of the previous scenic delights. Incidentally, one of the windmills previously mentioned appears to have been converted to domestic use. The further south the journey progresses, the more noticeable are donkeys and herds of goats. In the area of **Pera Melana** (82km) the surface of the thoroughfare becomes rather 'moth-eaten'.

From up above, a tantalising sighting is made of:
LIVADI (84km from Tripoli). From the main road, the access, signed to a fish taverna, is some way south of the settlement. The *Manolis Taverna*, of pleasing appearance, offers accommodation (Tel 22292). Throughout this green and pretty valley gulch, and coastal plain, are several more **Rooms**. They are spaced-out along the one, narrow, winding, cul-de-sac of a track. This terminates close to a terrace of fishermen's cottages, bordering a boulderous pebble shore, with small jetties protruding into the sea. Despite the presence of the accommodation, Livadi has firmly eschewed tourism.

At the south side of the Livadi headland, the main road shoots past a fishing community bordering more grey pebble beach, and yet one more hamlet. Beyond the latter, the road gently descends towards the lovely, fertile Dafnon River valley, unfortunately host to a fair amount of polythene agriculture. After the main route swings inland, up the river valley, a road junction signpost, overlooked by at least three ruined windmills indicates **Lakkos** (9km). But travellers needn't bother to detour, unless they wish to observe Greek farming of a rich alluvial plain, in some detail, or are turned-on by the sight of long, steep, sand and pebble beach. As the land is lower than the sea, the shore is the other side of a high sea wall, along which are spaced-out a couple of tavernas.

LEONIDIO (94km from Tripoli) Tel prefix 0757. At the outset to this inland village are a filling station, a Health Centre (or cottage hospital..., not a fitness club), and a *Rooms*, labelled 'Information'. Leonidio is a long, spaced-out 'High St of a village' along which are strung several restaurants, another filling station, an OTE, Post Office, a 'bit-of-a-square', a kafeneion, pharmacy, a National Bank and a grand, neo-classical Town Hall. Beyond the latter, the High St bridges the wide, summer-dry river-bed, which appears to split into two, with mature gum trees edging the road. If the river were full of running water, Leonidio would have a more French ambiance, than Greek.

Once over the river, the village effectively comes to an end, in a profusion of olive groves, in which nestle a restaurant, where English and French are spoken, and yet another filling station.

Beyond some intense agriculture, close to a lovely little chapel, are the outskirts of, and the steep road, to:

PLAKA (98 km from Tripoli) Will the real Plaka stand up? What on earth...? Well, Leonidio has 'stolen' the fishing port's name and identity. For example, the hydrofoil schedules do not list Plaka. Oh, no, they detail Leonidio, despite the fact that Plaka is the flying dolphin (hydrofoil) port of call. In fact it is one of a number of prettily located, if somewhat isolated ports and harbours spaced out, all the way down this eastern stretch of coastline.

It was a visit here that gave me the idea for a super method by which to explore this segment of the Peloponnese, namely to catch a hydrofoil at Zea Port (Piraeus), and speed along their flight path, not only to the islands of the Argo-Saronic, but the Peloponnese ports of Methana, Ermioni, Portoheli, Nafplio, Paralia Tiros, Leonidio, Kiparissi, Gerakas, Monemvassia, and Neapoli. Some of these locations are really most attractive, and 'off the beaten track'. It certainly is a thought.

The access road tumbles down through the old houses, past the *Taverna Virantes*, the modernish, three storey *Hotel Dionyssos* (Class D, tel 22379), where all bedrooms have en suite bathrooms, with a single priced at 3700/4000drs & a double 4700/5000drs, and to the right, around the end of the *Taverna Margarets*. This last named establishment overlooks the centrally located quay, quayside buildings, and the fishing boat harbour, the latter being enclosed by a substantial sea wall stretching to the right. Also in this direction is a crescent of pebble beach.

To the left is a wide sweep of clean, neat, gritty sand and pebble beach, the backshore of which is bordered by mature trees. Fixed to their trunks are 'No Camping' signs - which one discerns are 'meaningful'! To assuage any demand in this direction, there is an organised, enclosed area of packed flat mud to accommodate camper-vans and tents - more often than not totally ignored by visitors. It would appear that the locals have, from time to time, had to suffer a surfeit of wild camping.

Adjacent to the quay is supposed to be a *Disco Plaka*, whilst on the quayside is a periptero and close to it, fixed to one of the buildings, is an information board. Details hereon include the following:

Opening Hours

Shops	Mon, Wed & Sat	0800-1430hrs.
	Tues, Thurs & Fri	0800-1300hrs & 1700-2100hrs.
Post Office	Weekdays only	0800-1400hrs.
Bank	Weekdays only	0800-1330hrs.
Telephone office	Daily	0800-1500hrs.

Bus times
Leonidio to Athens

| Daily exc Sun | 0530, 0815, 1630hrs |
| Sun | 0815, 1630hrs |

Leonidio to Sparti

| Daily | 0600hrs |
| | returning at 1300hrs. |

In addition:
Hydrofoil timetables

Tues/Thurs/ Sat/Sun	1225hrs	Kiparissia, Gerakas, Monemvassia.
Tues	1155hrs	Kiparissia, Monemvassia, Kithira(island).
Wed	1140hrs	Kiparissia, Gerakas, Monemvassia, Kithira(island).
Sat	1140hrs	Kiparissia, Monemvassia, Kithira(island).
Tues/Thurs/ Sat/Sun	1550hrs	Tiros, Portoheli, Spetses(island), Hydra(island), Zea Port(Piraeus).
Tues/Sat	1820hrs	Portoheli, Spetses(island), Hydra(island), Zea Port(Piraeus).
Wed	1750hrs	Spetses(island), Ermioni, Poros(island), Methana, Aegina(island), Zea Port(Piraeus).

The *Hotel Dionyssos* and *Taverna Margarets* are under the same management. The taverna is a true representative of the old-time, family-run establishment, serving very reasonably priced, tasty, ample helpings. A meal, for two, of a plate of stuffed aubergines, a plate of meatballs with chips, a Greek salad, a plate of chips, 2 bottles of retsina, coffees and an ouzo will set a couple back some 2500drs. Certainly the locals are to be found here, in numbers.

All in all, Plaka is an excellent place at which to make a 'pit stop'. To the south is another pebble beach, which reminds me to point out that both shores have barrel roofed changing rooms.

POULITHRA (103km from Tripoli) This delightful, pretty, substantial fishing and farming village, 5km south and edging the same large bay as Plaka, is hard up against the Madara mountain range. Many of the houses and buildings are solidly built of dressed stone. Most maps give little idea of the size of the place.

Close to the outset of the settlement, on the right, are the *Hotel Kentavros* (Class D, tel 51214), the *House Katerina* and some apartments to let. In an orchard is the small, rather dead *Paradise Cafe-bar*, of tangible appearance, followed by a taverna, a mini-market and a hamburger/cheeseburger joint. But readers must not think that Poulithrais a tourist dominated, or even orientated location. It isn't.

The shore is a fairly narrow sweep of pebble, overlooked by a *Rooms*, in an attractive building, and the *Restaurant Akrogiali*. Where the High St/main road sets out on the steep, upward climb, from close by a popular, waterfront, local's kafeneion, in the direction of the inland 'massif', there is a concrete track which continues on along the shoreline, towards a small harbour.   Incidentally, the south end of the beach is kelpy, the sea is clean and the sea-bed is made up of big pebbles. Along this stretch is more accommodation - *Rooms Stagias*.

The ascending High St claws its way up the foothills of a mountain, for some 2 or 3km, past an impressive number of older, solid buildings, in amongst which is a grocer, to an upper village, where are another kafeneion, general store and a bar. Fortunately for the locals, taxis run up and down the asphalted hillside. The mountainsides are lovely and the ascent ends on a moorland vastness, which is surprisingly flat and rolling gorse-green.

A simple church, surrounded by a wall, and in the grounds of which are a lovely collection of trees, including cypresses, marks the outset of **Peleta village** (116km). Here, once again, are some pretty, four-square buildings, a bubbling kafeneion, and a very big church. Despite the maps indicating otherwise, the road is an 'all-red' affair, in much better condition than some of the previous route. But that is a 'too good to be true' state of the surface, as the road degenerates to a packed, scraped gravel and flint - all the way to **Kounoupia** (121km). Within the latter village is running stream water and the width of the carriageway narrows considerably, remaining unsurfaced, in places, all the way to **Mari** (124km). This settlement lies in a fertile, water-plenty, 'hidden' valley, which reminds one irresistibly of a French alpine location - if rather dry. The Byzantine styled church is large and rather new looking. Beyond Mari is a small chapel on a knoll.

The now-descending road really is quite roughly surfaced, coursing beside a river-bed, prior to cresting a saddle in the hillsides, and attaining the large village of **Ag Dimitrios** (136km), through which, as is often the case, the road is concreted. Beyond Ag Dimitrios, a left and then a right advances to the large settlement of **Lambokambos** (150km), around which, for a short distance, most of the roads are surfaced. Lambokambos is the road junction for access to the ports of Kiparissi, to the north, and Gerakas, to the south.

Heading north, first, makes for to the friendly, pretty, whitewashed village of **Harakas** (157km), wherein several kafeneions border the very narrow main street.

There are a number of attractive, hill-topping chapels, whilst the surface of the road 'chops and changes', in some places being concreted, in others metalled.

Where the route crosses from one gorge to another, an idea of the overall height above sea-level is gained, with a splendid glimpse out over the Mediterranean - way, way below. At a fairly dramatic bend, the road surface disappears. This is about where the line of the route allowsdistant views, to the north, along the undulating, but almost vertical mountainsides. These gracefully plunge beneath the surface of the sea. If the scenery is dramatic, so is the line of the road! To the immediate left is a steep cliff-face, whilst to the right is a precipitous drop.

The descent permits an almost Tyrolean view (if it were not for two bright red roofs) out over the extremely pretty, simple village of:
KIPARISSI (167km from Tripoli) Tel prefix 0761. The streets, in which are a couple of kafeneions, are steep and narrow. The various clock faces of the church show conflicting and incorrect information. The 'pedestrian difficult' fact that the church is separated from the cemetery, by a river, has been overcome with the construction of a bridge. The road becomes metalled, as the settlement is entered. At a fork is a sign *Paralia*, which leads to the harbour, whilst to the left is signed *Mitropoli*, which gives out to a huge sweep of beach, sweeping away to the north of the harbour.

PARALIA KIPARISSI (167km from Tripoli) The port has a whitewashed, Cycladean charm, and is as attractive as the upper village, if rather starker. The road drops to, and runs out on the quayside, close to which is a diminutive general store.
   To the right (*Fsw*) is a small, shingle, harbour beach, edging a beautifully clear sea, whilst round to the left is the referred-to, great swathe of fine, whitish pebble beach, bordering the deep bay. The harbour buildings spread out to the left, and amongst them is at least one *Rooms*, costing 3200drs for a double, with en suite bathroom. Further on round the sweep of the bay, almost at the far side, is a taverna with fine views. A narrow road leads to yet another beach.
   A small bus makes the journey to the port, probably tying in with the arrival and departure of the hydrofoils.

Ferry-boat timetable

Day	Departure time	Ferry-Boat	Ports/Islands of call
Thurs	1400hrs	Ionian	Gerakas, Monemvassia, Neapoli, Ag Pelagia (Kithira island), Githion, Kapsali (Kithira island), Antikithira (island), Kastelli (Crete).
Fri	2300hrs	Ionian	Piraeus.

Hydrofoil timetable

Day	Departure time	Ports/Islands of Call
Wed/Sat	1210hrs	Gerakas, Monemvassia, Kithira(island), Neapoli.
Tues	1225hrs	Gerakas, Monemvassia, Kithira(island), Neapoli.
Tues/Thurs/ Sat/Sun	1520hrs	Leonidio,Tiros, Portoheli, Spetses(island), Hydra(island), Zea Port(Piraeus).
Tue/Sat.	1750hrs	Leonidio, Portoheli, Spetses(island), Hydra(island), Zea Port(Piraeus).

One-way fare to Zea Port 3919drs; duration 3hrs 20mins.

Back at Lambokambos, the road to the south-east reveals a number of 'commanding height' round towers, probably 17/18thC look-out posts.
   The road becomes unsurfaced, yet again on a difficult bend, in addition to which there is a tricky bridge to negotiate. A river runs through the widely spaced-out, agricultural community of **Rihea** (160km), with many donkeys visible. Some of the house window frames are picked out in blue, whilst one of several kafeneions is a multi-wash of white, yellow and pink.
   This Gerakas descent is very different to that to Kiparissi, running down

a long, mountain bordered valley. **Ag Ioannis** (165km) is a tiny, simple hamlet, with a large church, set in olive groves and lots of field-enclosing stone walls. Where the surface becomes asphalted, almost at sea-level, alongside a large, marshy inlet of the sea, and some (Alikes) salt beds, is the onset of:

GERAKAS (172kms from Tripoli) The road edges the equivalent of a pretty Devonian river tributary, if an inexplicably hot Devonian river tributary! Apart from the heat, 'give-aways' might be the low-lying land, with no allowance for tide, and, in places, scummy, weedy shallows, into which jut rickety wooden piers. To the latter are tethered a number of craft, whilst set in the hillsides are a few new villas.

As the road snakes along beside the water's edge, into sight hoves the sleepy, island-like, extremely attractive main body of the settlement, across the street from the sea wall.

The first enterprise is the *Taverna Kavrogeraka*, followed by *Rooms/Taverna Kourouni*, a general store, open even on Sundays, the *Fish Taverna Ayra*, and the hydrofoil quay. Tireless, bespectacled Georgio and his family run the *Kourouni* (Tel 0732 59235). Their fresh smelling, en suite double rooms, in a building to the right *(Sbo)* of the cafe-bar taverna, cost 3000drs a night. Simple, traditional fishing village accommodation this might be, but there is a fridge and small sink. In addition, their taverna serves tasty, inexpensive, 'scrummy' fare. A meal, for two, of kalamares, a Greek salad, bread and 3 bottles of Amstel, costs about 1800drs. Drawbacks to this lovely location? A lack of beach, and the night-time mosquitoes - so keep the bedroom window closed, although most of them appear to have permanent netting.

All-in-all, a super spot to while away a day, a week, or two...

Ferry-boat timetable

Day	Departure time	Ferry-boat	Ports/Islands of call
Thurs	1500hrs	Ionian	Monemvassia, Neapoli, Ag Pelagia (Kithira island), Githion, Kapsali (Kithira island), Antikithira (island), Kastelli (Crete).
Fri	2200hrs	Ionian	Kiparissi, Piraeus.

Hydrofoil timetable

Day	Departure time	Ports/Islands of Call
Wed	1225hrs	Monemvassia, Kithira(island), Neapoli.
Tues/Thurs/ Sat/Sun	1325hrs	Monemvassia.
Tues/Thurs, Sat/Sun	1450hrs	Kiparissi, Leonidio, Tiros, Spetses(island), Portoheli, Hydra(island), Zea Port(Piraeus).
Wed	1650hrs	Kiparissi, Leonidio, Spetses(island), Ermioni, Poros(island), Methana, Aegina, Zea Port(Piraeus).

One-way fare to Zea Port 3919drs; duration 4hrs.

To save the long trek of returning to the main route, via Rihea, there is a coastal track, but, as the taverna owner said ..."The first five (km) are bad...". Without doubt, this choice of thoroughfare allows marvellous views along the coast, and across Ormos Kremmidi, to the towering peninsula of Monemvassia. Edging this bay is a splendidly rural fishing hamlet, a chapel, and a sunken tug, whilst the-till-this-point-boulderous shore is followed by a glorious sweep of several hundred metres of sand. The plage runs out on an outcrop of rocks, beyond which is..., even more sandy beach. Some of the backshore is backed by gorse supporting sand dunes, but shade is in short supply.

This delightful 'side route' joins a 'red' road, close to **Epidavros Limera**, an archaeological site. This junction is followed by one with an even 'more important' main road, bordering the south end of Ormos Kremmidi, and advancing past a now mainly rocky shoreline, signed *Pori Beach*. As the road forges on, it closes on the ever-bulking, impressive great lump of rock cutting off the southern end of the bay, connected to the land by a narrow causeway, and known as:

MONEMVASSIA (188km from Tripoli) Tel prefix 0732. The northern approaches are rather messy, passing by the *Malaysian Disco* and other rather recent developments, plonked down on the exposed inland slopes. These are about 100m distant from the backshore of a scrubbly, biscuit slab or rocky foreshore, with a 'bit of a' pebble beach and umbrellas, close to the causeway. These buildings 'house', for instance, the: *Hotel Kastro* (Class A Pension, tel 61413), where all rooms have en suite bathrooms, a single priced at 4000drs & doubles 6000/7000drs; apartments to let; *Angela's House Hotel* (Class D, tel 61418), offering single rooms with en suite bathroom for 4500/5000drs, double rooms sharing 5000/5500drs, & doubles en suite 6000/6500drs; *Rooms*; *Lekas Rent Rooms*; *Rooms*; a general store; more *Rooms*; *Rooms Bellasis*; *Villa Trugakos*; *Rooms*, *Hotel/Restaurant* Monemvassia (Class B Pension, tel 61381), with doubles sharing the bathrooms, costing 4000/5000drs, & with en suite bathrooms 5000/6000drs.

Beyond this 'rash of excitement' is the heart of the settlement, the east-west, angled High St, straddled by the modern village. To the south is the harbour, a disproportionately large quay, and another stretch of pebble. To the east, or forefront, rears-up an enormous outcrop of rock, and Old Monemvassia. The 'new' Monemvassia is linked to this island-like, Gibraltar of a promontory, by a kilometre long causeway.

New Monemvassia is shadeless and disappointingly Kosta'd - maybe still only half-way to the full horrors of a completely tourist raddled resort. But then it doesn't possess much of a beach, either side of the causeway, and what is available is mainly pebbly, with a rocky sea-bed, and the beach showers don't! The milieu is close to being that of 'Happy Hours', 'Kiss me quick' and 'Grab a Granny' hats, and 'wet T-shirt parties'. This is quite possibly accounted for by the high excursion coach trip rating of the location, with day-trippers arriving from far and wide.

Along or around the High St, are gathered: an OTE (signed, and about 100m off the main street), open weekdays only, between 0730-1500hrs, nearby which is a Community office; the Malvasia Travel office (Tel 61752); a supermarket; *Rooms*; the *Hotel S.Sophos*; the *Hotel Minoa* (Class C, tel 61209), where en suite single rooms cost 3015/4165drs & doubles 3990/ 5320drs, and opposite which are *Rooms*; a National Bank, close to which is the Police station; and a Post Office. The buses also 'rendezvous' on the High St, and daily connect to Molai (3 a day, weekdays, and 2 daily, weekends), from whence there are bus links to Sparti, Tripoli, Athens and Githion.

Around to the right (*Fsw*) from the National Bank are: more *Rooms*; the harbour; a general store; the *Hotel Acteon* (Class D, tel 61234), with pleasant balconies facing out over the harbour, where en suite singles cost 2570/3190drs, doubles sharing and en suite are charged at 3545/4430drs; a yachts' chandler & provender; a chemist; and a taverna. The town boasts a Medical clinic and benefits from both ferry-boat and hydrofoil services.

Ferry-boat timetable

Day	Departure time	Ferry-boat	Ports/Islands of call
Mon	1600hrs	Ionian	Neapoli, Ag Pelagia (Kithira island),Githion, Kapsali(Kithera island), Antikithera, Kastelli (Crete).
Tues	2100hrs	Ionian	Piraeus.
Thurs	600hrs	Ionian	Neapoli, Ag Pelagia (Kithira island), Githion, Kapsali (Kithira island), Antikithira Kastelli (Crete).
Fri	2100hrs	Ionian	Gerakas, Kiparissi, Piraeus.

Hydrofoil timetable

Day	Departure time	Ports/Islands of call
Tue/Thur/ Sat/Sun	1430hrs	Gerakas, Kiparissi, Leonidio, Tiros, Portoheli, Spetses(island), Hydra(island), Zea Port(Piraeus).
Wed	1635hrs	Gerakas, Kiparissi, Leonidio, Spetses(island), Ermioni, Poros(island), Methana, Aegina(island), Zea Port(Piraeus).
Tue/Sat	1705hrs	Kiparissi, Leonidio, Portoheli, Spetses(island), Hydra(island), Zea Port(Piraeus).
Wed/Sat	1255hrs	Kithera(island), Neapoli.
Tues	1310hrs	Kithera(island), Neapoli.

One-way fare to Piraeus 4881drs; duration 4hrs 40mins.

Old Monemvassia (Illus. 18)

Across the causeway, and to the left (*Fsw*) is a yacht harbour, whilst to the fore are a few dwellings, in amongst which is the *Kastro Pizzeria* cum filling station. Yes, the ...! The access road angles up the southern side of 'the rock'. About 100m along is a bathing area, with steps into the sea, and then Old Monemvassia Main Gate, let into the western fortified walls, which only allows pedestrian access.

Once through the gate, a narrow, cobbled street ascends through the medieval town, past rather glossy, well-heeled souvenir shops, and a few cafe-bars, set in the basements of vaulted buildings. Only the High St is thus cluttered, the rest of the Lower Town being old-time Greek alleys, bordered by domestic buildings, in various states of repair and disrepair.

The *Hotel Malvasia II* (Class A, tel 61323) offers en suite double rooms at 6850drs, otherwise 'Kastro' rooms are in very short supply.

The mediaeval village is made up of the Lower Town, above which is the fortified Upper Town, all originally Byzantine creations. Monemvassia was probably founded sometime between 600-700AD and

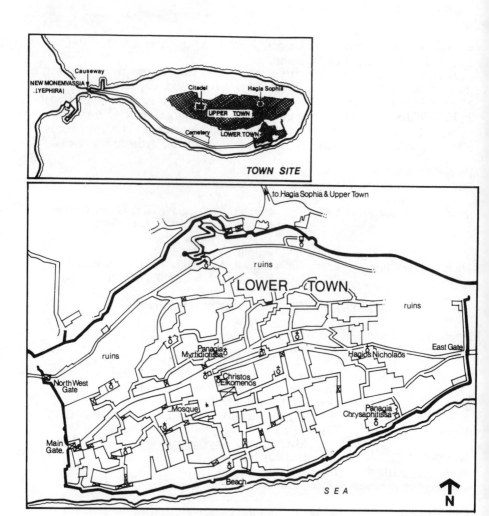

Illustration 18 Old Monemvassia

became a very important city state, reaching the height of its strategic importance in the Middle Ages - both as a military location and a trading centre. For instance, Monemvassia's Malmsey wine is supposed to have been famed throughout Europe.

Rulers of the island included the Pope (1460-64), the Venetians (1464-1540), the Turks (1540-1690), the Venetians again (1690-1715), and the Turks once more (1715-1821). In 1821, after the outbreak of the War of Independence, a rather dreadful massacre of the Turks preceded the final cessation to the nascent Greek state. In 1941, in the face of the advancing Germans, some 4000 New Zealand troops were evacuated from the town.

The location really is of coffee-table, picture-book quality, with a lot of the middle level restored, and with some of the Lower Town undergoing rebuilding. The Upper Town is worth the climb, even if little else but the walls remain intact, that is except for the remarkable Hagia Sophia Church. There aren't any toilets up there, but the views out over the Lower Town are breathtaking.

There is a most informative, yellow covered guide book available which is vital reading for those interested in anything more than a passing visit.

From Monemvassia, the tarmacadamed road continues on southwards along a boulderous coastline. This is yet another stretch of 'West Coast of Ireland' look-alike, with volcanic rock type formations thrusting into the sea, rather than there being an abrupt cliff-face.

At or about **Nomia** (192km from Tripoli), the coastal plain widens out, with the soil being very red and the shoreline remaining angled rock. Close to the junction of the coast road, with the Nomia road, is *Camping Paradise* (Tel 61123). Beyond the campsite are a couple of promising looking sand and pebble beaches. Turning up through the pretty, 'old and new' village, makes a steep, winding climb to the settlement of **Lira** (200km from Tripoli), where are clear signs for Neapoli. The road becomes unsurfaced 1km beyond Lira, all the way to the large village of **Elliniko** (206km from Tripoli). Here a Neapoli bus parks, but the road remains unsurfaced. Beyond Elliniko are magnificent vistas out over the Gulf of Lakonikos. The track is a 'bit of a sweat' with, as it descends, a lot of hairpin bends. Prior to finally joining the 'red' highway, is a short stretch of concrete, followed by yet more unsurfaced track. The main road allows views over a fairly large coastal plain, with Neapoli in the distance.

At **Ag Apostoli** (222km from Tripoli), where is a filling station, is the right-hand turning off to Elafonisos island, whilst straight on is the tree-lined, gently descending, 7km long road, past **Kampos Voion**, all the way to Neapoli.

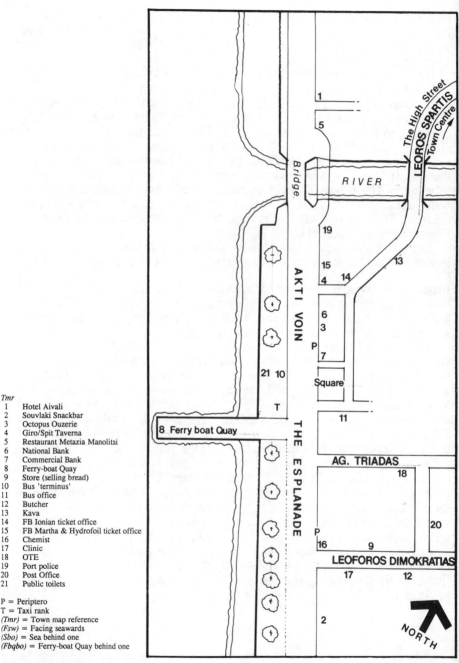

Tmr
1   Hotel Aivali
2   Souvlaki Snackbar
3   Octopus Ouzerie
4   Giro/Spit Taverna
5   Restaurant Metazia Manolitsi
6   National Bank
7   Commercial Bank
8   Ferry-boat Quay
9   Store (selling bread)
10 Bus 'terminus'
11 Bus office
12 Butcher
13 Kava
14 FB Ionian ticket office
15 FB Martha & Hydrofoil ticket office
16 Chemist
17 Clinic
18 OTE
19 Port police
20 Post Office
21 Public toilets

P = Periptero
T = Taxi rank
(Tmr) = Town map reference
(Fsw) = Facing seawards
(Sbo) = Sea behind one
(Fbqbo) = Ferry-boat Quay behind one

Illustration 19 Neapoli

8 NEAPOLI (Neapolis)

Illustration 19

VITAL STATISTICS Tel prefix 0732.

GENERAL Rarely, if ever, does Neapoli get much of a guide book mention, which is not only a pity, but mystifying. That is because this very Hellenic port and town is a most attractive seaside resort, with a five star beach. Furthermore, Neapoli is an extremely useful, if unheralded, springboard for Kithira Island, as well as a 'base camp' for an excursion to the superb, if little known island of Elafonisos. Despite this, Neapoli makes few concessions to tourism, with only a few postcards for sale. The town is based upon a long, pleasant, if somewhat featureless Esplanade, off which the main streets laterally branch.

ARRIVAL BY BUS There are Athens buses that route via Sparti and Molai, as well as the rumour of a direct Athens link.

ARRIVAL BY FERRY & HYDROFOIL Apart from the once, sometimes twice weekly, ferry-boat connection with Piraeus and Crete, there is a summer months only, hydrofoil link with Piraeus.

THE ACCOMMODATION & THE EATING OUT

The Accommodation Most of the town's hotels line the inland side of the Esplanade, north of the river bridge, starting with the:
Hotel Aivali (*Tmr* 1) (Class B)   Tel 22287
Directions: As above.
    Actually classified as a pension, in which all bedrooms have en suite bathrooms. Single rooms cost 2480/3570drs & doubles 3465/4580drs.

Hotel Limira Mare (Class B)   Tel 22208
Directions: As above, and going north.
    A massive, three storey hotel, at least half of which appears to be unoccupied and in a state of desolation. Maybe it is simply under construction! The en suite single and double bedroom rates are 5095/7800drs.

Still further north-west along the Esplanade are the *Hotels Stathiki* and *Aesodos*. Continuing to the northern outskirts, to where the extension of the High St loops back to join the main road, is a rather distant *Rooms*.

Back in the town, beside Ag Triadas St, is the:
Hotel Neapolis (Class D) 2 Ag Triadas   Tel 22339
Directions: As above.
    The en suite double bedrooms cost 4160/5065drs.

The Eating Out As would be expected, the few opportunities are spread along the Esplanade. These include, from the south, a souvlaki pita *Snackbar* (*Tmr* 2), an octopus *Ouzerie* (Tm*r 3),* a giro/spit *Taverna* (*Tmr* (*Tmr* 4), and the:

Restaurant Metazia Manolitsi (*Tmr 5*)
Directions: Beside the river bridge slip road, at the north end of the Esplanade.
    A family run restaurant, where the papa cooks and friendly Michelle, his Australian/Greek wife, serves. Michelle understandably, speaks excellent 'Grine'. On offer are excellent value meals, with, as an example, a repast, for two, of 2 'ginormous' plates of spaghetti with tomato sauce, a huge, delicious Greek salad, and a half litre of retsina, bread & service, costing 1540drs - and the quality was not sacrificed to size.

THE A TO Z OF USEFUL INFORMATION

BANKS There is an 'Esplanade' based **National Bank** (*Tmr* 6), as well as a **Commercial Bank** (*Tmr* 7).

BEACHES There is a tremendous sweep of fine sand beach to both sides of the Ferry-boat Quay (*Tmr* 8), with tiny pebble at the sea's edge and the first metre of the sea-bed. After the initial large step into the waters, the bottom angles steeply to a sandy bottom.

BREAD SHOPS Apart from a **Baker**, about 150m from the Esplanade and on the right (*Sbo*), there is a Store (*Tmr* 9) beside Leoforos Dimokratias which sells bread.

BUSES The buses 'terminus' (*Tmr* 10) beside the Esplanade. The unhelpfully manned (or in this case, 'womaned') KTEL Bus office (*Tmr* 11) borders a small, central square, the other side of the road.
    The print-out available is totally indecipherable, but most buses route via Molai. There is a daily Sparti service, which links with an Athens bus. In addition, I am of the opinion that there is a direct Athens connection, but...

Bus timetable.
Neapoli to Sparti, via Molai
Daily   0810hrs
Neapoli to Athens
Daily   0600hrs*
* *This is an uncertain possibility.*

CAMPING *See* Route descriptions.

COMMERCIAL SHOPPING AREA The best bet is the High Street, whereon are   shops offering almost everything. There is a **Butcher** (*Tmr* 12) on the right (*Sbo*) of Leoforos Dimokratias, and a **Kava** drink shop (*Tmr* 13) on the right (*Sbo*) of the outset of the High St.

FERRY-BOATS Apart from the familiar **FB Ionian**'s weekly visits, there is a little-known daily service from Neapoli to Kithira island, on the **FB Martha**.
    The **FB Ionian** ticket office (*Tmr* 14) is tucked away on a kink in the 'preamble' to the High St, whilst the FB Martha and Hydrofoils are handled from an Esplanade bordering location (*Tmr* 15).

Ferry-boat timetable*

Day	Departure time	Ferry	Ferry Ports/Islands of call
Mon	1300hrs	Martha	Ag Pelagia(Kithira island) (returning at 1400hrs).

Day	Departure time	Ferry	Ports/Islands of call
Mon	1800hrs	Ionian	Ag Pelagia (Kithira island), Githion, Antikithira, Kastelli(Crete).
Tues	1900hrs	Ionian	Monemvassia, Piraeus.
Thurs	1800hrs	Ionian	Ag Pelagia (Kithira island), Githion, Antikithira, Kastelli(Crete).
Wed/Thur/ Fri/Sun	1300hrs	Martha	Ag Pelagia (Kithira island), (returning at 1500hrs)
Fri	1900hrs	Ionian	Monemvassia, Gerakas, Kiparrisi, Piraeus.
Sat	0830hrs	Martha	Ag Pelagia (Kithira island).
	1830hrs	Martha	Ag Pelagia (Kithira island).

* Please note these are as read!*

HYDROFOILS A welcome, if sparse summer months service operates, calling two or three times a week.

Hydrofoil timetable

Day	Departure time	Ports/Islands of call
Tue/Sat	1530hrs	Kithira(island), Monemvassia, Kiparissi, Leonidio, Portoheli, Spetses(island), Hydra (island), Zea Port (Piraeus).
Wed	1500hrs	Kithira(island), Monemvassia, Gerakas, Kiparrisi, Leonidio, Spetses(island), Ermioni, Poros(island), Methana, Aegina(island), Zea Port (Piraeus).

MEDICAL CARE
Chemist & Pharmacy There is a Chemist (*Tmr* 16) beside the Esplanade. **Clinic** (*Tmr* 17). On the right (*Sbo*) of Leoforos Dimokratias.

OTE (*Tmr* 18). On the right (*Sbo*) of Ag Triadas St, and open weekdays & Sat 0730-1510hrs, Sun & holidays 0830-1330hrs.

PARKING The spacious Esplanade is available.

PETROL There is a High St filling station.

POLICE
Port (*Tmr* 19) Unfailingly distant from the Ferry-boat Quay, but at least on the same road!
Town In a High St office, in the heart of town.

POST OFFICE (*Tmr* 20) One street back from the Esplanade, and open the usual hours.

TAXIS Rank (*Tmr* T) close to the Bus terminus.

TOILETS The public toilet block (*Tmr* 21) is close to the Bus terminus, and is a 'semi-basement job', being half in and half out of the ground.

TRAVEL AGENTS *See* Ferry-boat & Hydrofoil ticket offices.

EXCURSIONS TO NEAPOLI SURROUNDS

Excursion to Elafonisos Island (13km) From Neapoli proceed to **Ag Apostoli**, where turn left at the crossroads. This is well signposted, with a ferry timetable indicated.

The road snakes across not overly attractive countryside, littered with a mishmash of agriculture and private houses. **Ag Georgios** hamlet is scrubbly and charmless, beyond which is **Vinglafia** (13km), nothing more than a ferry-boat way-station, set in messy heath and marshland. About 1km prior to the quay are a couple of restaurants, one with accommodation, and the *Restaurant Rooms Makros*.

The seashore to either side of the Elafonisos ferry quayside is shadeless and rather wild. To the left is a large sweep of sandy beach and backshore, hemmed in by heather clad dunes, which curves round to run out on a spit of sand. To the right is rocky and boulderous.

At the end of the quay is a concrete shed 'of a waiting room'. Apart from the 'scheduled' ferry that ploughs back and forth to Elafonisos, a caique makes the trip, and the *FB Martha*, listed under Neapoli as a Kithira island service, also appears to drop-in.

Ferry-boat timetable
Vinglafia to Elafonisos island.
Daily 0800, 1000, 1200, 1600, 1800, 2000hrs
NB If the ferry appears to have disappeared, the skipper is probably throwing in an extra round trip!

The ¼ hour crossing passes over a channel of water so clear it is not only possible to see the yoghurt cartons, but to determine their 'sell-by date'.

ELAFONISOS ISLAND Tel prefix 0732. The solitary settlement is the low-lying port, of the same name as the island, which spreads along the edge of a large, semi-enclosed cove. The vehicle ferry docks at the left-hand (*Sbo*) horn of the cove, whilst the buildings curve round towards the right-hand promontory, on which is built a distinctive, large church. From the far side of the latter, a 'town' beach, at right-angles to the port, stretches along a flat shoreline, running out on a distant, rocky, low cliff-face.

The passenger caiques berth at a small central quay, also utilised by the extensive, home-grown fishing fleet.

It is almost too passe to continually make comparisons, as I almost always do, but the island irresistibly reminds me of Angistri (Argo Saronic), and the fishing fleet of that based on Samothraki (NE Aegean).

The Ro-Ro Ferry-boat Quay is more a mole, the area around which is almost entirely covered with building materials, and wrecked machinery. From this dock, to the right (*Sbo*) advances past an isolated bakery, then along a track to the outset of the 'informal' waterfront Esplanade. This proceeds past a cafe-bar, followed by a modern, single storey office, from which the *FB Martha* tickets can be purchased, a local *Ouzerie*, above which is a *Rooms*, a small periptero, and a *Restaurant/Rooms*. The owner of the last mentioned establishment is Mr K. Papouleas (Tel 49261). He is an interesting, island born gentleman, who was a merchant ship navigator, and owns a number of accommodation possibilities around the island, charging double rooms from 4000drs a night.

Beside his building is a narrow lane, along which are: a souvenir shop, on the right (*Sbo*), which sells postage stamps; a pair of two storey buildings, on the left, in which are *Rooms* (the first having the telephone number 49240), one above a fast-food/rolls/sandwiches *Snackbar*, and the other over a general store.

Back at the waterfront, the other side of the narrow lane is a *Cafe-bar Ouzerie*, approximately opposite the passenger caique/fishing-boat quay. This is not only a very useful location from where to watch the comings and goings of the port, but serves a 'mean', if expensive plate of octopus. Continuing on along the Esplanade progresses by a couple of maybe/maybe-not establishments, to the *Restaurant Limanaki*, a popular fish taverna/restaurant. Hereabouts the harbour bends round towards the church (close to a sign requesting visitors to keep the island clean) and a cafe-bar. Around to the left (*Harbour behind one*) is the not-so-satisfactory length of 'town' beach. Not so..., well it is rather kelpy, with some rock, angled biscuit rock, and rubbish. A pity really. Bordering the backshore is the *Taverna To Kima*, as well as a two storey cubic block, in which is a *Rooms*.

As detailed, the port's church stands on very low promontory closing off the right-hand side of the harbour, and surrounded by a small garden. Standing by the church allows views along both the town beach and the spread of the pretty, busy, harbour.

Ferry-boat timetable - FB Martha.

Day	Departure time	Ports/Islands of call
Mon/Thur/Fri	1100hrs	Neapoli, Kithira(island).
Tue	1000hrs	Neapoli, Kithira(island), Githion.
Wed	1100hrs from Githion	Kithira island, Neapoli, Elafonissi(island).
Sat	0645hrs	Neapoli, Kithira(island), Githion.
Sun	1100hrs	Neapoli, Kithira(island).

The **FB Martha** may well be an Elafonisos island based boat.

To the left (*Sbo*) of the bottom of the Ferry-boat Quay are some crudely whitewashed signs 'To Simou'. These point in the direction of the south side of the island, to one of the most amazing beaches anywhere in Greece, let alone the Peloponnese. For those setting forth, it is necessary to leave the lone chapel to the right. At first, the route along the sand-dirt track is unprepossessing, if not downright off-putting. To the left is a rocky shoreline, whilst on the inland side passes by a quarry, a rubbish dump, and then low, unattractive, very exposed moorland hillsides. Those intending to walk the 3½km, would be well advised to pack a water bottle, or two. Yet another, even more unsightly rubbish dump occupies a low hillside to the right, and after a length or two of concrete slabs, the track's surface becomes rougher still.

At a fork, select the left-hand choice, which runs out on the reverse side of a series of rubbish bestrewn sand dunes. Once they have been scaled, there is revealed one of the most stupefying sights, in 'all of Greece'. For the panorama is one of a huge sweep of fine sand, edging a bay formed by low hills to the left and, to the right, an isthmus connected to a low, mountain sized outcrop of rock. This is the sand of the Caribbean - and one wouldn't be at all surprised to see Ursula Andress stroll out of the turquoise shallows (I always live in hope!).

There is so much sand, that it is blown half-way up the cliff-face of the huge outcrop, on the flank of which is a wooden, 'western cowboy' Cantina, that may, or may not be open. Once on top of the promontory, it is evident that there is yet another, even longer, glorious sweep of sea edging sandy beach, with the end of the island stretching away to the south-west, slowly lowering into the distant Mediterranean.

That the beaches have no shade, seems not to matter. About centre of the first bay is some gently shelving biscuit rock. It is almost impossible not to 'have a dip', and the sandy, gently shelving sea-bed goes on, and on..., forever. Take it from me, this is one of the wonders of the beach-worshipper's world.

ROUTE SIX (See Illus. 16).
Neapoli to Githion (87km) From the Ag Apostoli crossroads, to the north of Neapoli, both sides of the main route, approximately paralleling the north-west coastline, are bestrewn with rubbish.

After 30km, a side turning to the left, heads to the coast and:

ARHANGELOS (33km from Neapoli) This once-upon-a-little fishing hamlet is close to the base of a low peninsular of rock. There is a natural harbour, with some prominent rocks, and a pebble/fine grit shore.

The road decants onto a small square, edged by the rather blancmange-mould shaped, small, three storey, *Hotel Palatso*, with, on the left, a similarly configurated cafe-bar/ouzerie, the *Restaurant Margarita*.

At **Demonia** (33km), it is possible to take a minor road to the left, which becomes unmetalled, where an unbroken, shadeless length of grit and sandy shore hoves into view. The coastal plain is devoted to agriculture and moorland. Beside a river-bed is a path down to the beach.

About where the settlement of Palladianika comes into sight, the road is surfaced again. Immediately prior to Palladianika, a turning proceeds through orchards of olives and fruit trees, including oranges, south-west towards **Plitra** (47km) Here is a quite large, old harbour to the right, whilst continuing on, there is a newer harbour wall, beyond which are some sandy, dune-backed beaches. Access to the latter is achieved by angling right, through olive groves, before the seaside way-station of Plitra is reached. A couple of largish tavernas probably spring into life, at the weekends, for 'lets visit a country fish taverna' outings. Some new construction is under way.

Back at **Palladianika** (42km), there is a filling station and a Post Office. Once over a river-bed, the road enters **Asopos** (44km), another spaced-out, uninteresting settlement. Here select the coast road, which route climbs into low mountains, passing by a lot of side-of-the-road stacked rubbish. The agricultural countryside is predominantly olive groves and orchards of fruit trees.

The now descending road allows views of a rocky coastline promontory with a 'sort of' castle tower, beyond which is **Elea** (51km). The road narrows down through the village. Close to a T-junction is a taverna, whereat a left-hand turning. This leads to a short harbour wall, topped by a navigation light, which encloses a deep, narrow bay encircled by 'local' housing. On the nearside of the not unpretty bay is a restaurant, and at the far side, low red cliffs, and a 'bit of shore'.

At the Elea junction with the main **Molai** road, the route passes on northwards, across 'artillery range' countryside, here and there closing with the coast. In the middle of nowhere is a small, concrete quay, a few fishing boats, and an enormous restaurant! The predominantly brown rock has become red about where the route tracks inland, passing by the relatively new *Korgos Campsite*.

Prior to **Kato Glikovrisi** (62km) are more orchards. At a crossroads, beside which are the mandatory kafeneion, restaurant, filling station and a taxi rank, is the left-hand turning to the east. This crosses flat countryside, populated by most friendly inhabitants, in the direction of:

ELOS (70km from Neapoli). A thriving little village wherein, apart from the to-be-expected kafeneions, bursting at the seams with 'the chaps', there are a filling station, and mini-market.

Alongside a *Kafeneion*, with a sign 'OTE', is a left-hand side road which passes across flat fields of tomatoes, as well as fruit orchards, and grass, and by a folly..., or a castle..., or a ruined church..., or a factory. At the road's end is one of those extraordinarily Greek locations - a seaside, tin-shack shanty town, bordering a gorgeous sweep of sandy beach. Being a lee shore there is some kelp. Yes, a timber and tin resort, with numerous small fishing boats pulled up on the shore. There is a changing room, in an incongruous, 'neo-classical' building, with running water and showers, that work! There is also a public toilet, whilst propped up against the backshore taverna is a discarded Golden Starfish sign. Oh, ho, ho!

Why haven't *Thomsons* discovered this *Shangri-la*? Perhaps it's because this is the sort of location where property boundaries tend to be delineated by discarded fridges, and flattened-out oil drums!

From Elos, the route runs through **Panagristra**, which owns up to a filling station and a Byzantine church, of pleasant appearance, and over a bailey bridge that spans the widish, summer-dry Evrotas river-bed. On the far side, is the by-passed, busy, industrial, large village/small town of **Skala** (75km). This possesses an OTE and Post Office. On the Githion side of the settlement is a large sports ground.

From the east side of Skala a main road to the north leads to:
GERAKI (23km from Skala). This large village is rather off the beaten tourist track, and why not stay that way you may ask? The why not, is that

about 4km to the east of the settlement are the remains of medieval **Geraki**, a castle state conceived by the Franks, and one of fifteen such baronies set-up in the Peloponnese. It was soon acquired by the Byzantines. The castle was built in 1254, adjacent to which are a number of small churches, in various states of disrepair, one or two of which date back to the 12thC AD. A few of them possess interesting frescoes (Ag Athanasios & Evangelistria) and shrines (Ag Georgios). The site is a 'poor mans' Mistras (*See* Sparti Excursions, Chapt. 10). To locate the 'keeper of the keys' ('phylax') enquire at one or other of the village's modern main square kafenions, at the nearby Post Office, or in and around the site. Once located, he will mount his motorbike and lead 'clients' to at least five of the wonderful Byzantine churches. From the village, it is possible to drive half-way up the hill, and walk the rest of the way, in approximately ten minutes.

Travellers can proceed directly from Geraki to Sparti, but, for the purposes of the route description, return to Skala. Continuing to the west, much of the land (from as far back as south of Kato Glikovrisi) around the bottom of the 'U' of Lakonikos Gulf, appears to be reclaimed, with agriculture predominant.

About 5km beyond **Skala** is a posh, seaside shanty resort, edging a sandy shore. Posh? Well, yes, as some of the buildings appear to be prefabricated! Further west are a few sandy coves, one or two of which are popular with caravanners and camper-vans alike. A shipwreck hoves into view, a wrecked, fire-damaged coaster, beam-on to a long, if narrow, gritty sand shore. At the far end is a ruined castle tower topped headland. Beyond this is a 1930s, circular, lido type building, with bungalows for rent and a restaurant bar, and below which is a broad sweep of beach.

Almost around the corner, and to the left, is Githion.

Vathia tower houses

A Monemvassia back street

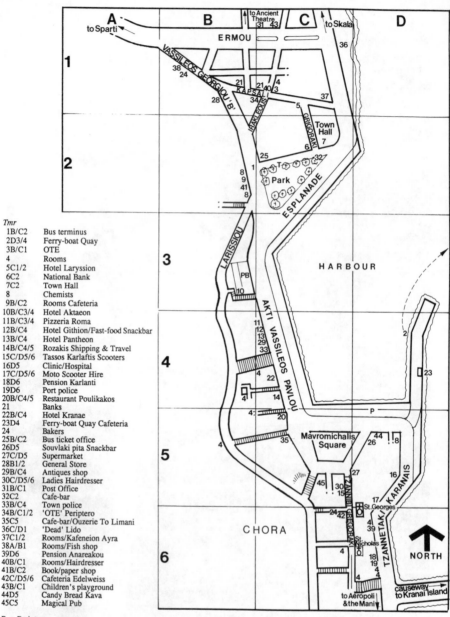

P = Periptero
T = Taxi rank
(Tmr) = Town map reference
(Fsw) = Facing seawards
(Sbo) = Sea behind one
(Fbqbo) = Ferry-boat Quay behind one

Illustration 20 Githion

9 GITHION (Githio, Gythion, Yithion)

Illustration 20

VITAL STATISTICS Tel prefix 0733.

HISTORY Githion, in ancient times, was the port for the Spartan empire, and still is the harbourage for the once mysterious region of the Mani* (*See* Places & Events...).

Mythologically of interest, around the 'corner' from the Ferry-boat Quay (*Tmr* 2D3/4) is the elongated, pine tree shaded islet of Kranai (or Marathonisi), now joined to the Esplanade by a walled causeway. It is said, that in a boat offshore of Kranai, the unprincipled Paris (of Troy) had his wicked way with one Helen. Yes, she of the face that... In any case, back to the salacious bit. This was a teeny-weeny bit unchappish, as Helen was married to another, one Menelaus, apart from which, it was one of those acts of 'nooky' that had far-reaching effects, setting in motion the apocalyptic Trojan War.

Despite Kranai's diminutive size, this islet experienced a remarkably expansive slice of history. For instance: it was the site of the ancient city of Kranai; it was a Phoenician trading post; and the Spartans constructed the town of Las, with many shrines and temples, the archaeological remains of which are still extant. Perhaps most interesting, to the modern-day visitor, is an endearing, and enduring structure that we would call a 'folly', but was actually a refuge tower, a life or death relic of the Mani of yesteryear. The building has been restored to house a folk museum. It once belonged to the Mavromichalis family, who gained national fame through the War of Independence achievements of General Petrobey Mavromichalis. This family acclaim was equally matched by notoriety, when one of their number assassinated the first Greek president, Ioannis Kapodistras, at Nafplio in 1831. For further Kranai thoughts *See* Places & Events of Interest.

GENERAL This spacious, very clean, pleasant port is spread out along the west side of a bay, at the foot of Mt Larysion. Despite the island harbour, village ambiance, Githion is rather larger than at first appears to be the case, thus less intimate. The north end, especially in the area of the Town Hall, is reminiscent of Ag Konstantinos, on the east Central Greece coastline, whilst the south sector is similar to Paralia Kymi, Evia island.

ARRIVAL BY BUS There is a daily bus to Athens, via Sparti, as well as connections to Kalamata, Monemvassia and, naturally, Sparti.

ARRIVAL BY FERRY A Piraeus based ferry-boat docks two or four times a week. It proceeds to Kastelli (Crete), via the islands of Kithira

*Essential reading is Mani, by Patrick Leigh Fermor, Penguin Travel Library. Also try The Flight of the Ikaros Eagle, by Kevin Andrew, Penguin.

(Kapsali) and Antikithira, and calls in on the way back fom Kastelli to Piraeus, stopping off at a number of east coast Peloponnese ports.

THE ACCOMMODATION & EATING OUT Githion is extremely well-endowed with accommodation, as it is with run-of-the-mill restaurant/tavernas. The latter mainly border the Esplanade, spaced out from the north to the south of the waterfront.

The Accommodation There is a very satisfying mix of hotels and *Rooms*. Radiating out from the area of the Bus terminus (*Tmr* 1B/C2) are:

Rooms (*Tmr* 9B/C2) Akti Vassileos Pavlou   Tel 22654
Directions: South along V. Pavlou, from the Bus terminus, and above a cafeteria, alongside a pharmacy.

North from the Bus terminus, along Odhos Irakleous, crossing over Kapsali St, and on the other side, is a *Rooms* (*Tmr* 40B/C1, tel 23005), above a hairdresser, and:
Rooms (*Tmr* 4C1)
Directions: As above, just beyond the OTE (*Tmr* 3B/C1).
   A neat, very nice looking, three storey house, part-clad with a lovely spread of bougainvillea.

Hotel Laryssion (*Tmr* 5C1/2) (Class C) 7 Grigoraki   Tel 22021
Directions: Proceed east along the well tree'd park, and at the first side-street, Odhos Grigoraki, turn left between the National Bank (*Tmr* 6C2) and the Town Hall (*Tmr* 7C2). The hotel is on the left.
   A very swish, five storey building in which all rooms have en suite bathrooms. A single room costs 4500/5500drs & doubles 5500/7000drs.

Just around the corner from the *Laryssion*, east along Kapsali St is a *Rooms,* above the old-fashioned *Kafeneion Ayra* (*Tmr* 37C1/2).
   To the left along Kapsali St, from the *Laryssion*, runs into Leoforos Vassileos Georgiou 'B', on the left (*Sbo*) of which is a *Rooms*, above a wet fish shop (*Tmr* 38A/B1).

Advancing south along Akti Vassileos Pavlou, and on the right is:
Hotel Aktaeon *(Tmr* 10B/C3/4) (Class D) 1 V. Pavlou   Tel 22294
Directions: As above. An old-fashioned, provincial hotel, almost stretching from the Esplanade to the narrow street above and behind, which courses along the steep hillside. Some of the front, ground floor is occupied by shops and the entrance is up a very sheer flight of steps, on the south side of the building.
   The ground floor rooms at the back are on the same level as the Esplanade-facing, first floor bedrooms, the latter having grandiose balconies, from which there are superb harbour views. Bedrooms share the bathrooms, singles costing 3500drs & doubles 4500drs.

Further along the Esplanade is the *Pizzeria Roma* (*Tmr* 11B/C3/4), with a sign in the window for *Gellys Apartments & Rooms*. Next door is the:

Hotel Githion (*Tmr* 12B/C4) (Class A) V. Pavlou   Tel 23523
Directions: As above, and with a glitzy fast-food establishment set in the ground floor.
   Only quite swish, with en suite double rooms costing 5500/6500drs.

Don't miss the rather lovely example of an overhanging balcony, to the south of the *Githion*, prior to the very smart:

Hotel Pantheon (*Tmr* 13B/C4) (Class C) 33 V. Pavlou   Tel 22284
Directions: As above, and a most modern, four storey building.

Friendly and spotless, though the bedrooms with the best views, overlooking the harbour, inevitably suffer from night-time traffic noise. All rooms have en suite bathrooms, singles & doubles priced at 5650/7900drs.

Continuing south along the Esplanade passes by a very wide flight of steps, on the left of which, about half-way up, is a *Rooms* (*Tmr* 4B/C4). A metre or so further along the Esplanade is the:

Hotel Kranae (*Tmr* 22B/C4) (Class D) 15 V. Pavlou   Tel 22249
Directions: As above.

'Air Conditioning' - and well it may be. All rooms have en suite bathrooms, with singles priced at 4400/5000drs & doubles 6100/6700drs. A few paces further south is a narrow, stepped alley which climbs to a 'bit of' a rabbit-warren, in which is a *Rooms* (*Tmr* 4B/C4/5).

Beyond Rozakis Shipping (*Tmr* 14B/C4/5), the office of one of the most important men in town, and of whom more later, is yet another steep, stepped alley and *Rooms* (*Tmr* 4B/C4/5).

The Esplanade parallels the waterfront wall, round to the left (*Town Hall behind one*) to the busy, if small, Plateia Mavromichalis. Branching off from the west of the square, alongside the *Cafe-bar/Ouzerie To Limani* (*Tmr* 35C5), is yet one more narrow lane that 'steps up' to Odhos Larissiou, whereon more *Rooms* (*Tmr* 4B5). South of the same square are a number of narrow streets, one of which is Odhos Tzannibi Gregoraki that gently climbs towards the prominent St Georges Church. On the right (*Harbour behind one*) is Tassos Karlaftis Scooters (*Tmr* 15C/D5/6, tel 24001), at No 16, and in the window of which are various signs extolling the virtues of their accommodation. The latter is some 80m south, along Odhos T Grigoraki, towards the smaller St Nicholas Church, opposite which is a lane, on the left of which is:

Karlaftis Rooms (*Tmr* 4C/D6) T. Gregoraki St
Directions: As above.

Traditional 'island' rooms at average prices.

Backtracking to the previous lateral lane off Odhos T Gregoraki, opposite St Georges Church, is the *Cafeteria Edelweiss* (*Tmr* 42C/D5/6) on the corner. Next door is a Baker (*Tmr* 24C/D5/6), with *Rooms* above, whilst close by is *Koursouris Rooms*.

It has to be pointed out that rising up the mountainside, from approximately between the two Tzannibi Gregoraki churches, is a lovely, if messy Old Chora, with one or two immediately notable, fine edifices, one a beautifully stone carved, three 'belfry high' tower. Another 'for instance', immediately across the street from St Nicholas Church, is a Corfu style, elegant building, with delicate fretworked balconies.

Continuing south on T. Gregoraki St, and on the left, on the corner of a wide flight of marble steps, with nicely crafted water gullies on each side, which descends to the waterfront, is a *Rooms* (*Tmr* 4C/D6). Further south on T. Gregoraki St leads to *Gellys Apartments* (Tel 24426), on the left, *Stella's Apartments*, on the right, and still further on, the *Pension Sarantia*.

Back to Plateia Mavromichalis (*Tmr* C5) and following the Esplanade round to the east, beyond the Ferry-boat Quay, advances past a line of restaurants. In amongst these is the *Pension Kolokotroni* of very smart appearance, and next door to the Clinic/Hospital (*Tmr* 16D5). South of Moto Scooter Hire (*Tmr* 17C/D5/6), is a *Rooms* (*Tmr* 4C/D5/6), next door to which is *Pension Anareakou* (*Tmr* 39D6).

Continuing south is the:
Pension Karlanti (*Tmr* 18D6) T. Karanais   Tel 22719
Directions: As above.

Comes well recommended, as a lovingly cared for, spotless, and homely consideration. Double rooms sharing cost 3500drs, and with en suite bathrooms 4500drs.

The other side of the Port police office (*Tmr* 19D6) are a couple of side-by-side *Rooms* (*Tmr* 4D6).

For more accommodation and campsites *See* Route Seven.

The Eating Out The majority of the fish tavernas are lined up, bordering the inland side of the Esplanade, between the Ferry-boat Quay (*Tmr* 2D3/4) and the Clinic (*Tmr* 16D5). Starting at the north end of the stretch, first off is the *Trata Restaurant*, followed by: a chemist; the *Paloppoia*, or *Sea Tide Restaurant*, where a meal for two of whitebait, taramosalata, 2 red snappers, Greek salad & a bottle of Apelia cost 4900drs; the *Faros*; the *Dolphin*; another *Faros*, all the above with awning-covered quay wall terraces, across the Esplanade; the *Pension Kolokotroni*; the *Kibubu*; and lastly the *Akrogiali Restaurant*, which is a rather imaginatively decked-out with a half-boat cum Chinese pagoda(!), as part of the display.

Back at Plateia Mavromichalis, there is a 'tasty looking' Souvlaki pita *Snackbar* (*Tmr* 26D5), on the Ferry-boat Quay side of the square.

There are plenty of zacharoplasteions and kafeneions spread throughout the town, but apart from the fish tavernas, fairly centrally located is the *Cafe-bar Ouzerie To Limani* (*Tmr* 35C5) and the:

Restaurant Poulikakos (*Tmr* 20B/C4/5) Akti V. Pavlou.
Directions: Across the harbour wall from the change of direction in the Esplanade, from east/west to south/north. The establishment is alongside a narrow, stepped alley, the other side of which is Rozakis Shipping & Travel.

Average fare at reasonable prices, considering the place is an absolute hang-out for everybody and anybody catching a ferry, but no itemised bills.The management spend their time attempting to get punters to sit at their tables, across on the square. A meal, for two, of one plate of stuffed tomato & green pepper (500drs), roast beef (700drs), zucchini (450drs), a kortaki retsina (200drs), almost a loaf of bread & service (50drs each), cost 1950drs.

Another possibility is the *Pizzeria Roma* (*Tmr* 11B/C3/4), whilst at the far, north end of Githion, along the Skala road, is a 'tempting' fish taverna, housed in a cut-stone, two storey building. Quite convenient to the Bus office is a *Cafeteria* (*Tmr* 9B/C2), whilst another *Cafeteria* (*Tmr* 23D4) handily 'lurks' on the Ferry-boat Quay. There is an 'appetising' *Zacharoplasteion,* immediately to the north of the *Hotel Laryssion* (*Tmr* 5C1/2).

THE A TO Z OF USEFUL INFORMATION
AIRLINE OFFICE There isn't an Olympic office, but our 'old friend' **Rozakis Shipping & Travel** (*Tmr* 14B/C4/5 - *See* Ferry-boat Ticket Offices) is a 'hot potato' in this field of activity. Mind you, the nearest, and only Peloponnese airport is at Kalamata!

BANKS The **National Bank** (*Tmr* 6C2) is to the north of the port, and cashes Eurocheques. In the same area are some two or three more banks, one the **Ioniki**, another an **Agricultural Bank** (*Tmr* 21B/C1). If all else fails, including the Post Office, proceed to **Rozakis** (*Tmr* 14B/C4/5), noting he charges up to 4% commission.

BEACHES At the north end of the port is a 'dead' restaurant/lido project (*Tmr* 36C/D1), once a fenced-off section of pebble beach and now a shambles. The main beach, a broad sweep of shadeless grey sand, with a pebbly sea's edge and sea-bed, is almost exactly 1.6km north-east of town. Further east from that climbs past a 1930s, circular, headland-topping restaurant, to reveal, down below, another stretch of gritty sand beach, also lacking any shade. This foreshore is, in the main, angled rock. The most noteworthy item is the 'past sell by date', but upright, rust-flaked and fire-ravaged merchant ship, hove-to at the water's edge.
   The best beaches are to the south of Githion, spread along the first four kilometres or so of the coastline. (*See* Route Seven).

BICYCLE, SCOOTER & CAR HIRE Close by Plateia Mavromichalis, is **Tassos Karlaftis 'Super Cycle Moto For Rent'** (*Tmr* 15C/D5/6). Bordering the Esplanade, south of the Ferry-boat Quay, is **Moto Scooter Hire** (*Tmr* 17C/D5/6, tel 22853). Average daily scooter hire rates are 2000drs, with rather unusually, a 15drs surcharge per kilometre for those who exceed 100km. Hours of business are 0900-1300 & 1700-2000hrs, and a day's hire is considered to be between 0900-2000hrs, not a 24hr span.

BOOKSELLER Close to the Bus terminus is an excellent foreign language **Bookshop** (*Tmr* 41B/C2), from whence are sold overseas newspapers. There is a Souvenir/Newspaper shop in the front of the *Aktaeon* (*Tmr* 10B/C3/4), but printed matter doesn't get any cheaper.

BREAD SHOPS There is a **Baker** (*Tmr* 24B1) in the 'northern quarter', close to the junction of Leoforos Vassileos Georgiou 'B' and Odhos Kapsali. Just to balance matters up, there is a **Baker** (*Tmr* 24C/D5/6), to the south of Plateia Mavromichalis.

BUSES The Bus office (*Tmr* 25B/C2) borders Akti Vassileos Pavlou, across the road from a park planted with numerous trees.
   An extensive service allows links with a number of pivotal Peloponnese locations, as well as Athens.

Bus timetable (Mid-season)
Githion to Athens (Athens Terminal: 100 Kifissou St, tel 5124913)
Daily   0830, 1200, 1550, 1750hrs
Return journey
Daily   0800, 1130, 1430, 1715hrs
One-way fare 3000drs; duration 5½hrs.
Note, that Patras port connects with Kalamata, not Githion.
Githion to Sparti
Daily   0600, 0730, 0845, 1215, 1515, 1900hrs
Return journey
Daily   0900, 1200, 1530, 1830, 2130hrs
One-way fare 400drs; duration 1hr.
Githion to Kalamata (via Sparti)
Daily   0730, 1215hrs
Githion to Kalamata (via Areopoli/Itilo)
Daily   0600, 1300hrs
Return journey
Daily   0515, 0730, 1300hrs
Duration 2½hrs.
Githion to Gerolimenas (South Mani, via Areopoli)
Daily   1300, 1930hrs
One-way fare 650drs; duration 2hrs.
Githion to Monemvassia
Daily   0845hrs
Return journey
Daily   1115hrs
One-way fare 750drs; duration 2hrs.
Githion to Caves of Dirou (Mani)
Daily   1015hrs
Return journey
Daily   1245hrs
Githion to the 'Campings' (Beaches & campsites south of Githion)
Daily   0600, 1015, 1300, 1930hrs
One-way fare 120drs.

CHILDCARE There was a children's playground cum dodgem car park (*Tmr* 43B/C1) beside Odhos Ermou, at the north end of town, but it has been made into a car park!

COMMERCIAL SHOPPING AREA Plateia Mavromichalis (*Tmr* C5) is bordered by shops, mainly vendors of fish, as well as fruit & vegetables. On the left (*Harbour behind one*) of Odhos Tzannibi Gregoraki, which climbs away from the south side of Mavromichalis Square, is an old-fashioned **Supermarket** (*Tmr* 27C/D5). Continuing south, the far side and alongside a one-hour photo-processor is another **Supermarket**.
    At the north end of town, Leoforos Vassileos Georgiou 'B' is lined with shops of all sorts, including a dusty, inexpensive **General store** (*Tmr* 28B1/2), and a **Supermarket**, opposite the **Fish shop** (*Tmr* 38A/B1). Another 'late hours' **Supermarket** is immediately to the south of the *Hotel Laryssion* (*Tmr* 5C1/2). There is an unusually named Kava, the **Candy Bread Drink shop** (*Tmr* 44D5), close to the outset of the Ferry-boat Quay. There are several peripteros (*Tmr* P).
    Although the usual antique/gift shop would not be included in the guides, it is a joy to list the excellent **Kostas Vreto Antique** shop (*Tmr* 29B/C4)), next door to the *Hotel Pantheon*. The door sign advises 'All things we sell in this

antique shop are original, not copies or imitations'. Open for business Weekdays between 1100-1400 & 1800-2200hrs, but closed Sundays.

DISCOS Close to the Moto Scooter outfit (*Tmr* 17C/D5/6) is the **Kousaros Music Club**, an extremely smart disco. Another, rather more down-market option is the **Magical Pub** (*Tmr* 45C5), south of Plateia Mavromichalis.

FERRY-BOATS The very old-fashioned **CF Ionian**, makes a two or four times a week visit, depending on the season. This ship has second-class, 4 berth cabins, in which male and female passengers are kept segregated. It does at least ensure that the chaps can enjoy the sleep of the just, whilst the women and (screaming) children are quite rightly kept apart - in purdah. The time of night of the outward sailing, en route from Piraeus to Kastelli (Crete), results in little or no food or drink being available at the snackbar.
    Another boat is the **Delfini** which offers day-long cruises on Wed, Fri & Sun, departing at 0830hrs for Kithira island and returning at 1930hrs.

Ferry-boat timetable (Mid-season)

Day	Departure time	Ferry-boat	Ports/Islands of Call
Mon	2200hrs	Ionian	Kapsali (Kithira island), Antikithira island, Kastelli (Crete).
Tues	1500hrs	Ionian	Ag Pelagia (Kithira island), Neapoli, Monemvassia, Piraeus (M).
Thurs	2200hrs	Ionian	Kapsali (Kithira island), Antikithira island, Kastelli (Crete).
Fri	1500hrs	Ionian	Ag Pelagia (Kithira), Neapoli, Monemvassia, Gerakas, Kiparissi, Piraeus(M).

One-way fares Githion			
to Kapsali	600drs; duration	3hrs	
to Kastelli	2900drs;	6hrs	
to Ag Pelagia	600drs;	2hrs	
to Neapoli	1250drs;	4hrs	
to Monemvassia	1825drs;	5hrs	
to Piraeus	3000drs;	13hrs	

FERRY-BOAT TICKET OFFICES Only the ubiquitous 'Mr Big', the splendid Theodore Rozakis Esq, who runs:

Rozakis Shipping & Travel (*Tmr* 14B/C4/5) 6 Akti V. Pavlou Tel 22207 *Directions*: Towards the south end of the waterfront Esplanade.
    This old-fashioned, brown painted, wood panelled office is the lair of the mature (okay, well-advanced in years) Mr Rozakis, who is very helpful, knowledgeable and speaks excellent English. He not only acts for the **Ionian**, but many other ferry-boat companies throughout Greece, in addition to Olympic Airways, as well as exchanging money - at a cost of 4% commission. An activity, once strictly prohibited, was the storage of luggage, but this stricture seems to have been relaxed. The office opens daily, between 0800-1300 & 1630-2100hrs.

HAIRDRESSERS There is a **Ladies Hairdresser** (*Tmr* 30C/D5/6) beside Odhos Tzannibi Gregoraki, south of Plateia Mavromichalis.

LAUNDRY There is a **Dry Cleaners** immediately to the south of the Baker (*Tmr* 24B1) on Leoforos Vassileos Georgiou 'B'.

LUGGAGE STORE A waiver might be granted to those who purchase tickets, by Rozakis Shipping & Travel (*Tmr* 14B/C4/5).

MEDICAL CARE
Chemists & Pharmacies They are comparatively plentiful, with a couple (*Tmr* 8B/C2) close to the Bus terminus and another (*Tmr* 8D5) across the way from the outset of the Ferry-boat Quay.
Clinic/Hospital (*Tmr* 16D5) A large building bordering the Esplanade, south of the Ferry-boat Quay.

OTE (*Tmr* 3B/C1) At No 8, close to the junction of Kapsali and Irakleous Sts. The office is a bit of a muddle and only opens Weekdays, between 0730-2100hrs. To compensate, diagonally across from the OTE is a Periptero (*Tmr* 34B/C1/2) advertising 'We have a telephone with a measurer'!

PARKING Not a problem.

PETROL There are a couple of filling stations spaced out around the town.

PLACES & EVENTS OF INTEREST Many of the Harbour Esplanade buildings are of the older, two or three storey variety. Odhos Larissiou which approximately parallels the waterfront Esplanade, but higher up, on the hillside, has some extremely interesting architecture dotted about along its length. Towards the south end, in the area of the Churches St Georges and St Nicholas, is the old, hillside Chora.
    Beside the Sparti road into Githion are Roman bits and pieces, including a sarcophagus, which realignment of the road appears to have literally 'thrown-up'. To have an overall view of the port and bay, why not climb Mt Larysiou, on which is an ancient acropolis, and into the foothills of which is tucked the town and port.
Ancient Theatre At the north end of town, turn off Ermou St, west of the Post Office (*Tmr* 31B/C1), on to Odhos Archaiou Theatrou. At the doo-hickey Army Camp jink to and follow the track round to the left. The Odeion is a lovely, if small, but largely unsung site, with much of the stone seating in place.
Museums
Archaeological Museum A new building is planned but ..., for the moment the exhibits are in store.
Kranai Museum The old Mavromichalis family mansion is now a museum. The doors are open every day between 0900-1300 & 1700-2000hrs, admission is free, there is a small, but sparkly-clean coffee bar inside, and a smiley girl oversees the exhibits - mainly photographs.
Kranai island I am indeed fortunate that a correspondent has been kind enough to pen some further thoughts in respect of this location. And thus, without further ado, and very little editing, I repeat his thought-provoking comments: "No, the island looks no better at sunrise than at sunset, though an early morning stroll to the lighthouse and back has its rewards. ...the best time to visit would probably be midnight, when it would be easier to ignore the mass of litter, strewn about the place. More difficult to ignore are the hordes of German camper-vans, parked everywhere, despite the prominent No Camping signs. These happy, touring Huns probably cannot conceive that these prohibitory notices apply to them, and their grotesque, three storey mobile bedrooms-on-wheels, festooned with mountain bikes and windsurfing equipment".
    My informant goes on to write that any possible romantic atmosphere,

accruing to the   island (through the mythological associations), is completely dissipated by the thought of the jolly German couples 'doing' a 'Paris and Helen',   within the confines of their mobile vans! Well, there you go - one nation's comment is another's...! Naturally, I absolutely and totally dissociate myself from these xenophobic comments.

POLICE
Port (*Tmr* 19D6) Their office borders the Esplanade, close to the Kranai/Marathonisi islet causeway.
Town (*Tmr* 33B/C4) The 'cop-shop' edges Akti Vassileos Pavlou, is some 75m north of the 'U' of the harbour, and is easily identifiable by the presence of a circular, traffic style sign on the edge of the pavement.

POST OFFICE (*Tmr* 31B/C1) On the far, north side of Ermou St. There is a post box let into the facade of the *Aktaeon* (*Tmr* 10B/C3/4), whilst another is attached to the wall of the Akti Vassileos Pavlou Bookshop (*Tmr* 41B/C2).

TAXI (*Tmr* T) There is a major Rank (*Tmr* T C2) north of the park.

TELEPHONE NUMBERS & ADDRESSES
Hospital (*Tmr* 16D5)	Tel 22001
Police, town (*Tmr* 33B/C4)	Tel 22271
Taxi Rank (*Tmr* T C2)	Tel 23400

TOILETS It is necessary to patronise the Bus and Ferry-boat ticket office facilities, or any one of the kafeneions, tavernas or restaurants.

TRAVEL AGENTS & TOUR OFFICES *See* Rozakis Shipping & Travel, Ferry-boat Ticket Office.

ROUTE SEVEN (Illus. 21)
Githion to The Mani (145km) The huge Sangias mountain range protrudes like a thick finger, into the Mediterranean. This constitutes the area known as the Inner or Deep Mani, about which have been written many hundreds and thousands of words. The unmarked boundary stretches from Itilo, on the west coast, past the 17thC Turkish **Fort Kelefa**, across to Ageranos, on the east coast. That fortress indicated the limit of Turkish authority, and the most southerly point of their advance. They were never able to conquer the Inner Mani, and feared the inhabitants, who they granted both autonomy and privileges - a unique state of affairs. Beyond that line is the Outer Mani, the northern extremity of which is bounded by another invisible frontier, curving round from western Kardamili to eastern Githion.

The Inner Mani inhabitants, who were effectively isolated from the rest of the Peloponnese, for many centuries, were supposed to have retained an individual patriarchal nature and character. Practically, this segregation only came to end in comparatively recent times, during the last century. A deadly tradition of extended family and or inter-village blood-feuds developed sometime in the 14thC - not to end until the 1870s, when they were finally put down by government troops. These intercine campaigns lasted for decades, and resulted in the development of the unique tower houses, from which the combatants blasted away at each other. The society reminds me irresistibly of the old Scottish clan structure, and the Mafiosa.

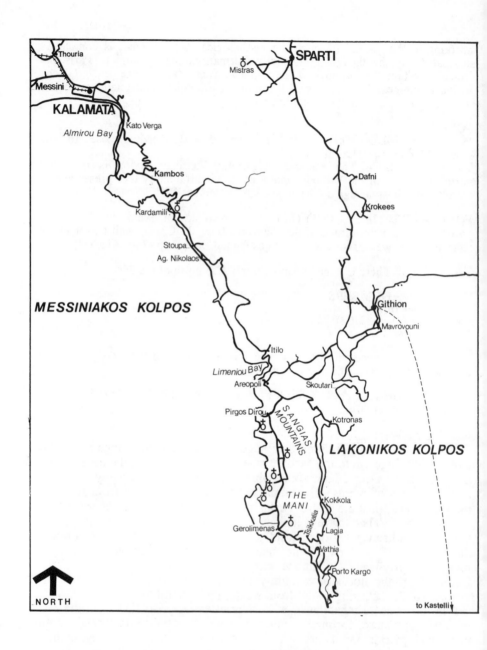

Illustration 21 Routes Seven, Eight & Nine

Certainly, the history and nature of the people, and the region, has resulted in a German love-affair with the Mani, so much so that they are to be found in each and every nook and cranny of the peninsula.

The southern outskirts of Githion, en route to Mavrovouni, are littered with accommodation possibilities. These include: *Rooms Kalorathokos*; *Pension Katerina; Calypso Apartments*; the *Hotel Milton* (Class C, tel 22091), where all rooms have en suite bathrooms, a single priced at 4200/5000drs & a double 4800/5500drs; *Rooms*; and *Pension Red Rose*.

Hereabouts the route is on the heights between Githion and the next coastal resort. *Rooms Monsina*, is followed by *Rooms, Pension Rooms, Pension Paradise* (Tel 23960), the *Taverna Tardentra*, and then the by-passed, off-beat little village of **Mavrovouni** (circa 3km), wherein some three tavernas.

To one side of the route, is a sign to '*Rooms by the Beach*' and a *Fish Taverna*, indicating a sharp left-hand, unmade turning down to a back-shore dirt track bordering a gorgeous sweep of fine grit beach. This is up to 30m wide and must go on southwards for several miles. Admittedly, there is not a lot of tree cover, but any number of saplings have been planted. To the left (*Fsw*) is the *Rooms* (Tel 014137166), and the restaurant is damned smart. A very nice location, if a little remote.

Returning to the main route, the road runs distant from, but roughly parallel to the shoreline, for some 4km. Access tracks lead off to the left, to various, often invisible businesses, amongst which are the: *Villa Drossia*; the *Gold Bird Discotheque*; a Mobil filling station, to the right; *Rooms* (Tel 22757); the *Ocean Pub*; *Cavo Grosso Bungalow Camping*; a single storey pension, to the right; the well organised *Camping Meltemi* (Cat A, tel 22833); *Spiders Dancing Disco* (the what...?); a shed-like mini-market, boasting a metered telephone; *Hellenic Githion Camping* (Cat C, tel (0703) 23441), from whence the horse riding activities that have been presaged by a sign or three; a Shell filling station; the '*On the Road*' *Cafe-pub*, on the right and with a pub type sign (but where do they conjure these names from?); *Main Beach Camping* (Cat C, tel 23450), and the '*Shoreline Country Tavern*'. Beyond these delights, the road swings inland, shakes-off the ramshackle development and crosses over a water bearing river-bed (7km). The countryside is pleasant, with some hills and a 'hint or three' of the famous Mani towers. About 8km from Mavrovouni, a glance or even a 20min scramble up a reasonable path may be well worthwhile, in order to look over the hill-topping ruins of the **Castle of Passava**, built by the Franks in 1254. To gain the heights, as it were, park opposite the taverna at the outset to **Hosiari** village. Some 100m back along the road is a track which leads up the slopes. The castle walls allow stunning views.

A left-hand turning makes off towards **Ageranos** (15km), past the *Taverna Hanover*, outside which is an imperative sign 'Stop, sit down' (see what I mean about the Germanic influence?). Beyond a *Rooms*, is *Camping Porto Ageranos* (Cat C, tel 22039), and the rather unattractive, four storey *Hotel Belle Helene* (Class B, tel 0733 93001), with all bedrooms having en suite bathrooms, singles priced at 6570/7885drs & doubles 8190/9810drs. The pleasant, fine grit of beach stretches back to the left (*Fsw*), around the curve of the bay to the north.

Rather than return to the main road, it is possible to climb away to the right from Ageranos on a concrete slab surface, past a nicely restored tower, alongside a church, with another tower to one side, about where the road's surface runs out. This area is off the beaten-track and the signposting is almost non-existent.

There are lovely views out over **Skoutariou Bay** and the backing plain. The 3m wide sweep of fine gritty beach, broken up by a chapel-topped low knoll, plunges quite steeply into the sea. This track, from which a minor turning makes off to a nearside settlement of working buildings, joins the worn concrete surfaced Skoutari-Kalivia road. To the left (*Facing south*) leads to the out-of-the-way settlement of **Kalivia** (20km), which is quite a way above sea-level. The *Taverna Petros* looks after the 'inner traveller'.

From **Skoutari**, the Githion to Areopoli road climbs on to fairly massive, if featureless mountainsides. There is evidence of bygone terracing - how the peasants must have worked! The town 'tip' heralds panoramas out over Limeniou Bay, and arrival at:

AREOPOLI (24km directly from Githion) Tel prefix 0733. The main road bypasses this agriculturally pleasant, if rather rambling and messily attractive market town. Due to the configuration of the road round the Mani peninsular, which is almost a peripheral rectangular circuit, Arepoli is effectively the gateway to the Mani.

The outskirts, the fields of which are seemingly cluttered with larger than usual cows, contain the *Pension Areopoli* (Tel 51302), the *Pension Gouthis*, a filling station, *Rooms* (Tel 51454), a fairly modern snackbar/restaurant, the village school, a repair garage, a supermarket, the *Pub Drama*, in a restored, dressed-stone building, and the *Pub Disco*, lurking behind some bamboo in an olive tree grove. There is also a Health Centre.

The modern-day village is spaced out around a surprisingly large square, in the centre of which is a statue to the memory of the War of Independence hero, Petro Mavromichalis. In and around this plateia, the buses pull-up, there is a Post Office, supermarket, pharmacy, an OTE (open Mon-Fri 0800-1500hrs), an old-fashioned kafeneion, *Nicholas Corner Restaurant*, a *Cafeteria Pizza*, next door to which is the *Taverna Simovar*, a butcher, hairdresser, taxi rank, zacharoplasteion, the *Europe Cafeteria/Pizza/Restaurant Grill*, and a very modern, two storey *Pension* (Tel 51340). Both the main tavernas offer basic, but reasonably priced fare. Buses connect to the 'outside world' of Itilo, Kalamata, Githion, as well as the Mani villages of Gerolimenas, Vathia and Tsikkalia.

The older, more medieval village 'shambles' around the church square and boasts one or two ancient shops, that is their contents and owners are both ancient. Amongst these are a baker, National Bank, General store, a *Rooms*, and the *Hotel Mani* (Class C, tel 51269), with en suite singles priced at 3550/4120drs, doubles sharing 3810/4850drs & doubles en suite 4965/5495drs. The referred-to, very pretty church is extensively restored, with a powerfully painted interior and an interesting bell tower. Close byis the most intriguing, NTOG sponsored *Pyrgos Kapetanakou* (Class A Pension, tel 51233), rather reminiscent of a Spanish parados, with bedrooms costing 4550/9200drs a night. There is a pretty garden and I am advised "...it is a great place to stay".

Prior to departing Areopoli, the smaller 18thC Ag Ioannis Church is reported to be worth a visit, if only to see the numerous 'strip-cartoon' frescoes that 'plaster' the walls.

From Areopolis, south along the west side of the Mani, the route flies across the increasingly barren mountains, devoid of much, if any, vegetation, with the coast away to the right. The first village is **Kalou**, which sports a few towers. Here a BP filling station reckons it is the last garage at which to be able to fill-up, only to be followed by yet another filling station, complete with a forecourt souvlaki shack!   The next settlement is:

PIRGOS DIROU (31km from Githion) As will be observed at ensuing villages, there is a Mani blight - that is the unsympathetic nature of much of the ugly, 'post war' housing. Here as elsewhere, there is a Chora of an older village, somewhat distant from the new development.

The fame of Pirgos is based upon the 4km distant, coastal caves, thus there are a two storey, 1960s *Rooms/Restaurant*, and the *Hotel Diros* (Class C, tel 52306), where all bedrooms are en suite, with singles priced at 5000/6000drs & doubles 6500/7500drs. On a paved square is a statue to a local hero, added to which the village boasts a Post Office, a baker, supermarket, and the *Restaurant Music Bar Antania*.

A well-signed turning indicates the curving, winding direction, to the right, down to:

Spilia Dirou (35km) This choice of road reveals quite a deep bay and a pebble shore. Almost at the bottom of the descent is the newish *Pension Panorama* (Tel 52280), followed by a coach park.

There is a vehicle barrier, to bar further progress, and a single storey entrance/ticket office building, with public toilets. Without doubt this natural phenomenon is worth a visit and admission to the cave and underground lake costs 1400drs. Opening times are 0800-1500hrs, between Oct-May, and 0800-1800hrs, June-Sept. Visitors are not allowed to carry bags or use a video camera, but can take photographs. If they swim or 'circulate' it is at their own risk. To avoid the crowds, that cascade out of the endless stream of tour buses, drop in, early in the morning.

Returning to the main road, there is a *Rooms*, almost immediately beyond the 'Caves' turn-off. The route runs due south, along a narrow plain, with the coast to the right, and the steep-sided mountains to the left. Many of the older buildings are in ruins, there are a noticeable number of towers and cemeteries, and the present-day, squared-off, pre-stressed concrete constructions can only offend the eye. The villages of **Ag Varvara, Kouloumi** and **Vamvaka** are followed by a crossroads, close to a tower, with **Mina** clearly visible on the inland side, and an unattractive seaside hamlet off to the right. The latter location is:

MEZAPOS (44km from Githion). This is accessed along a surface of concrete slabs, set down on a barren countryside, scattered with towers. There is a kafeneion and a couple of rural tavernas, one signed 'Taverna Seafood', at which a meal, for two, of 2 plates of fish, Greek salad & ½litre of apo varelli rose wine costs 4700drs. The natural sea inlet has probably been carved out by the winter flood waters that course down the boulderous, stony, pebbly, rubbish-littered river gulch. The cove is bordered by a couple of large pebble shores. These are hemmed in by cliff-faces of aggregate-type rock, in which are one or two sea caves.

The settlement is set in a much larger bay, formed by a tongue of land, the Tigani (or frying pan shaped) headland, encircling the sea side of the configuration. The latter is whereon are the ruins of the **Castle of Maina**, erected by William de Villehardouin, in 1248. This William is the same chap who constructed the fort at Mistras, and captured the Monemvassia fortress, all at about the same time. In 1262, after three years in captivity, poor old de Villehardouin had to cede all three castles, as way of a ransom, to his captors, the Byzantines. For those who don't fancy the scramble all the way out there, a boat trip might suffice. The owner of the already detailed *Taverna Seafood* offers a ride on his fishing boat - for a price. A one hour voyage around the headland, and on down the coast, to view the tiny Odiyitria Church, inaccessibly built into a cliff face, costs 7000drs - after a certain amount of negotiation.

At **Kita** (48km) is a cafe-bar ouzerie, named *The Heart of Mani*, with the word heart depicted by a heart... Oh dear! The WC's of the latter establishment register a healthy 7.5 on the Richter scale. Apart from a scattering of towers, there is a Chora off to the left, whilst to the right is signposted the settlement of **Kounos**. A couple of kilometres further on, and to the left is an unsurfaced track to **Ano Boulari**, close to the foothills of the Sangias Mountain range. Immediately above the hamlet is the 11thC Ag Stratigos Church, with Roman columns supporting the dome.

At a fork in the main road, with Vathia to the left, a sign to the right indicates the direction for:
GEROLIMENAS (51km from Githion) Tel prefix 0733. One of the only 'genuine' Mani fishing boat and resort villages, and peaceful 'to boot'. In addition to these attributes, Gerolimenas is one of the chosen repositories, a holder for the keys to some of the more notable Inner Mani churches, for the mechanics of which, read on. Although I am a proponent of the Messinia region (*See* Route Ten, Chapt. 11), vis a vis the Mani, it has to be admitted that the Mani scores hand-over-fist for those visitors with a love of small, beautiful Byzantine churches - the Mani has a surfeit.

The narrow bay is to the right (*Fsw*), whilst the rest of the village dog-legs down to the left. The backshore of the comparatively short stretch of mixed pebble, steeply shelving shore is across a wasteground. Jammed up against the backshore is the three storey, modern *Hotel Akrogali* (Class E, tel 54204), where a double room, sharing the bathrooms, costs 3600drs, but some German friends of ours were charged well in excess of these rates, for an en suite bedroom, with a balcony, looking out over the bay.

A meal here, for two, of squid served in wine sauce, a Greek salad & retsina cost 2700drs.

The sea's edge is rather greenish, with some tar, and the beach is about 5/6m wide. The right-hand side of the bay is blocked off by steep mountainsides, whilst the left-hand, village side is rocky. In amongst the delightfully old, 'High St' buildings, which edge the left-hand side (*Fsw*) of the bay, is a Post Office, alongside which is the *Taverna Orama*. Then, across a narrow alley, is a well-worth-a-visit 'village shop', *Katas Dimakanikonidon*, with a Santorini-like, barrel roof, and which is stuffed 'to the eaves' with almost all and everything, some of it dating back to the War of Independence! A cafe-bar is followed by the two storey, older building of the *Hotel/Restaurant Akrotaenaritis* (Class E, tel 54205), costing some four hundred drachmae a night less than the *Akrogali*. Beyond a jink in the street are a number of derelict houses.

Returning to the Post Office, this is where the 'keeper of the keys' for many of the area's Byzantine churches is to be located, at 1000hrs, Mon-Fri. He will join 'searchers after the churches' and their wonderful frescoes, in their vehicle, navigate to the chosen destinations, and patiently wait for the visits to be completed. There's service for you.

Without a doubt Gerolimenas is worth a visit.

The countryside bordering the road to Vathia, is majestically mountained, and, as at a number of other Hellenic locations, rather reminiscent of the south-west coast of Ireland.

About 1½km beyond Gerolimenas, is *Rooms/Taverna The Waves*, followed by the 'likeable' village of **Alika** (54km), the entrance to which is flanked by a pair of towers. At the bifurcation of the ways, to the right advances to the southern end of the peninsula, passing by an unnamed hamlet, a sea inlet, an outcrop of towers, a nice, chisel-sided rocky cove, filled with turquoise clear sea, to the outskirts of:

VATHIA (60km from Githion) Tel prefix 0733. This is THE Mani village - *to ena meghalo*. The arresting settlement juts up from a barren, colourless mountain slope, commanding the approaches, and is dominated by a cluster of lofty, gaunt, sombre grey stone and slate, tower-houses, the upper walls of which are pierced by the occasional slot and narrow aperture. Some of the towers have been converted, by the NTOG, into 'traditional pensions', which include the: *Pyrgos Exarhakou*; *Pyrgos Giannakakou*; *Pyrgos Keramidia*; *Pyrgos Mitsakou*; *Pyrgos Papadongona*; & *Pyrgos Tselepi*. Their shared telephone number is 54244, and the universal en suite double room rate is 6250/10500drs. Some have a cafeteria, open all day, and restaurant, open evenings only, between 2000-2200hrs. The menu range tends to be limited.

For those who choose to stay here, the benefits are tranquillity, wonderful sunsets, beautiful vistas, and an eerie sensation of being lost in a timeless environment.

Beyond Vathia are stunning views back along the coast. Here and there, boulderous lumps dramatically hang on to the mountainsides, but unfortunately the roadside is littered with plastic rubbish. Rounding a particular point allows an eye-catching sight of a large bay 'driven' into the rolling, once terraced, now barren, mountain face, a bay around which are spaced at least three shadeless coves, edged with dirty brown sand and pebble beaches.

The road now runs along the top of a headland peninsula, allowing views out over both sides of the coast. These vistas stretch out as far as **Cape Tenaro**, or Matapan. This is the southernmost point of mainland Greece, and, via a sea cave, one of mythology's legendary entrances to Hades. Those who have boundless energy (and are quite mad) can follow the 6km track from Porto Kargo, through **Mianes**, to the tip of the cape, and live to tell the tale that 'they have been to hell, and back'!

Up on the left mountainside is the rebuilt hamlet of **Ahillio**, divided by a gulch, up which profusely grow cypress trees. The track drops down to the left-hand side of the cape, to the lovely setting in which resides the natural harbour, tiny fishing hamlet of:

PORTO KARGO (65km from Githion). The informal, fairly narrow seashore is more pebble, than beach. Once down at sea-level, the location is rather scrubblier than the first glimpse, from up above, would indicate.

There are now three tavernas bordering the backshore. Their aim is to appeal to the better-heeled visitor, most of the staff speaking English and wishing diners to consume plates of fish. The furthest of the trio, the *Taverna Porto*, even has an art gallery, Lordy, lordy! On the other hand, they serve bottled beer, not cans, and kortaki retsina. A meal for two, at the *Taverna Akrothiri*, the middle one of the three, of excellent kalamares, swordfish, Greek salad, patatas & 2 bottles of kortaki retsina cost 3900drs.

Beyond the furthermost taverna is a two storey, recently constructed, apartment block, which probably heralds the beginning of the end for this, to date, idyllic location. Despite the 'No Camping' sign, there is the inevitable tent, or two.

Back at the main route, from Alika, the road to the left climbs steeply past spaced-out **Tsikkalia** village. Across a gulch, Mani towers are ranged along the hillside, similar to Cyclades or Cretan windmills. Beneath them, the mountain slopes are totally terraced - the setting is rather like a gigantic amphitheatre, with the terracing representing the seating. The situation allows splendid views over the distant coastal plains, and the south-east coastline.

The road continues to ascend windingly up the mountain, now with views back over the Vathia towers. Once the heights are scaled, the route runs along, close to the mountain tops, through the be-towered but messy, rubbish stacked village of **Lagia** (64km). Apart from a sleazy kafeneion-cum-local store, there is an individual church belfry and clock tower, from which the tops appear to have been removed, as well as quite a number of roofless buildings. Those that do possess roofs, are tiled, Skopelos style, with grey stone slate. The vistas from the village are splendid, looking out over the sea and to the north, along the eastern coastline.

Further on, as the road descends, into sight comes the eye-catching spur of rock, capped by the fishing village of **Ag Kiprianos**. Where the route drops to near sea-level is:

KOKKALA (73km direct & anti-clockwise from Githion) At the southern end is a white, small pebble beach, set in a cove, the sea-bed of which is also pebbly, and a nicely restored church. In fact, there is much new building taking place, in amongst the rubble of the old.

The village is tourist orientated, and visitors can take their pick of: *Restaurant Loulines*, where are served 'Greek foods in pot pan, in oil'; the welcoming, blue arrow indicated *Monara Restaurant*, to the right and run by a young couple; the *Pension Kokala*, next door to which is the *Restaurant Kavomataras*; *Georges Restaurant*; and a bakery. Further 'attractions', spaced out along the widespread High St, include yet another *Restaurant Kokala*, a cafe-bar, a taverna, a sign indicating the presence of a telephone, and the *Georgios Restaurant*. At the north end is more beach, but rockier, pebblier and longer, with a lovely little chapel at the far side.

In a cleft, high above the village, are some tower houses. Beside the roadside is an unprepossessing hillside cemetery, without a retaining wall, just a number of prefabricated, square block mausoleums.

Close to a roadside hamlet, in amongst the fire-damaged hillsides, is the *Taverna O Georgios*, followed by a cluster of buildings that make up **Nifi** (87km). In amongst these is a pleasant looking *Pension*. To the right is a sign indicating a beach taverna, where there is a cove in which are moored some fishing boats.

Drimos is a small hamlet, above which are even more tower houses, whilst the route continues in a northerly direction, beside the large Kolokithias Bay. At the head of the latter, is the yet distant, attractively sited, cape-topping village of Kotronas, beneath which is a tear-drop of an islet, connected to the shore by a thin slither of pebble. But prior to that the road enters **Flomochori** (107km), wherein the main square is edged by a *Cafe-bar Taverna* and the *Mani Kafeneion*, close by which are four towers. Hereabouts, olive groves and trees reappear. At a T-junction, Kotronas is signed to the right and Athens(?) to the left - perhaps Areopolis would be more appropriate. Turning right, the attractive countryside road leads to:

KOTRONAS (110km anticlockwise from Githion) I own-up to voting this one of, if not the most attractive, where-I-would-wish to stay of the Mani villages. It brings to mind one or two of the more appealing, east coast, Peloponnese hydrofoil ports.

At the approach are a number of towers, one of which looks like a castle keep, and which is butted on to a domestic dwelling. Close to the village entrance is a side-street baker. On the right is a small taverna, followed by a Post Office, a shop, the *Taverna Mani* and *Pension Adolphia*, both down a side-street, and a small chapel. Beyond the latter is a *Rooms*, and then the concrete surfaced, tree shaded, village square, alongside and overlooking the fairly large fishing boat quay. To the left

(*Fsw*) of another concrete quay, is a small, large pebble beach, with some seaborne rubbish, bordering an attractive, large bay. Where the street slopes down to the waterfront is a *Fish Taverna*, where, at one sitting, it is possible to eat every item on the menu! A meal, for two, of 2 plates of kalamares, a Greek salad, patatas & kortaki retsina cost 2800drs. Next door is the three storey, swept-up, modernish but pleasant *Rooms Restaurant Sylvia* (Tel 53246), owned by Petros Kousonas. Here a double bedroom, with en suite bathroom, costs 3500drs a night. Beyond the pension is a cemetery and a little chapel, with a prefabricated concrete bell tower, and a small warehouse cum dwelling.

This route now proceeds back to Areopolis, via the villages of **Loukadiki** and **Himara,** up a lovely valley set between the upper, nicely vegetated and agricultural mountain slopes.

ROUTE EIGHT (*See* Illus. 21)
Githion to Sparti & Mistras (47km) There are plenty of filling stations on the way out of town, and the roadsides are intermittently lined with gum trees. As the route progresses there is a singularly attractive, if stark, not very high range of mountains to the west. Closer to Sparti the road runs up a valley between two mountain chains.

Methoni Castle

Well Vicar, we ran out of bricks and stone. **Xilkastro**

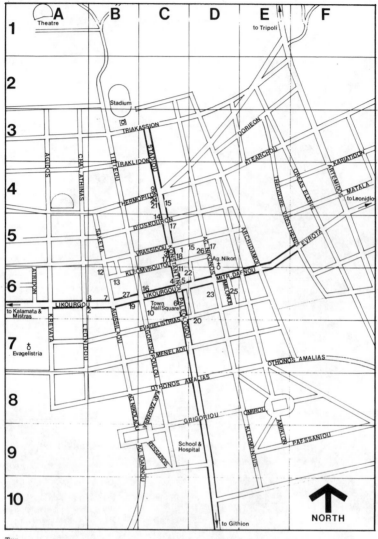

Tmr
1C/D5	Main Bus terminus	16B/C6	Olympic office
2A/B6/7	Mistras Bus terminus	17	Banks
	/Zacharoplasteion Select	18C5/6	Supermarket
3C5	Hotel Menelaion	19B/C6	Kava/breadshop
4C6	Hotel Lakonia	20C/D6/7	Fish shop
5C/D5/6	Hotel Maniatis	21C4	Clinic
6C6	Hotel Panhellinion/Ionian Bank	22C/D5/6	OTE
7B6	Hotel Anessis	23D6	Archaeological Museum
8A/B6	Hotel Kypros	24C4	National Gallery
9C4	Hotel Cecil	25D/E6	Town police
10B/C6/7	The Town Hall	26C/D5	Post Office
11C5/6	Cafeteria Villa	27B6	Sparta Travel
12A/B5/6	'Tasties'		
13B6	Souvlaki Zestifolia	(Tmr) = Town map reference	
14C4/5	Restaurant Elysee		
15	Bakers		

Illustration 22 Sparti

10 SPARTI (Sparta)

Illustration 22

FIRST IMPRESSIONS Wide, open layout; a pleasant town.

VITAL STATISTICS Tel prefix 0731. The population is some 12,000.

HISTORY Despite an 'overwhelm' of history, there are few remains of the ancient civilisation that gave us the modern-day word 'Spartan'. The ancient city was forged from a number of local communities, in about 1000BC, and over the next six centuries built - and lost a Peloponnese empire. The success was achieved by exercising a strict military regime, starting with the males at the age of 7 years - an ancient Hitler Youth!

GENERAL The reason for the spacious look and feel to the city, is that it was constructed as late as 1834, with very wide, often dual carriage streets and avenues.

ARRIVAL BY BUS Sparti is a major epicentre for Peloponnese bus services with a wide choice of destinations. It seems a pity that the main bus terminal is some distance from the local Mistras (historical site) service.

THE ACCOMMODATION & THE EATING OUT
The Accommodation From the fairly central Main Bus terminus (*Tmr* 1C/D5), most accommodation borders the main, north-south'ish avenue, Konstantinou Paleologou, or is to the west of it, as far as the Mistras Bus terminus (*Tmr* 2A/B6/7). Closest is the:

Hotel Menelaion (*Tmr* 3C5) (Class B) 91 K. Paleologou   Tel 22161
Directions: West of the main bus terminus, facing on to the main avenue.
    This is one of the oldest of Sparti's hotels, but has been given a face-lift, and is now one of the smartest in town. All bedrooms have en suite bathrooms, a single priced at 5095drs & a double 6380drs. The bath water might be ice-cold, from both taps! A truly authentic Spartan touch.

Further south along Leoforos K. Paleologou are the:
Hotel Lakonia (*Tmr* 4C6) (Class C) 61 K. Paleologou   Tel 28951
Directions: As above, and on the right (*Facing south*).
    Single bedrooms sharing the bathrooms cost 3000/4000drs, & en suite 4000/5000drs, whilst doubles sharing cost 4500/5500drs, & en suite 6000/7000drs.
And the:
Hotel Maniatis (*Tmr* 5C/D6) (Class C) 72 Paleologou/Likourgou Tel 22665
Directions: Diagonally across the main avenue, from the Lakonia.
    All bedrooms have en suite bathrooms, with singles priced at 4250/5095drs & doubles 5315/6380drs.

From the crossroads of Leoforos K. Paleologou and Odhos Likourgou, and continuing south, on the right is the:

Hotel Panhellinion (*Tmr* 6C6) (Class D) 43 K. Paleologou   Tel 28031
Directions: As above, with the rear of the hotel facing the town's Main Sq. A rather splendid building, with wrought iron balconies and the entrance from Leoforos K. Paleologou where there are apparently three storeys, whilst from the Main Sq there appears to be only two storeys!

Only double rooms available, sharing the bathrooms, at a cost of 3800drs.

Back at the main crossroads, and heading west up the quite steeply ascending, wide Odhos Likourgou 'perspires' towards the Mistras Bus terminus (*Tmr* 2A/B6/7). On the right are the:
Hotel Anessis (*Tmr* 7B6) (Class D) 60 Likourgou St   Tel 21088
Directions: As above, and a three storey, 'Colonels' pension type of set-up.

All bedrooms share the bathrooms, with a single priced at 2120/2280drs & a double 2480/2890drs.
And the:
Hotel Kypros (*Tmr* 8A/B6) (Class E) 72 Leonidou/Likourgou Sts   Tel 26590
Directions: As above, and at the junction of Leonidou & Likourgou Sts, in a small, two storey Victorian building.

A youth-hostel flavoured, E class establishment, where, naturally, all bedrooms share the bathrooms, with the doubles priced at 3545drs.

Hotel Cecil (*Tmr* 9C4) (Class D) 1 Stadiou St   Tel 24980
Directions: At the north end of the avenue, in a three storey, older building.

All bedrooms share the bathrooms, with a single priced at 2215drs & a double 3545drs.

Camping *See* Excursion to Mistras.

The Eating Out Most of the town's eateries are ranged up and down Leoforos K. Paleologou, and around the Town Hall Sq (*Tmr* C6/7). The east side of the latter is a 'crowd' of restaurant tables and chairs, on awning shaded terraces, whilst even the rather baroque Town Hall (*Tmr* 10B/C6/7) is bordered by cafe-bars. A coffee at a Main Sq establishment is expensive, but will be 'smartly' served, with iced water.

A local popular eaterie is the main avenue edging *Cafeteria Villa* (*Tmr* 11C5/6) and in the same block, at the Kleomvroutou St end, is a small, promising-looking basement taverna. To the west, in the general area of the Mistras Bus terminus, are *Tasties* (*Tmr* 12A/B5/6), a favoured cafe-bar, if possessing an unlikely name, and *Zestifolia* (*Tmr* 13B6), a souvlaki snackbar.

Close to the junction of Leoforos K. Paleologou & Dioskouron St, is:
Restaurant Elysee (*Tmr* 14C4/5)
Directions: As above.

Previously a 'Big Mac' fast food restaurant, but now reputably serving some of the best food in town. A meal for two of lamb in lemon sauce, a casserole, Greek salad & local wine cost 3900drs.

On the right of the southern, Githion approach to Sparti, is a family-run taverna, the sign for which advises 'The best in town, speaking English, garden. Come in, we're open'.

Incidentally, the Baker (*Tmr* 15C/D5), on the same side of the street as the Main Bus terminus, serves an inexpensive tiropites.

THE A TO Z OF USEFUL INFORMATION

AIRLINE OFFICE (*Tmr* 16B/C6) Despite the lack of any airport, there is an Olympic office. Maybe the authorities are thinking ahead.

BANKS The **Commercial Bank** (*Tmr* 17D5), beside Ag Nikonos St, changes Eurocheques, whilst the **Bank of Crete** (*Tmr* 17C5/6) borders the main avenue, as does the **National Bank** (*Tmr* 17C4/5).

BOOKSELLER A good shop, selling English books and newspapers, is beside Konstantinou Paleologou, across the way from the *Hotel Panhellinion* (*Tmr* 6C6).

BREAD SHOPS There is a Baker (*Tmr* 15C/D5) close to the Main Bus terminal, on the same street, and another (*Tmr* 15C4) towards the north end of Leoforos K. Paleologou.

BUSES An excellent service serving a widespread number of destinations.

1. **Main Bus terminal** (*Tmr* 1C/D5).
Sparti to Athens (100 Kifissou St) via Argos & Korinthos.
Daily   0830, 0930, 1300, 1500, 1700, 1930hrs
Return journey
Daily   0800, 0930, 1130, 1430, 1530, 1830, 2015hrs
One-way fares to Argos   1200drs; duration 2½hrs
                  Korinthos   1550drs;   "   3 hrs
                  Athens   2500drs;   "   4½hrs
Sparti to Tripoli
Daily   0750, 0915, 1130, 1500hrs
One-way fare 550drs; duration 1 1/3hrs
Sparti to Neapoli, via Molai
Daily   0645, 1200, 1700, 1930hrs
One-way fare 1500drs; duration 4hrs
Sparti to Monemvassia, via Molai (where change)
Daily   0645, 1130, 1330hrs
One-way fare 850drs; duration 2½hrs
Sparti to Kalamata
Daily   0900, 1430hrs
One-way fare 350drs; duration 2hrs
Sparti to Krokees & Skala (south-east of Sparti)
Daily   0650, 1130, 1330, 1700, 1930hrs
Sparti to Githion
Daily   0900, 1200, 1530, 1830, 2130hrs
One-way fare 420drs; duration 1 hr.
Sparti to Pirgos Dirou (Mani Caves), via Githion (where change) **& Areopoli**
Daily   0900hrs

2. **Mistras Bus terminal** (*Tmr* 2A/B6/7)
Sparti to Mistras (Historical Site).
Daily   0650, 1000, 1710, 2040hrs
Sun & hols   0900, 1200, 1615, 1700, 2040hrs
Return journey
Daily   0700, 1015, 1730, 2055hrs
Sun & hols   0900, 1730, 2055hrs (yes 5 out, 3 in!).
One-way fare 120drs; duration 15mins.

BUS OFFICES The main office (*Tmr* 1C/D5) edges the street in which the buses park. Within is a largish cafeteria and luggage store, whilst in the basement are some Richter 10 toilets. The informal Mistras bus office (*Tmr* 2A/B6/7) is, in actuality, the *Zacharoplasteion Select*.

CHILDCARE There is a children's playground in a park to the left of Odhos Likourgou (*Tmr* A6/7), beyond the crossroads with Leoforos Leonidou.

COMMERCIAL SHOPPING AREA It is necessary to shop around - sorry! In fact, there are numerous peripteros, supermarkets and shops. The main avenue and lateral streets of M. Dafnou/Likourgou are fertile areas. For instance, there is a good **Supermarket** (*Tmr* 18C5/6) beside Leoforos K. Paleologou, whilst on Odhos Likourgou is a **Kava** drink shop (*Tmr* 19B/C6), where bread is also sold.
   The older quarter, gathered-up at the Town Hall end of the streets of Evagelistrias and Gortsopoulou (*Tmr* C7) offers possibilities. Beside Evagelistrias St, but the other, east side of the main avenue, is a wet Fish shop (*Tmr* 20C/D6/7). There is a fruit & vegetable street market at the top, west end of Odhos Kleomvrotou (*Tmr* B5/6).

ELPA The office is west along Odhos Likourgou, and on the right, prior to the main junction of the Mistras and Kalamata roads.

HAIRDRESSERS Ladies salons are plentiful.

LUGGAGE STORE The Main Bus office (*Tmr* 1C/D5) has a facility.

MEDICAL CARE
Chemist & Pharmacies There is one close to the main avenue supermarket (*Tmr* 18C5/6).
Clinic (*Tmr* 21C4). On the left-hand side of the north end of the main avenue, near to the National Gallery.
Hospital (*Tmr* C/D9). Beside the main avenue, at the southern end of town.

OTE (*Tmr* 22C/D5/6). From the 'main' crossroads, in a street parallel to and one to the east of Leoforos K. Paleologou. It is opposite a park, and opens daily between 0600-2400hrs.

PARKING Despite the wide, spacious streets, parking can be a teeny-weeny problem. It is often necessary to choose a distant side-street.

PETROL Filling stations are evenly spaced out along the main avenue.

PLACES & EVENTS OF INTEREST
Museums.
Archaeological (*Tmr* 23D6) Open daily 0830-1500hrs, Sun & hols 0930-1430hrs, closed Mon. Admission costs 400drs. Items of note on display are votive ritual masks and the bust of one Leonidas, a renowned Spartan warrior king. This latter 'chappie' has a 'statue prominent', at the top end of Stadiou St (*Tmr* B3), which is a continuation of Leoforos K. Paleologou.
National Gallery (*Tmr* 24C4) The full title is the Alexander Suitsos Museum Koumantaros Art Gallery. Officially open Tues-Sat, 0900-1500hrs, Sun & hols 1000-1400hrs, and closed Mon, but..., the times are variable! Exhibits

are mainly paintings by 19thCEuropean artists, as well as some   modern Greek 'daubers'.

Ruins The archaeological sites, mostly to the north of the town are pretty disappointing.

Ruminations (or Odds & Ends) A building facing the Town Hall (*Tmr* 10B/C6/7) is signed the 'Lakonian Aero Club' - I bet that's a bit of a whiz!

POLICE The town police (*Tmr* 25D/E6) are tucked away on Odhos Hilonos. The officers hand out a skimpy, A5 sized town plan, produced by courtesy of a main avenue, Kodak one hour photo shop, next door to the *Cafeteria Villa* (*Tmr* 11C5/6).

POST OFFICE (*Tmr* 26D5) A surprisingly small office, for a town of this size. Apart from the usual weekday hours, the office may well open Sat, 0730-1400hrs, & Sun, 0900-1330hrs.

TAXIS Rank here and there, with the main concentration alongside Leoforos K. Paleologou, either side of the main crossroads with Dafnou/Likourgou. The cabs are distinctive because the official colour is red, with white lids.

TELEPHONE NUMBERS & ADDRESSES

Hospital (*Tmr* C/D9)	Tel 28671
Police (*Tmr* 25D/E6) 8 Hilonos St	Tel 26229
Town Hall (*Tmr* 10B/C6/7)	Tel 24852

TRAVEL AGENTS & TOUR OFFICES Mainly lined-up west along Odhos Likourgou, prominent amongst which is **Sparta Travel** (*Tmr* 27B6).

EXCURSIONS TO SPARTI SURROUNDS

Excursion to Mistras (6km) At the main road junction of the Mistras/ Kalamata junction is an oldish house festooned with vines. The Mistras road is a lovely route, running alongside a summer-dry river-bed, bordered by gum trees and other foliage. Passed by is the *Pub Sunrise Napkin* (?), beyond which the river-bed becomes a bit of a mess. At the fruit orchard surrounded village of **Paliologou** (1½km), and off to the left, beyond a filling station, is *Camping Mistras* (Cat C, tel 22724). This is reputed to 'have every possible facility', as well as a swimming pool.

At the far side is the Stalig Luft-like *Camping Castle View* (Cat C, tel 93384), which it may be, as in the village is a sign to a German bistro-bar!

MISTRAS (Mistra, Mystra) (5km from Sparti) Tel prefix 0731. The whitewashed, quite pretty village is signed 'welcome to Mystra', alongside a large chapel and small church (or a small church and tiny chapel, or...). Attractions include the *Old House Dance Pub* (oh dear), and the 1950s, four storey *Hotel Vyzantion* (Class B, tel 93309), where en suite bathroom singles cost 4500drs & doubles 6200drs. Close by is a craft shop. As would be expected, there are a number of tavernas and *Rooms*, with a few kafeneions, a shoemaker(!) and a tourist shop, spaced about, in and around the 'regular', old-tree shaded village square. There is running water, but tourism has killed the place off.

The village and the descending High St inexorably head towards a

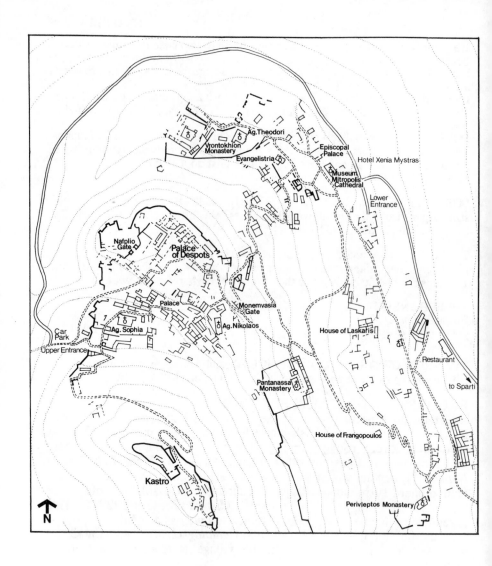

Illustration 23 Mistras Archaeological Site

one-way system around a hero's statue, and the bottom of the extremely steep climb up and around the almost island-like, mountain-hugging:

Mistras Archaeological Site (Illus 23) (6km from Sparti) Open Mon-Fri, 0800-1900hrs, Sat/Sun & hols 0830-1500hrs. Admission cost 1000drs, and keep the ticket stub to allow entrance to both the castle and the town. Allow some three hours for a good look round, wear a hat and pack some drink (although there are drinking water fountains at both entrances), as the location becomes insufferably hot by mid-morning.

The fascinating ruins of the Byzantine town, and one-time capital, are an outstanding testament to medieval Hellenic life.

The access road passes by the abundantly tree'd, lower slopes, over a river, by a sign forbidding camping, the *Miramara Restaurant-bar* cum souvenir shop, the lower entrance to the site, and the *Xenia Mystras*. Incidentally, the latter was only ever a taverna/bar, but appears to now be 'dead'. This is where the public buses stop, despite which the upper entrance is still further on up the mountainside. The car and coach park is littered with camper-vans, and during the day must accommodate 'most of the excursion buses in all of Europe'.

As visitors continue the heart-attack-inducing ascent, the main gate is straight ahead, whilst the upper castle entrance is further up round to the right. I prefer to go on up to the very top and 'fall down' to the bottom exit/entrance gate, by way of the castle.

It is worth bringing supplies of food, as well as drink, for despite there being drinking water close to both upper and lower gates, snacks and drinks at the entrance cantinas are not cheap. For those who have not packed provisions, a few metres down from the aforementioned bus stop is the recommended *Taverna Magrakaki Anna*. A meal, for two, of stuffed tomatoes, moussaka, a Greek salad & a litre of white wine, from the barrel, costs 3400drs. Who was thirsty then?

The castle was built by a Frankish prince in 1249, to help guard his territory. When the Franks were overcome, Mistras and the surrounding area were made over to the Byzantines, in 1263. In 1265 they were at the receiving end of a major assault, and this outpost of their Empire contracted so much, that they retreated into the hill-top castle, and the city state came about.

Mistras remained a sentinel of the Byzantine culture, and way of life, until 1459 (when the Turks captured the site). It was during these two centuries that the religious, intellectual and artistic aspects of the settlement flowered. Hence the extraordinary number of magnificently basilica'd, domed and frescoed churches, monasteries and palaces, which edge the ever so narrow streets, lanes and alleyways. It is a help that the layout is adequately signed.

Life after the Turks followed the 'norm', with the Venetianstaking over between 1687-1715, after which the Turks returned, until the Albanians set fire to the town. By 1834 it was deserted, once and for all.

From Mistras village it is worth returning to Sparti, via Ag Ioannis. On the outskirts is accommodation (over a restaurant), as well as more restaurants, two of which serve souvlaki.

At **Parori** village, keeping to the right of the two roads (rather than the left-hand Sparti turning), leads to an attractively tree shaded square, alongside a waterfall, gathered around which are a church and three rural tavernas, one of which advertises rainbow trout. The eateries are possibly only open in the evenings.

Ag Ioannis marks the bottom of the dog-leg back to Sparti and offers excursion coach drivers the last 'home-straight' opportunity to unload their human cargo at a plane tree shaded square, for a traditional Greek lunch/high tea/evening meal!.

Excursion to Geraki (38km). If setting out from Sparti, select the Tripoli road for about 2km, and, after crossing a bridge, turn right for Geraki. For details of the medieval city state *See* Geraki, Route Six

ROUTE NINE (*See* Illus. 21)
Githion to Kalamata via Itilo and Stoupa (109km) For the first part of the journey follow **Route Seven to Areopoli**.

Proceeding in a north-westerly direction, from Areopoli the road descends steeply to sea-level, to the nearside of the Bay of Limeniou. Here a slip road angles down to:
LIMENI (26km from Githion) This settlement turns out to be a surprisingly twee, St Ives-like, extensively restored fishing village, clinging to the hillside. The almost Norman style church, is actually a castle built by Petrobey Mavromichalis (*See* History, Githion, Chapt. 9), and recently restored by the NTOG. Above Limeni is an extremely smart, sympathetically built, Mani-style development.

Prior to visiting, callers might like to have a wash and brush up! More useful advice would draw attention to a sea edge taverna, in a marvellous setting, and from which are superb views. A meal for two of kalamares, Greek salad, 2 ouzos & a kortaki retsina cost 3150drs. The WC measures 8 on the Richter scale. A fish taverna, at the right-hand (*Fsw*) end of the village, offers accommodation.

Around the bay is:
SKALA (or Neo) **ITILO** (29km from Githion) Tel prefix 0733. The main road bypasses this settlement, which is positioned on the edge of a coastal plain circled by tall mountainsides. An older, fishing hamlet is at the south end, whilst the more recent, seaside resort is spaced out along a bay, beside a long 'Esplanade'. This runs parallel and some 100m distant from the main road. The shoreline is pleasant enough, with a sandy sea's edge but a pebbly mid and backshore. Due to the prevailing winds, the beach 'attracts' some kelp and seaborne rubbish.

Peter Vosdelakis runs the *Taverna Meros*, as well as a backshore cafe-bar restaurant. He is a friendly, interesting character with an Athens shoe shop and a little bit of property in Australia. A meal, for two, of boney but tasty garfish, a large Greek salad, 'moreish' bread, a large bottle of retsina, and 2 coffees cost us 3000drs (and we had a couple of ouzos on the house).

To the north of the *Meros,* and also on the inland side of the beach
Esplanade, is the four-square *Hotel Itilo* (Class C, tel 51300), where all
bedrooms have en suite bathrooms, with a single priced at 6310/7570drs &
doubles 7570/9085drs. Further on, about where the Esplanade rejoins the
main road, is a *Rooms/Cafe-bar,* and almost at the far, north side of the
bay there is signed *Captain Vassilikas Rooms & Taverna,* whereat 'fresh
fish and meat at all times'.

The road climbs and zig-zags steeply up the far mountainside from
'seaside' Itilo, passing by the hillside **Dekoulou Monastery.** It goes without
saying that the backward views are splendid. At the top of the ascent is:
ITILO (31km from Githion) Spelt as Oitilo, the name dates back to the
Homeric era. It was also known as Vitylo, and was once the capital of the
Mani. The far side of a ravine, to the east, between two folds in the
mountains, is the 'perfectly formed' **Kelefa Castle,** with castle keeps on at
least two corners (*See* Route Seven, Chapt. 9). Beside the thoroughfare is
a *Taverna Pub Garden,* and beyond a drinking water fountain, a *Rooms* in
a quite smart, two-storey building.

The roadsides are almost country lane-like, with stone walls, trees, groves
of olives, cows-a-munching, grass-a-growing, and fields-a-fielding. A
number of hamlets and villages are dotted along the route. These take in:
Ag Nikon (43km), a nice, dressed-stone village, with a pretty church,
whereabouts the, in places, poorly surfaced road passes through fairly
massive mountains, with much evidence of ancient walling; and **Langada**
(48km), which has several Mani-like towers, a pretty little Byzantine
church, a souvlaki shack and double headed fountain. In **Thalames,** around
a bend in the road and on the left, opposite a large, possibly now unused
school, is the unexpected, 'private enterprise' *Popular & Historical
Museum of the Mani.* Many of the exhibits are to do with other matters
than the Mani, such as Byron and the War of Independence, and the house
is worth visiting. The village of **Nomitsis** (52km) appears to have an
inordinate number of churches, several of them Byzantine and 'sporting'
interesting, if not unique, bell towers. Less than a kilometre on is **Platsa,**
which also boasts an oldish Byzantine church.
      The route now descends to about sea-level, to ford a river-bed, beyond
which is a turning to the left, advancing to:
AG NIKOLAOS (60km from Githion) The Stoupa overflow of *Sunmed*
holiday-makers will, without doubt, alter the basic characteristics of this
to-date somewhat scrubbly, if picturesque fishing-boat port cum low-key
seaside resort.
      Rooms and taverna/restaurants are scattered throughout the settlement.
Beyond the *Taverna To Lemani* is a small harbour, home for some resident
ducks. A meal for two at the *Lemani* of stuffed tomatoes, octopus, Greek
salad & kortaki retsina cost 2700drs. Apart from a few shops, there is
asupermarket, Post Office, *Pension Pharos, Rooms Sakis* (Tel 54259), as
well as *Rooms* (with private bath). The latter is housed in a building
resembling a Cretan windmill - a windmill that, at a superficial glance,
appears to have some machine gun nests built into the rear of the building!

A filling station marks the northern end of the settlement, close to where the loop road rejoins the main route.

One of the most interesting points about Ag Nikolaos is that there is a sea-hugging, tarmacadam road that backtracks to the south. The initial wildish bit of coast is dominated by a pumice type rock. In this is set an 80m long, wide, grey sand beach, the backshore being thickly planted with tamarisk trees, throughout which are a colony of 'wild' campers - and thus much dirt and litter. Beyond an outcrop of rock is a smaller cove of beach, bordered by a two storey *Pension*. The still metalled road continues on, past a tiny chapel edging the now boulderous shore. In amongst the varied scattering of domestic dwellings, one in the style of a Mani tower, another Spanish villa-like, are *Rooms*, close to a tiny harbour. The suburban development finally dribbles to an end, probably because the inland cliff-face has inexorably narrowed down towards the rocky sea-shore. Set into the sheer rock face are two or three caves, but the absence of an entrance fee extracting attendant signifies they are not worth a visit. To the right, between the road's edge and the sea, is a DMV - a deserted 'medieval' settlement of strange, little, barrel-like houses.

After some 3 or 4km, the road finally narrows down through thickly vegetated domestic front gardens, to run out in **Trahila**, a small, harbour village, the inhabitants of which are particularly friendly.

For those who make the trek to this well and truly off-the-beaten-track location, there are *Rooms*, in a particularly smart building, as well as more accommodation, for details of which, it is necessary 'to enquire at the tower of the village'. Apart from a couple of tavernas, there is a cafe-bar/grill house. The stone flagged 'High St' edges the harbour.

Inland of Trahila there appear to be even more rock caves. One drawback to any increasing tide of tourism is the lack of a beach. Another deterrent is the siesta-wedded nature of the contented inhabitants. It is to be hoped that they will not crack under the to-be-regretted, ever-creeping proximity of the package storm-troopers.

Returning to the main route, not 2km north of Ag Nikolaos is:
STOUPA (62km from Githion) Tel prefix 0721. Probably as a result of a combination of the attractiveness of the location, the somewhat English country village ambiance, and the small bay packed with a 100m of beautiful, golden, if gritty sand, Stoupa has been selected for an outright onslaught of villa-style, package holiday exploitation.

Close to the turning off the main road is: a bakery; a sign advising 'For a House to Rent by the Sea, ask Thanissis'; on the right, the modern, two storey *Hotel/Restaurant Stoupa* (Class C, tel 54308), where all bedrooms have en suite bathrooms, with a single priced at 4700/5650drs & doubles 5650/6750drs; followed by the *Hotel Lefktron* (Class B, Pension, tel 54322), where the prices are similar to those of the *Stoupa*.
Despite the air of quiet suburbia, necessary for a successful tourist resort,it is not unusual to observe a young shepherd (or shepherdess) herding the family's goats and sheep along the still country lanes.

South of the beach Esplanade is the Stoupa Athletic Centre, at which can be played outdoor tennis, as well as volley and basket ball. In amongst the trees are *Rooms* (Tel 54365) and a taverna, and immediately prior to the waterfront is a video shop. Apart from the aforementioned beach, away to the left is a small harbour, one side of which is formed by a man-made wall. The low-key Esplanade offers scooter and car hire, a souvenir shop, a taverna offering 'Information local houses rent', a supermarket and several *Rooms*, as well as pedaloes for hire. Where the street starts to circle back round the village it passes by Rest Estate Stoura, *Rooms*, a *Sunmed Hotel* (that offers excursions to various Peloponnese locations), *Rooms*, the Mirthos Disco Club, and a taxi rank.

As the road heads back towards the main route, it sweeps by a *Rooms/Taverna* and *Camping Kologria*, close to another, if much smaller, golden sand beach.

Two kilometres north of Stoupa is the Mirthos Club, as well as a *Pension* - in the middle of nowhere. A sign points to *Camping Delfinia*, which overlooks a stony beach headland.

A large bay, with a rocky islet just offshore, heralds:
KARDAMILI (72km from Githion) Tel prefix 0721. A substantial, prosperous, old village. The main road/High St is edged by dressed stone buildings, many of them a pretty pinky-brown, and parallels the some 100m distant, rocky shore.

Many of the residents speak 'American' or 'Canadian', and obviously have relatives in the respective countries, or have lived in North America. Most importantly, it is the home of one of my hero's - Patrick Leigh Fermor. So, if you observe a large, overweight, bearded poltroon, with a big backside, lurking on street corners, it might well be me, trying to catch a glimpse of the master - similarly to some lovelorn, ardent swain mooning about outside the garden fence of his 'fancy of the moment'. Don't get me wrong, there's nothing like that about my admiration. It is simply that I wish I had been fortunate enough to experience some of his adventures and travels, and that I were able to write with a quarter of his skill. One can dream!

The outskirts are heralded by a spot of pebble beach, followed by: the smart *Hotel Kalamitsi* (Class B, tel 73131), spread through an olive grove and with a delightful private beach, where en suite singles cost 6950/7560drs & doubles 8400/9480drs; the prettily located *Pension Pelateki* (Tel 28095), up to the right; an apartment block *Rooms*; lots of flowers; a bridge; and, to the left, a doo-hickey harbour. There are any number of signs for *Rooms*, a Post Office, opposite which is a bakery, and numerous souvenir shops festooned along the main drag, as is an overseas newspaper shop and *Rooms/Taverna Lela*. A 'blowout' at *Lela's,* for two, of 2 fish soups, stiffado, veal with potatoes, gigantes, a Greek salad & Naoussa Boutari wine totted up to 5180drs, and my informant stated that he voted it one of the top ten taverna's - in all of Greece. That is praise, indeed. Opposite and on the right of the latter is a Rent A Vespaoutfit (Kardamila Fotis, tel 73564; Stoupa Fotis, tel 73564; Orathina, tel 54533/54011) - 'Wild Mani is nearer by renting a Vespa', at a cost of some 2500drs a day. Next along is a filling station, a number of kafeneions, a taxi rank and a small public garden, overlooked by a pleasant accommodation block. Kardamili (Morgan) Holidays is close to the Post Office, and is owned by Nick Morgan, a friendly Brit, who gives a good currency exchange rate, organises tours to all the right places, and is a most helpful mine of information.

On the sea side of the aforementioned public garden is a block of 'firmly shut' toilets, whilst a side-street descends to an insignificant quay, edged by sea-washed boulders. This reminds me to point out that there isn't a waterfront Esplanade, just a number of lateral streets off the High St, which wander down to the rocky shore, some through a mess of backyards and orchards. Beside the last mentioned, public garden side-street, and on the left is the *Restaurant/Taverna Kiki*. Here a quickly served, hot meal, for two, of 2 veal & chips (750drs and a great lump of meat, probably goat), 1 green beans (350drs), 2 Amstel beers (175drs each), bread (awful) & service (75drs each), cost a total of 2350drs. The menu is 'tourist unimaginative', but the portions are plentiful.

For those who can stand the exhaust fumes, a 'local atmosphere' High St cafe-bar, worth a recommend, is the *To Kentro*, where a Nes meh ghala, without saucer, cost 150drs. Incidentally, the chairs here are not the traditional wicker, back-of-the-leg-biters, but red, shiny, modern plastic jobs.

Continuing north-west along the High St, from the public garden, one passes by a dentist, the Police station, opposite a church on the left, and two supermarkets cum grocery stores. Once over a summer-day river-bed, there is a sign to the left for *Camping Melitsena*, of which more soon, then the village school, and a few Mani-like towers, on the inland side of the road.

The lack of any 'town' beach is ameliorated, if distantly, by following the sign for *Camping Melitsena*, down a some 1½km long turning off the main route, alongside the new school. Almost immediately there are a group of three *Rooms*, in pension-like buildings, of pleasant appearance, followed by a cafe-bar, with a garden, set in the 'bundy'. The dirt track initially parallels a rocky coastline, followed by a very broad sweep of pebble, in which are 'here and there' hunks of sand, a shore that has been awarded (yet another) Golden Starfish. To the inland side of the track are tree bordered smallholdings, with a beach hut cafe-bar set in a grove of olives. The north end of the beach is marked by more rocky coast, *Kardamila Beach Cafeteria Bar & Restaurant*, and finally by the entrance to *Camping Melitsena* (Cat C, tel 73461), set on a low cliff. From the campsite steps lead down to the sea.

Returning to the main route, looking back over Kardamili, from above, one can enjoy an attractive scene, with the village almost a headland site, set in a veritable sea of olive trees.

The main road crests the mountainside to reveal a most pleasing panorama - a sweep of land broken up by hilltops, at least three of which are capped by castle keeps, and a range of mountains shutting off the right-hand, inland side.

From **Kambos** (87km) the road steeply serpentines down past a couple of campsite signs, one for *Camping Avia* (Cat B, tel (0721) 41780), which are both 'on the beach', away to the left, prior to revealing a sight of Almirou Bay, and yet distant Kalamata.

From a backward-angled junction (102km), a 9km long, coastal road heads south to end up at **Kitries**. This route is dotted with suburban seaside resorts servicing Kalamata. The first of these is the pretty location of **Avia**, with a pleasant grove of tamarisk trees edging the backshore of a pebble beach, with beach showers. Next along is 'another' Avia', but only having a 'splash of' pebble beach, because this not-so-attractive village is built over a sea-lapped cliff edge. The following village is a 'carbon copy Avia', actually **Paliochora**, where is a sign for *Furnished Rooms*. This settlement is a little distant and above the shoreline. The next along 'Avia-like', **Ag Krogiali**, has *Rooms*, the already referred-to, swept-up *Camping Avia*, and the modern *Apollon Apartments*, up on the right, overlooking the sea.

The road now curves round and drops down to border the narrow, pebble shoreline of end-of-the-line **Kitries**. Whitewashed tamarisk trees are scattered along the low sea wall of the roadside. Round to the right (*Fsw*) is a smidgin of sandy/pebble beach. Although I felt 'undistinguished' best described the spot, others have suggested that 'delightful' and 'capable of inducing contentment' would be more appropriate. You simply cannot please all of the readers, all of the time. A valued correspondent reports that an idyllic lunch for two, at the quay end fish taverna, of grilled octopus, 2 large fish, fried patatas & a Greek salad, preceded by 2 ouzos accompanied by mezes, and helped down by a litre of kortaki retsina was billed at 6200drs. Idyllic! I'm surprised they could remember what they ate, let alone where they were!

The main route swiftly proceeds to Kalamata.

Ain't going nowhere - a static exhibit in Kalamata park. Sometimes its difficult to tell an exhibit from a live one...

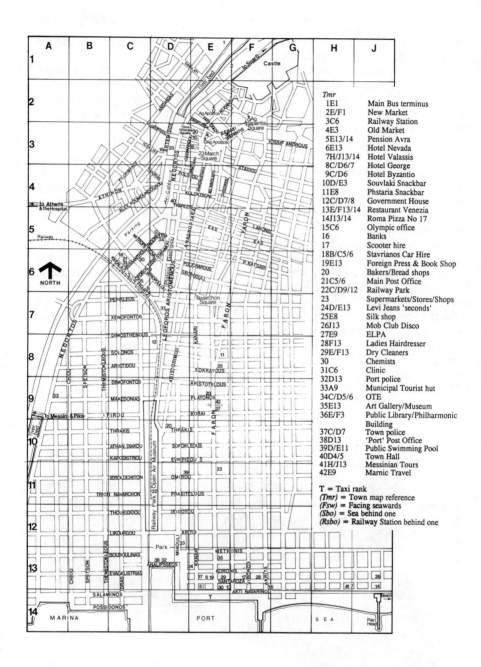

The map legend reads:

Tmr
1E1	Main Bus terminus
2E/F1	New Market
3C6	Railway Station
4E3	Old Market
5E13/14	Pension Avra
6E13	Hotel Nevada
7H/J13/14	Hotel Valassis
8C/D6/7	Hotel George
9C/D6	Hotel Byzantio
10D/E3	Souvlaki Snackbar
11E8	Phstaria Snackbar
12C/D7/8	Government House
13E/F13/14	Restaurant Venezia
14J13/14	Roma Pizza No 17
15C6	Olympic office
16	Banks
17	Scooter hire
18B/C5/6	Stavrianos Car Hire
19E13	Foreign Press & Book Shop
20	Bakers/Bread shops
21C5/6	Main Post Office
22C/D9/12	Railway Park
23	Supermarkets/Stores/Shops
24D/E13	Levi Jeans 'seconds'
25E8	Silk shop
26J13	Mob Club Disco
27E9	ELPA
28F13	Ladies Hairdresser
29E/F13	Dry Cleaners
30	Chemists
31C6	Clinic
32D13	Port police
33A9	Municipal Tourist hut
34C/D5/6	OTE
35E13	Art Gallery/Museum
36E/F3	Public Library/Philharmonic Building
37C/D7	Town police
38D13	'Port' Post Office
39D/E11	Public Swimming Pool
40D4/5	Town Hall
41H/J13	Messinian Tours
42E9	Marnic Travel

T = Taxi rank
(Tmr) = Town map reference
(Fsw) = Facing seawards
(Sbo) = Sea behind one
(Rsbo) = Railway Station behind one

Illustration 24 Kalamata

FIRST IMPRESSIONS Initially, apparently a souless, way-station of a city - which grows-on a visitor, with time.

SPECIALITIES Silk worms & the silk trade; trains.

VITAL STATISTICS Tel prefix 0721. The population is some 42,000.

HISTORY Despite its modern-day importance to the region, there is very little evidence of historical interest. The remains of the Kastro (*Tmr* F/G1), first constructed in 1208, are to the north of the Old Quarter.

GENERAL The rather sterile appearance has not been helped by the fact that Kalamata is the second largest Peloponnese city, and has recently been struck not once, but twice by earthquakes. The worst was as recently as 1986, when many buildings were reduced to rubble, the port facility suffered, about 10 people were killed, and about 12,000 inhabitants were made homeless. In 1989/90 another tremor kept everyone on their mettle.

To view the worst of the damage caused by these latest upheavals, it is only necessary to visit the Old Market (*Tmr* 4E3), and the encircling lanes, much of which was 'rubbled' in the devastation. The byeways and shops remain a mute testament to the destructive forces that hit the settlement. It is planned to convert much of the area into craft and cultural workshops, with a bias to the region's traditional silk industry.

The street naming is poor, and probably because it is so unsightly, the concrete lined river-bed, visible at the Main Bus terminal (*Tmr* 1E1), is bridged-in for much of its length.

ARRIVAL BY AIR The airport is 8km distant, just prior to the River Pamisos, and within a kilometre of Messini Town outskirts. An Olympic bus makes the connection to Kalamata. A direct Gatwick (UK) flight operates once a week.

ARRIVAL BY BUS The Main Bus terminus (*Tmr* 1E1) is 1½km from the Railway station (*Tmr* 3C6), is the the same again from the waterfront Esplanade, and is a long, hot trudge to most places.

ARRIVAL BY FERRY Kalamata should be a ferry-boat port, but is not. (What does he mean..., should be a...?).

ARRIVAL BY TRAIN The Railway Station (*Tmr* 3C6) is about midway between the Esplanade and the Bus terminal. It is conveniently close to the main avenue, Leoforos Aristomenous. The station complies with the 'standard' Peloponnese design.

THE ACCOMMODATION & THE EATING OUT

The Accommodation East along the waterfront Esplanade, Akti Navarinou, are a number of hotels. In addition, there are a couple of opportunities in the street parallel to and one back from the Esplanade, in the area of the Port (*Tmr* D/E/F14), as there are close to the Railway Station (*Tmr* 3C6).

Pension Avra (*Tmr* 5E13/14) (Class C) 10 Santaroza   Tel 82759
Directions: Santaroza St is north of, and runs parallel to Akti Navarinou. The clean building is two storeys high, with a flat roof.
    Only offers double bedrooms, sharing the bathrooms, at a cost of 3100/3700drs.

Diagonally across the street from the Avra is the:
Hotel Nevada (*Tmr* 6E13) (Class E) 9 Santaroza   Tel 82429
Directions: As above, in another pleasant, but three storey building.
    Run by a diminutive lady, Sophia, with all bedrooms sharing the bathrooms, a single priced at 2060/2620drs & doubles 3030/3760drs.

Further east along and bordering the Esplanade is the more modern:
Hotel Valassis (*Tmr* 7H/J13/14) (Class C) 95 Navarinou   Tel 23849
Directions: As above.
    As befits a modern C class hotel, all bedrooms have en suite bathrooms with a single costing 5500/6500drs & a double 6500/8500drs.

Hotel Haicos (Class C) 115 Navarinou   Tel 82886
Directions: As above, and further east, beyond the pier head.
    Similar prices to the *Valassis*.

Next door is the:
Hotel Plaza (Class D) 117 Navarinou   Tel 85590
Directions: As above.
    Less expensive, but should be, as the bedrooms share the bathrooms, with a single costing 4270/4790drs & doubles 5200/6650drs.

Another three blocks east and prior to a large church is the:
Hotel Flisvos (Class C) 135 Navarinou   Tel 82282
Directions: As above.
    All bedrooms have en suite bathrooms, with a single priced at 6000/7280drs & doubles 7630/9500drs.

East of a large church bordering the Esplanade, beyond a couple of narrow, lateral lanes is the:
Hotel Nedon (Class B pension) 153 Navarinou   Tel 26811
Directions: As above.
    En suite bedrooms with each bedroom, singles charged at 6000/7280drs & doubles 7270/9100drs.

Even further to the east, there are the: *Pension Tathia*; the three storey, family style, D class *Hotel Alexandrion* (Tel 26821), where en suite single costs 5890/6720drs & doubles 6720/8415drs; and the glitzy, three storey *Hotel Elite* (Class A, tel 25015) where singles are charged at 10400/12400drs & doubles 13000/15400drs.

Close to the Railway Station (*Tmr* 3C6) are the:
Hotel George (*Tmr* 8C/D6/7) (Class E) Dagre/Frantzi Sts   Tel 27225
Directions: To the right (*Station behind one*), in a two storey building, with the addition of a third, a distinct possibility - if all the rooftop reinforcing bars are any indiction...
     Clean with bathroom sharing double bedrooms costing 3430/3830drs.
And the:
Hotel Byzantio (*Tmr* 9C/D6) (Class C) 13 Sidir Stathmou   Tel 86824
Directions: The six storey, modernised building is to the front of the Railway station, along Leoforos Sidir Stathmou, at the junction with Iatropoulou St.
     The 'going' rates.

Camping Almost at the far eastern end of the Esplanade are three campsites, the: *Camping Hotel Patisla* (Cat C, tel 29525), 350drs a head and per tent, set in a garden, and in front of which is a smart, art deco building; *Camping Elite* (Cat C, tel 80365), 500drs per head and per tent, down a turning alongside the *Hotel Elite*; and *Camping Fare* (Tel 29520).

The Eating Out The eateries tend to be located in widely spaced-out groupings. For instance, close to the Old Quarter is a row of roadside (Leoforos Nedontas) edging cafe-bars (*Tmr* D4), whilst on the south side of Plateia Dios Ithomata, up against Odhos Germanou, is a souvlaki pita snackbar (*Tmr* 10D/E3), where a 'handful' costs 120drs.
     Mind you, the 'best souvlaki in town' is to be found at *Phstaria Snackbar* (*Tmr* 11E8), noticeable for its window-mounted Coca Cola advert. They do a roaring trade, with up to five girls serving, at any one time. A 'slick' souvlaki and chips costs 110drs.
     The hub of the town's cafe/volta society stretches along Leoforos Aristomenous, from Plateia Georgiou (*Tmr* D5/6) as far south as Government House (*Tmr* 12C/D7/8). A Nes meh ghala costs 150drs.
     Understandably, the majority of the restaurants and tavernas are ranged along the Esplanade, from the *Restaurant Venezia* (*Tmr* 13E/F13/14), at the west end, all the way eastwards past the large church. Unfortunately, no one establishment is outstanding. For a typical, 'rural' style taverna meal, why not try the:

Nea Kalamata Taverna
Directions: East of the pier head, beyond the church and the *Hotel Nedon*.
     A meal, for two, of roast beef & chips (750drs each), a Greek salad (400drs), 2 Amstel beers (150drs each), bread & service (50drs each), added up to a total of 2300drs.

A more anodyne alternative is the:
Roma Pizza No 17 (*Tmr* 14J13/14) 113 Navarinou
Directions: Across the Esplanade from the pier head. Despite the title of this 'chain' restaurant, it is Canadian backed.
     A meal, for two, of the best, all 'swinging & dancing' house pizza (1500drs) and 2 Henninger beers (150drs each), cost 1800drs.

A TO Z OF INFORMATION
AIRLINE OFFICE (*Tmr* 15C6) Open Mon-Fri, between 0900-1700hrs. The Olympic bus sets out 70mins prior to flight departures and costs 100drs.

Aircraft timetable
Kalamata to Athens
Daily   1955, 2045hrs
Sun   1705, 1755hrs
Return
Daily   1840, 1930hrs
Sun   1550, 1640hrs
One-way fare 8000drs; duration 50mins.

BANKS (*Tmr* 16) There are a couple in the area of the Old Quarter, the Commercial Bank (*Tmr* 16D/E3) and the Ergobank (*Tmr* 16C/D3), whilst there is a National Bank (*Tmr* 16F/G13/14) beside the Esplanade.

BEACHES The not over-wide, gritty, grey sand beach certainly stretches a long way to the east, bordering the Esplanade, all the way. There are beach showers and much of the backshore/Esplanade is shaded by tamarisk trees.

BICYCLE, SCOOTER & CAR HIRE The bulk of the establishments are grouped around the area behind the Port Esplanade, and include a **Rent A Scooter/Motorbike Firm** (*Tmr* 17E13) beside Odhos Kanari, and nearby **MotoWork Scooter Hire** (*Tmr* 17F13) on Odhos Vironos. **Rent A Car Stavrianos** (*Tmr* 18B/C5/6) is beside Nedontos St, fairly close to the Railway station, whilst **Manyatis Rent A Car** is across Iatropoulou St from the Main Post Office (*Tmr* 21C5/6). **Hertz** are based at KNS Travel, 186 Faron St.

BOOKSELLERS The **Foreign Press & Book Shop** (*Tmr* 19E13) borders Odhos Faron, close to the Port Esplanade. It is 'strong' in English language newspapers, but 'weak' on books.

BREAD SHOPS These are rather widely scattered throughout Kalamata, with a **Bread** shop (*Tmr* 20D/E2/3) bordering Plateia Dios Ithomata, another (*Tmr* 20D9/10) at the junction of Aristodimou and Thrakis Sts, with a **Baker/ Zacharoplasteion** (*Tmr* 20E9) at the crossroads of Platonos and Faron Sts.

BUSES The main terminus (*Tmr* 1E1) is a rather sterile, if not a horrid, concrete-hot, tin shed roof, permanent looking, temporary set-up! The tin shed toilets, which lack toilet paper, are of the 'starting block' variety, very smelly, and in the midday sun must become pretty steamy. The cafe-bar/ticket office is also pretty steamy!
    The back of the buildings edge the unattractive, summer-dry, concrete lined river-bed. A meccano-like Bailey bridge allows foot passengers easy access to the top end of the massive, equally concrete, modern Market (*Tmr* 2E/F1).

Bus timetable - main services
Kalamata to Athens (100 Kifissou St) via Megalopoli, Tripoli, Argos & Korinthos.
Daily   0445, 0630, 0900, 1000, 1030, 1200, 1400, 1600, 1830, 2245hrs
Return journey
Daily   0800, 0845, 1100, 1230, 1400, 1500, 1700, 1900, 2100, 2330hrs
One-way fare to   Athens   2850drs; duration 4½hrs
                  Megalopoli   500drs
                  Tripoli   850drs
                  Argos   1400drs
                  Korinthos   1860drs

Kalamata to Patras, via Pirgos
Daily   0830, 1400hrs
One-way fare to   Patras   2250drs; duration 4hrs
                   Pirgos   1300drs;   2hrs
Kalamata to Sparti
Daily   0915, 1430hrs
One-way fare 650drs
Kalamata to Itilo (for Areopoli & Githion)
Daily   0730, 1300, 1730hrs
Kalamata to Messini
Daily   0630-2200hrs, every ½hr
Kalamata to Filiatra
Daily   0600, 0830, 1345hrs
Sun/hols   0830, 1400hrs

The (blue) Buses No 1 & 2, are town services with No 1 drifting down to, and along the Esplanade, thence back to the terminus (70drs to anywhere).

CHILD CARE There is a children's playground, with swings and tyres, in the Railway Park (*Tmr* 22C/D9/12), which is in itself a children's delight (*See* Places & Events ...).

COMMERCIAL SHOPPING AREA The Old Quarter Market (*Tmr* 4E3) is an excellent 'hunting' ground. Lots of the buildings hereabouts are in a pitiful state, many clapped together with corrugated iron, some fenced off. Close to the small Byzantine Church Ag Apostolio (*Tmr* E3) is the most inexpensive **Tapestry** shop in Kalamata. The west side of Leoforos Nedontos is a singular row of temporary, single storey shops (*Tmr* 23D3). There is a very large, very swept-up **Supermarket** (*Tmr* 23E10/11) beside Faron St, and another sizable one (*Tmr* 23D/E12/13) alongside Odhos Miaouli, near the port.
     Close to the latter is the quite amazing **Levi Jeans**, 'seconds' warehouse (*Tmr* 24D/E13). Not only are the prices eminently reasonable, but the range of display and choice is enormous. Open the usual shop hours.
     The **New Market** (*Tmr* 2E/F1) is an extensive, raised, double-sided building, either side of a central square. The retail shops are on the east side of the complex and the toilets are comparatively clean.
     The only traditional **Silk** shop (*Tmr* 25E8) still in business is besides Odhos Faron. It used to be combined with a factory workshop, but sadly the latter activity has been discontinued.

DISCOS At the eastern end of the Esplanade is the air conditioned **Disco Dodina**, whilst further on, close to *Camping Hotel Patista*, is the ever-so smart, and expensive **Disco Palladium**, where entrance costs 1000drs including the first drink. Another possibility is the **Mob Club Disco** (*Tmr* 26J13).

ELPA (*Tmr* 27E9) The office is beside Faron St.

HAIRDRESSERS There is a **Ladies Hairdresser** (*Tmr* 28F13) on the north side of Santaroza St. I'm sure there are more, but ....

LAUNDRY A Dry Cleaners (*Tmr* 29E/F13) is beside Santaroza St.

MEDICAL CARE
Chemists & Pharmacies A Chemist (*Tmr* 30C/D5/6) is conveniently adjacent

to the Railway station, and another (*Tmr* 30E/F13/14) to the Port Esplanade.
Clinic (*Tmr* 31C6) Beside Odhos Chrissanthou, close to the Railway station.
Hospital The facility is some way along Odhos Athinon (*Tmr* A4/5), to the
west of the town, on the left of the Athens road.

MUNICIPAL TOURIST OFFICE (*Tmr* 33A9) A most extraordinarily
positioned hut, in the western outskirts, on the right of the Messini road, by
the river-bed. The facility is under the control of Georgou Lacos Michael, a
pleasant, slim, helpful, young gentleman, who speaks sufficient English. 'Did
you know'... the inclusion of 'lacos' in a person's name indicates that they hail
from the Mani? He explains away the apparently strange location of the office
by advising that the 'powers that be' consider this road is the major highway
into Kalamata, along which will troop all the visitors to the town! What a 'load
of gollies' - most visitors are deposited at the Bus terminus (*Tmr* 1E1) or the
Railway station (*Tmr* 3C6), and even those who fly-in will be whisked by on
an Airways bus, to be set down at the Olympic office (*Tmr* 15C6). Whatever,
the Tourist office opens daily, between 0930-1400hrs & 1800-2030hrs. The
town map available is an unsatisfactory, spidery scrawl and Mr Michael's pool
of knowledge is selective. For instance, he appears to know little or nothing
about the Kastro. Incidentally, the Faron St office is administrative only, and
not for the punters.

NTOG *See* Municipal Tourist Office

OTE (*Tmr* 34C/D5/6) The doors open weekdays, between 0600-2400hrs, and
weekends 0600-2300hrs.

PARKING No problem, except perhaps on either of the busy main avenues, or
the narrow lanes of the Old Quarter.

PETROL There are several filling stations beside the Port Esplanade.

PLACES & EVENTS OF INTEREST
Churches The 18thC *Ag Ipapantis Cathedral Church* (*Tmr* F2/3), the 13thC
Ag Apostoli Church (*Tmr* E2), and *Ag Apostolio Church* (*Tmr* E3) are all in
the Old Quarter, close to Plateia 23rd March. The latter square is 'yet
another' Greek location where it is said that the local patriots first gathered,
and, swept on by an unstoppable tide of nationalistic fervour, overwhelmingly
voted to uprise and overthrow the oppressive Turkish yoke, thus causing the
onset of the War of Independence (1821-1829). I write 'yet another', as
throughout one's travels it is not uncommon to have pointed out this square,
or that building, which was THE SPOT at which the momentous decision was
taken, that at last galvanised the Greeks into a country-wide revolt, resulting
in their regaining the sovereignty of their nation. Yes...!
Kastro (*Tmr* F/G1) The existing structure was built in 1208, on the site of
previous Mycenean and Byzantine fortifications. During the summer a
cultural show is staged in the grounds.
Museums The contents of the Archaeological museum were removed to Sparti,
when the building was irretrievably damaged in the recent earthquakes.
Art Museum & Gallery (*Tmr* 35E13) A pleasant display of mainly modern
Greek paintings.
Railway Museum & Park (*Tmr* 22C/D9/12) This represents an equally
imaginative treatment of the, now disused, port railway facilities, as that of

Nafplio. Here the emphasis is on an extensive, if static display of antique railway engines and rolling stock. Mind you, I am not entirely sure that I have not observed similar trains - still in use. The lineal garden park stretches from south of the existing Railway station, towards the port. The pleasantly tree, shrub and bush planted area has a stream running down its length, and there is a children's playground.

The first exhibits are some Athens Metro-style wooden carriages, built in 1904, and until comparatively recently working the Athens to Piraeus line. It is a pity that many of the labels and signs explaining the function of the various displays are now illegible. Continuing south, next along are some rolling stock and track maintenance plant, spaced out along the original track and sidings. These are followed by the nub of the layout, a number of trains and shunting engines gathered around the old port railway station and buildings. There is a cafe-bar let into the east side of the old station, as well as a bandstand, and further south a small lake. Without doubt, the park is well worth a ramble, and it is possible to clamber in, on and around the 'exhibits'.

Public Library & Philharmonic Building (*Tmr* 36E/F3) In the Old Quarter.

POLICE
Port (*Tmr* 32D13) Unusually, bang-on the port quayside. Almost invariably these offices are tucked away, well out of sight of the waterfront!
Town (*Tmr* 37C/D7) The one-way road system in and around the Railway and Police stations, makes it rather difficult to find one's way into the police offices.

POST OFFICE There are two. The main Post Office (*Tmr* 21C5/6) is located close to the Railway station, whilst the other one (*Tmr* 38D13) is down by the port. The main office not only opens weekdays, but Saturdays between 0730-1400hrs and Sundays 0900-1330hrs.

SPORTS FACILITIES There is a stadium to the east of the map, along Odhos Eas (*Tmr* G5/6), and a public swimming pool (*Tmr* 39D/E11). Whilst in the area of the swimming pool, around the corner is a small church set down bang in the middle of Odhos Evripidou. Strange!

TAXIS (*Tmr* T) They rank beside the port and at the Railway station (*Tmr* 3C6), amongst other city locations.

TELEPHONE NUMBERS & ADDRESSES
Bus terminus (*Tmr* 1E1)	Tel 22851
ELPA (*Tmr* 27E9) 155 Faron St	Tel 24100
Hospital	Tel 85203
Municipal Tourist Office (administration only) 221 Faron St	Tel 22059
Olympic office (*Tmr* 15C6) 17 S. Stathmou St	Tel 22376
Police (*Tmr* 37C/D7)	Tel 23187
Town Hall (*Tmr* 40D4/5)	Tel 28000
Taxi (radio)	Tel 21112

TOILETS *See* Bus terminus (*Tmr* 1E1), New Market (*Tmr* 2E/F1) and the Railway station (*Tmr* 3C6).

TRAINS Kalamata is the end of the line for both the clock and anticlockwise Peloponnese railway tracks. The building has a cafeteria, toilets and a cold drinking water machine.

Train timetable
Kalamata to Korinthos (anticlock) & Athens, via Tripoli & Argos.
Daily Dep.   2256, 0640, 1035, 1515hrs
Tripoli   0140, 0932, 1328, 1817hrs
Argos   0302, 1045, 1450, 1936hrs
Mikines   0312, 1059, 1501,   - hrs
Korinthos   0402, 1159, 1552, 2035hrs
Athens   0543, 1355, 1742, 2219hrs
Kalamata to Korinthos (clockwise) & Athens, via Pirgos & Patras.
Daily Dep. 2025, 0810, 1340hrs
Kiparissia   2221, 1007, 1532hrs
Pirgos   2343, 1146, 1656hrs
Patras   0200, 1408, 1910hrs
Egio   0246, 1456, 1952hrs
Diakofto   0304, 1515, 2014hrs
Xilokastro   0353, 1607, 2104hrs
Korinthos   0407, 1646, 2145hrs
Athens   0628, 1900, 2342hrs
Return
Athens to Kalamata (clockwise), via Argos & Tripoli.
Athens Dep.   0730, 0930, 1430hrs
Korinthos   0922, 1111, 1623hrs
Mikines   1011,   - 1714hrs
Argos   1022, 1210, 1726hrs
Tripoli   1147, 1327, 1855hrs
Kalamata   1438, 1549, 2148hrs
Athens to Kalamata (anticlock), via Patras & Pirgos.
Athens Dep.   0650, 1000, 2128hrs
Korintho   0848, 1200, 2326hrs
Xilokastro   0926, 1235, 0041hrs
Diakofto   1015, 1329, 0052hrs
Egio   1033, 1347, 0111hrs
Patras   1117, 1445, 0154hrs
Pirgos   1342, 1655, 0405hrs
Olympia   1449, 2036,   - hrs
(branch line)
Kiparissia   1507, 1818, 0523hrs
Kalamata   1702, 2013, 0717hrs
One-way fare to Athens 3570drs; duration 7hrs (clock)/10½hrs (anti).

TRAVEL AGENTS & TOUR OFFICES Some firms are gathered along the
Esplanade, which number includes **Messinian Tours** (*Tmr* 41H/J13, tel 20704),
at No 93 Akti Navarinou. This office specialises in boat trips and handles the
MY Delfini, which indulges in daily, height of summer months cruises. An
eight hour excursion, down the Messiniakos Gulf, to the Dirou Caves costs
3500drs a head. Unfortunately, the tour office owner is a large, blonde,
supercilious Greek. A better bet, for friendly, well-organised service, is
Marnic Travel (*Tmr* 42E9, tel 24000), at 147 Faron St, where they also
exchange currency.

EXCURSIONS TO KALAMATA SURROUNDS
Excursion towards Sparti (some 54km). Those who fly direct to Kalamata,
might wish to proceed to Sparti and Mistras, a choice of route which
proceeds through the Langada Pass, or Gorge, one of the most spectacular

Peloponnese scenery locations. The road advances approximately north-east, up the River Nedon valley, prior to angling off to scale the Taigetos mountain range. There are a number of refreshment stop settlements, such as **Artemisia** and **Tripi**, but why not avoid the summit-adjacent *Tourist Pavilion*? To the left of the gorge is where the Spartans were in the habit of ridding themselves of sick and weakly children, by throwing them over the edge. As a father, I'm not sure that the custom should have ended, or be restricted to the sick ...!

Once over the saddle of the mountains and through the gorge, there are lovely views of Mistras, through massed olive groves.

ROUTE TEN (Illus. 25)
To Killini via Koroni, Methoni, Pilos, Olympia & Pirgos (306km) This route initially takes in the Messinia province and a square shoulder of land that juts down into the sea. The latter is an area that should make Mani-lovers weep, as it is arguably the most attractive locality of the Peloponnese - and that is a big statement to back-up.

The route out of Kalamata passes by a pottery factory, in addition to the more usual car breaker's yards, and the Levi jeans factory complex. The road runs alongside the main railway line for a time, then past the part-military, part-civil airport, symbolised by a strange metalwork structure hanging above the entrance. Almost immediately beyond the airfield is the swampy, summer-running River Pamisos, into which the locals appear to dump most of their rubbish.

Messini (10km) has a disused railway station and messy industrial outskirts, and bears no relationship to its namesake - Ancient Messene. To visit the latter is a 27km detour, for which turn right, in modern Messini, heading north up the valley of the River Pamisos, through **Triodos** and **Eva**. At **Lambene** follow the sign for Ithomi, by turning left, and then north again, for the pretty, lush hamlet of **Mavromati**. This is within the grounds of:

Ancient Messene (Ithomi) The city was built in BC 369, as part of a defensive chain of fortified cities, subsequent to the Spartans being defeated, at Leuktra, in BC 371.

Apart from the small odeion, and the astonishing nine kilometres of wall, perhaps the most remarkable item is the Arkadian Gate, to the north of the site, and reputed to be one of the best preserved city gates in Greece. From the village to the summit of Mt Ithomi, which is more correctly a ridge, takes about 1½hr. Legend states that Zeus was born on this mountain top, by a spring, so it can come as no surprise that there was a human sacrifice altar, no doubt a gathering place for festival worshippers in those far off days. Close to the spot stands the abandoned **Monastery of Vourkano** (16thC), which in 1712 founded, or mothered the other **Vourkano Monastery**, some 20mins walk south of the Laconian Gate. The latter monastery is a crowded place of annual pilgrimage to venerate the Assumption, on 15th August. The various vantage points allow marvellous views out over the region.

Returning to the road west of Messini, at **Analipsis** village (17km) is a

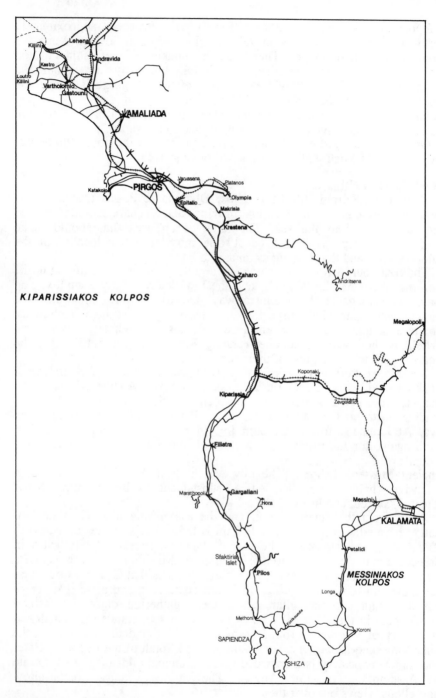

Illustration 25 Route Ten

turning to the left, signed *To the Beach & Club Aquarius*. This leads to a massive, village bungalow complex that has annexed a great chunk of the beach and backshore. Despite which, there still remains an enormous sweep of gritty sand 'plage', with some pebble, stretching away to the right (*Fsw*). The sea-bed, of bigger and bigger pebble, steeply shelves. The nearside of the *Club Aquarius* is delineated by a man-made, sea-inlet, the mouth of which is protected by a rock mole. The somewhat shadeless shore must continue on for several kilometres, as far as **Paralia Velika**, access to which is from the inland village of **Velika** (20km). At that beach is a restaurant/beach bar and *Camping Velika* (Cat C, tel 0722 24789).

At **Rizomilos** (22km) the main road crosses over to the west coast of the Peloponnese, to Pilos, whilst 'our' route turns left, with a view out over the village and a 'U' shaped bay, south, down the coast towards:

PETALIDI (27km from Kalamata). Tel prefix 0722. The outskirts of this old, rural, seaside Greek resort are marked by a sign for the *Venus Disco Club*, beside the road, followed by *Camping Petalidi Beach* (Cat C, tel 31154), furnished flats, and *Camping Zervas Beach* (Cat B, tel 31223), the last three being down a track to the left.

Beside the pleasant High St are the *Steak House Cafe Bar*, *Romantica Rooms*, another *Rooms*, *Bungalows for Rent*, *Cafe Croissant*, a super-market, baker, a BP filling station, a dairy products shop, more *Rooms*, a cooper, a mini-market, with a metered telephone, and a Post Office. The High St spills out on to a very large, rectangular, one-way traffic square, around which are spaced a Rent A Motorbike firm, a bank, butcher, baker and a taxi rank. There are also a few gift shops and a ladies hairdresser. A number of the residents are American and Canadian speakers.

A sample of the extremely reasonable prices at the main square *Cafeteria/Pizzeria/Chrissos Snackbar* are: a breakfast of bacon & eggs/ham & eggs/ sausage & eggs with coffee, tea or milk 650drs; plain omelettes   250drs; cheese or sausage omelette 450drs; ham & cheese omelette 500drs;   special omelette 550drs; spaghetti Neapolitan 300drs; spaghetti bolognese 450drs; special spaghetti 550drs; spaghetti carbonara 550drs; bacon/ham or special pizza 550drs; moussaka 580drs; beefsteak Viennese 750drs; fried   squid 500drs; weiner schnitzel 700drs; and fried shrimps 950drs.

To one side of the grassy waste of the square is a church. To the right (*Fsw*) slowly curves the old-fashioned, dirt surfaced, spacious village waterfront, to which are moored some fishing boats. To the left, the waterfront also curves round. In this direction, there has been a desultory attempt to create a smart, formally paved area, followed by some steps down to a continually running drinking water fountain, all bordered by nice old houses. Beyond these a broken ramp of concrete descends to the nearside of an 80m long beach, edged by the gardens of various homes, and a *Rooms*. The mid-shore is pebble and sand, the foreshore and immediate sea-bed are sand, whilst the sea-bed becomes progressively more pebbly. Beyond a spur of concrete patio and a few houses, is another sweep of pebbly beach.

On the south side of the main square is a Camping Gaz store, as well as a backyard farmer who corrals his turkeys beside the road. I vote Petalidi on to an impressive list of splendid locations in this region, to which travellers should head.

The route parallels the coastline for a while, past a sign for the *Eros Beach Snackbar*, a 'bit of pebble beach' (similar to a number dotted all the way along this road), *Eros Beach Camping* (Cat B, tel 31208), all on the left, and on the right, the *Camping Sun Beach* (Cat C, tel 31200). The lengths of shore from which to bathe are separated by low cliff and rock.

A *Rooms* and 'Real Estate shack of a house' heralds the outset of the hamlet of **Kalamaki** (31km) close to a rickety sign indicating a 200m track to a campsite. At about the point where there is the view of a long length of shore, and a *Rooms*, is the 'German flavoured' hamlet of **Hrani** (34km). In fact, it is a very nice, yellow sand, pleasantly tree-shaded beach, bordered by a scattering of holiday villas, low-rise apartments and houses for rent, in amongst groves of olives. They are serviced by the *Supermarket/Cafe-bar/Information/Bungalows/Paradise Supermarket* - phew! Towards the south end of this lovely spot, the shore is steeply inclined and still a bit wild. Access to the beach is marked by a crudely drawn sign for *Socrates Apartments*, whilst another board indicates a *Pizza Restaurant*. Along the main road are the *Villa Fragos* and more *Rooms*.

The agricultural countryside is pleasing, despite the intrusion of some plastic farming. Opposite a filling station is a strip of golden sand and pebble beach, as well as flats and bungalows to let, with some of the gardens beautifully planted with bougainvillea.

The commencement of **Longa** (38km) and the low-rise, old village of **Ag Andreas** (39km) is marked by the *Hotel Longa Beach*, with the main town up to the right, on a low, olive tree covered hill, with 'snatches' of villas here and there. Rates for the *Longas Beach* (Class C, tel 0725 31583), where all bedrooms have en suite bathrooms, are 5500/6500drs for singles & 6800/8000drs for doubles. Signs in the trees indicate the *Hotel Renaissance* and the *Hotel Angelos* (Class C, tel 0725 31368), the latter only offering double rooms sharing the bathrooms, at a cost of 3000/5200drs. The shore is about 50/100m distant. In addition to a couple of tavernas, there are *Rooms* (Tel 31268), a High St, a filling station and a taxi rank. A track cuts down to a sizeable caique harbour, and, beyond an outcrop of rock, some tree shaded, sand and pebble beach to the left (*Fsw*). To the right, beyond the *Holiday Disco Cafeteria Restaurant*, is another sweep of more pebbly, if similarly tree edged beach, which runs out on a spit of land. The closer one progresses towards the far end, the lower droop the branches of the trees.

South of Ag Andreas is a summer time, water-bearing river bed. In the busy, small, but outstretched village of **Harokopio** (45km), the indistinct signposting laggardly points the way through lovely countryside to:

KORONI (51km from Kalamata) Tel prefix 0725. On the way along the peninsular are a number of houses bearing 'For Rent' signs, and the swept-up *Camping Koroni* (Cat C, tel 22119), which boasts a swimming pool and water sports. The lovely view from the approach reveals an

Italian-like, terracotta roofed fishing village, a large harbour and smart waterfront, overlooked by the ruins of a castle. The Malta-like, narrow streets climb, wind and descend through the settlement. Koroni is a chic location, even boasting a better class of souvenirs, and popular with the in-the-know, smarter French and Italian tourists.

A small store is signed as the bus station and there is a taxi rank. Apart from *Rooms*, and an antique shop, the *Hotel Panorama* (Class D, tel 22224), is to the right, at a fork in the road. Descending towards the waterfront, the twisting lane of a street passes by grocers, a bank, bread shop, more *Rooms*, and an 'information inside' sign on a souvenir shop.

Alongside the pleasant Esplanade running away to the right (*Fsw*), towards the harbour, are a possible over-kill of gift shops, as well as the *Hotel/Restaurant Flisvos* (Cat D, tel 22238), where en suite doubles cost 5000drs, a pizzeria, the port police, and towards the far end, a nicely old, if small, paved plateia. Here are *Rooms*, reached through a colonnaded archway, and the square is bordered by attractive, stone walled buildings in which is a baker 'bread making', and an Agricultural Bank, which does not indulge in exchange transactions. Still further on, the castle walls stretch down to the sea's edge. The builders of the castle were 'early day Greens', or simply lazy, as they recycled as much of an on-site, ancient settlement's masonry as they could rake up. The beach is no more than a smidgin of mainly pebble, set in a rocky cove, overlooked by *Rooms*. Probably one of the best, and certainly the most popular of the seafront tavernas is the *Parthenon*, where a meal, for two, of 2 plates of kalamares, aubergines, briam & retsina cost 3050drs.

Away to the left is a fairly narrow crescent of shore rimmed by sharply rising hillsides. The seas around Koroni are clean, even if the sea-bed tends to encourage the growth of sea-grass.

Despite the undoubted attractiveness of the port/resort, this would surely not be sufficient to entice the class of tourist to be found here? And nor is it. To fully comprehend the appeal, take the left-hand fork out of Koroni, in a southerly direction, towards **Vasilitsi**. This leads by the Gallic named *Hotel de la Plage* (Cat B, tel 22401), to the left, where en suite singles cost 6560drs & doubles 8450drs, a restaurant, a football pitch, on the right the *Manni Beach Camping* (Cat C, tel 22130) and, to the left, the raison d'etre - an enormous bay's length of magnificent beach. It has to be admitted that there is a narrow band of small pebble in the first metre of the otherwise sandy sea-bed, and, unfortunately, an extensive beach shower area has had the water turned off. At the far end of the attractively tree shaded backshore is the *Restaurant Limenaki*. The 2/3km distance from Koroni explains the extensive number of taxis - 'in town'.

Without doubt, Koroni is an ideal destination for the Mediterranean lover - note, not the committed, 'warts and all', indigenous Grecophile, for there is bound to be a boutique here and there. Even the countryside reminds one of Tuscany, with a similarly coloured soil.

Heading west towards Methoni, after some 11km a viewpoint is reached allowing a lovely sea panorama over the offshore islands of **Shiza** and **Sapiendza**, as well as the coastline. Furthermore, back to the left can be snatched glimpses of Cape Akritas, off which is the islet of **Venetiko**.

Edging a chisel shaped, large cove is the settlement and harbour of:
FINIKOUNDA (70km from Kalamata) Tel prefix 0723. The approaches
across the plain, along the narrow, old main road are highlighted by some
'plastic' agriculture, a disco sign, and a water ski/windsurfing school. The
latter operates from a small, sandy cove blocked off by a (eastern)
headland, the other side of which is the small, flat bay on which stands the
pretty, once-upon-a-time fishing village of Finikounda.

The road angles and descends, past a schloss-like tourist hotel, to the
outset of an Esplanade High St, edged by a slim, gritty sand sweep of
beach. There are: *Rooms* (Tel 71306); the well-run, charmingly staffed
Hotel Finissia (Class C, tel 71358), where en suite singles are priced at
3500/7000drs & doubles 5500/8500drs; a *Falcon Sailing* sign; any
number of *Rooms*; the *Hotel Finikounda* (Class C, tel 71208), where
en suite single rooms cost 4500/6000drs & doubles 5500/7000drs; and the
Disco Memory.

The village has a vehicle parking lot, by the church, and a one-way
traffic system. Smack in the middle of the place is a filling station, whilst
on the west side is the harbour. Apart from the to-be-expected restaurant
grills, more *Rooms*, a travel agency, taxi rank, various shops, a number of
signs in English (no doubt due to the presence of *Falcon Sailing*, which
include the admonishment 'Please keep the area clean'), there is a
back-street baker.

An establishment serving 'breakfast, lunch & dinner', is called *To
Kyma*, where the service is rather desultory, and a meal for two of
souvlaki, moussaka, briam, Greek salad & a litre of barrel rose wine costs
3200drs. A preferable eaterie, on the grounds of location, service, quality,
and the variety of the menu, is the *Taverna Elena*. It is rather hidden away,
amongst olive trees, on the promontory to the right (*Fsw*) of the bay. A
meal for two of beetroot in sauce, baked aubergine salad, stuffed
aubergines, briam, lamb in lemon sauce & a house red wine cost 4100drs.

For my sensibilities, it is unfortunate that Finikounda has been
discovered, even if only by a minority interest package-holiday clientele.
The plus side is that it has not yet been Kosta'd, by either the 'cocktail and
adultery set' or 'low-brew larger louts'. Since my original research,
tourism has resulted in the creation of two 'bright' pastry shops. The
smaller is the *Gardenia*, where 2 Greek coffees cost 300drs, and which
offers 'fizzi drings' and a pastry 'trunk'! The huge, garishly-lit opposition,
straddling the High St and spilling over on to the backshore, is
appropriately named *Medusa* - no doubt in fond memory of the gorgon of
the same name, whose hideous appearance turned any onlooker into stone!
Two coffees & 2 sticky cakes are charged 800drs.

Beyond the west headland of Finikounda cove is a great sweep of a bay,
and in amongst these outskirts are some *Rooms*, and about ¾km out of
town a couple of discos.

The route continues to wind along an old road, across flat, intensively
farmed land, past a sign for *Camping Ammos* (Cat C, tel 71262), close to
sand dunes, followed by a jolly big factory. The campsite is adjacent to a

fairly wild shoreline and the a jolly nice beach, bordering the long bay, to the west of Finikounda. Incidentally, a Pilos bus routes around this hump of land. The road now climbs away from the coast, heading inland through the little village of **Kamaria** and larger **Evangelismos**, beyond which is:

METHONI (86km from Kalamata) Tel prefix 0723. This is quite a large village, if not a small town, dominated by a sizable castle, topping a low horn of land projecting into the sea, with a domed chapel at the tip, and **Sapiendza** island, just offshore.

The Finikounda/Koroni approach tracks through plastic greenhouses to a fork alongside a *Rooms*. To the right leads up into the main settlement, whilst to the left continues past *Camping Methoni* (Cat D,   tel 31228), several *Rooms* and furnished apartments, to the right-hand side   of the middle of the bay, on the east side of Methoni.

To the left (*Fsw*) sweeps a mainly pebble shoreline lacking any shelter, edging low-lying land. To the right crosses a river outfall, to sweep along the wide, if somewhat cluttered town beach, beyond which is the wonderful sight of the imposing castle walls rising up from sea-level. This shallow shelving, tree shaded shoreline is bounded by a small jetty to the left, and a large, rocky mole stretching out into sea, from the middle of the eastern castle wall flank. There is a working beach shower,   a children's park with swings, and pedaloes, as well as a sign indicating the accolade of the Golden Starfish. The award is certainly deserved, as the sand is, without doubt, golden.

From the edge of the backshore angles a plateia bordered by the *Hotel Alex* (Class C, tel 31219), where en suite singles cost 5000/6000drs & doubles 6000/8000drs, a taverna, the *Hotel/Restaurant Rex* (Class E, tel 31239), where bathroom sharing doubles are priced at 3170/3800drs, and the rather smart (and) expensive *Methoni Beach* (Class B pension, tel 31544), where en suite doubles cost 10400/12500drs.

The town beach continues on round, past a backshore taverna, to the foot of the fortifications, on the way to the castle wall mole. The walls effectively shelter the shore from the prevailing winds, making swimming and sunbathing most enjoyable.

Methoni Castle Entrance is free, daily between 0830-1900hrs. The Venetian fortress is built over a promontory with the sea on three sides. The landward flank was once protected by a sea-filled, but now dry moat, still   crossed by a stone bridge. On the village side of this bridge is a coach and car park.

The first section of the castle is surprisingly well-preserved, with a number of prominent Lion of St Mark carvings, whilst the middle of the great wall enclosed area is a 'bit of a waste-ground', in the centre of which is a singular Greek, Roman or Byzantine column. It is rather unfortunate that much of the western wall sea-erosion has remained unrepaired. On the other hand, it is to be applauded that the Sea Gate, the causeway, and the   classical, Venetian octagonal tower/Turkish Bourzi fortified islet have been so effectively restored.

On a historical note it may be of interest that the Turkish forces captured the castle and town, from the Venetians, in 1500, after a long siege, and, as their habit - massacred everyone. The Venetians recaptured it in 1686, only to lose it once again, to the Turks, in 1715.

Leaving the castle by way of the hibiscus tree lined High St, very close to the walls are the old style, two storey *Hotel Iliodyssion* (Class D, tel 31225), where all rooms share the bathrooms, singles priced at 2000/2500drs & doubles 2600/3000drs, and the slightly more modern, *Hotel Castello* (Class D, tel 31300), with en suite singles costing 4600/6250drs & doubles 5200/7200drs. These establishments are followed by: the *Hotel Aris* (Class D, tel 31666), with en suite singles priced at 5000/6000drs & doubles 6000/7500drs; the *Hotel Finikas* (Class D, tel 31390), with en suite singles charged at 3865/5040drs & doubles 5905/66850drs; the *Hotel Albatross* (Class D, tel 31160), where en suite singles are priced at 4800/5800drs & doubles 5800/7000drs; a Post Office; filling station; pharmacy; a Rent A Motorbike establishment; and, alongside a pool-cum-ping-pong games hall, a Y-junction. To explain, those arriving from Pilos will come down the main stroke of the Y to this fork. To the right, which this description has traversed from the castle, is signed 'Beach Fort', whilst to the left (or from the castle, actually back around to the right) is signed 'Shopping Centre'!

Down the 'Shopping Centre' street is a taxi rank, an Agricultural and a National Bank, both on the right, a number of kafeneions and ouzeries, a barber's, travel agency, all sorts of shops, some *Rooms*, and the *Hotel Dionysos* (Class E, tel 31317), where singles sharing cost 1500/2200drs, doubles sharing 2200/3200drs, & doubles with en suite bathrooms 2500/3500drs.

Apart from, or perhaps because of the flowering tree lined streets, the multiplicity of balconies, the castle and the splendid beach, Methoni is yet another super location.

From Methoni, the road to the north crosses over high hills (or very low mountains), with views of the far horizon, circled by mountains, and closer, the town and port of:
PILOS (98km from Kalamata) Tel prefix 0723. From above, the elongated **Sfaktiria island** shuts off the sea side of the Bay of Navarinou, giving the impression of an inland sea.

The left-hand side of the main road runs beside the arched walls of the 'Kamares' (part of an ancient aqueduct), prior to descending quite steeply by a filling station, on the right, the three storey, if small *Hotel Levanti*, to the left a sign for the 'Kastro' (or Neokastro), and a travel agent, to decant on to the surprisingly lovely, spacious main square, bordering the port. This is Plateia Trion Navarkhon, which is extensively planted with trees, some lime, some plane, two of which are very large indeed. Around the circumference of the square are spaced out some six peripteros. There is a memorial, erected in 1927, to commemorate the Admirals' Codrington, de Rigny and Von Heyden. They were respectively the commanders of the British, French and Russian fleets, at the Battle of Navarinou, which took place in the bay, in 1827. The square, around which the road is 'one-way'd', is bordered by colonnaded buildings beneath the arches of which the pavement is routed. The 18thC, western Mediterranean look to the solid, cut-stone buildings is because the town was constructed by the French, in 1829. That explains it!

Around the square, from left (*Fsw*) to right, are spaced: the Town police (Tel 22316); *Rooms* above a cafe-bar; a National Bank; the Bus station (at the far, south-west corner), close to a filling station; a dual carriageway; a pharmacy; the old style, three story *Hotel Trion Navarhon* (Class D, tel 22206); and, on the far, east side, several gift shops. The periptero closest to the Bus terminus sells stamps.

Climbing the dual carriageway, from the back of the square, ascends past the Post Office. Beyond the latter is a left turning, alongside a three storey *Pension* (Tel 22748), which leads to another, 'suburban' square, where turn right. The OTE opens the old-fashioned, weekday hours of 0730-1500hrs, and is on the right.

Bus timetable
Pilos to Athens (100 Kifissou St)
Daily   1000, 1400hrs
Return journey
Daily   0930, 1500hrs
One-way fare 3400drs; duration 6½hrs
Pilos to Kalamata
Weekdays   0635, 0800, 0900, 1100, 1245, 1400, 1530, 1800, 2100hrs
Sun/hols   1100, 1400, 1615, 1800, 2100hrs
Pilos to Kiparissia
Weekdays   0700, 0900, 1100, 1350hrs
Pilos to Gargaliani
Weekdays   0700, 0900, 1100, 1315, 1615hrs
  & Sat.
Sun/hols   1100, 1615hrs
Pilos to Methoni & Finikounda
Weekdays   0600, 1015, 1415, 1840hrs
Sat   1100, 1415hrs
Sun   1415hrs
Pilos to Kallithea
Weekdays   0600, 1100, 1330, 1630hrs
Sat   1200hrs

From the Main Square around to the left (*Fsw*), between the corner of the port and the office of the Town police, is a wide, substantial Esplanade that cuts past the Port police, a pocket handkerchief of sand, the *Hotel Navarinon* (Class D, tel 22291), where single rooms sharing the bathrooms cost 1900/2200drs & doubles 2500/3000drs, the *Hotel Nilefs* (Class B pension, tel 22518), with en suite singles priced at 4170//4630drs & doubles 5095/6485drs, and Sarientza Travel. Opposite a large, concrete swimming platform are a number of now deserted lido buildings. The Esplanade continues on almost to the foot of the lower castle walls, to a bluff on which is set down the smart *Hotel Karalis Beach* (Class B pension, tel 23021), where en suite single rooms cost 8500/9000drs & doubles 9500/10500drs.

The inland side of Sfaktiria island is a series of steep escarpment faces having a saw-edged appearance. Trip boats circumnavigate Sfaktiria, at a cost of 550/650drs per head, and the skippers of the craft attempt to gather together a boat-load, prior to departing. Enquiries should be made at the quayside cafe-bars.

Ascending a side-street from the back, east side of the Main Square, a sign reveals the presence of a certain 'Verouhis Service Auto & Boat Engine Repairs - Tel 22988 - Rent Motorbikes'. One up from the square, and to the left is a street (approximately paralleling the eastern plateia flank), which contains a ladies hairdresser, as well as a 'bit of a' sidewalk fruit & vegetable market, a dry cleaners and a baker.

It is impossible to depart from Pilos without elaborating about the archaeological and historical connections of the now uninhabited **Sfaktiria island**. There is evidence of Mycenean and Neolithic remains. The Spartans fought a rearguard action in 425BC, for some 70 days, but failed to live up to their legend of fighting to the last man, as a number surrendered. The island was fortified over the centuries, and in 1278 the medieval **Pailaiokastro** was erected. This was occupied, variously, by the Genoese, pirates, the Venetians, and the Turks. It's importance as a fortification was eventually superseded by **Neokastro Castle**, the construction of which was carried out by both Venetians and Turks, during their respective 'tenancies', on the western headland overlooking modern-day Pilos.

The island has various statues to heroes of the War of Independence, more especially in respect of participants in the Battle of Navarinou. This was a naval engagement fought between a combined naval fleet of ships from Gt Britain (when we were great), France and Russia, and a Turko/Egyptian navy. At the Treaty of London (1827) it was agreed by the Great Powers that they should uphold the emergent Greek nations autonomy, despite the continuing presence of the Turks. Admiral Codrington was the allies senior officer, commanding a total of 27 boats (12 British, 8 Russian and 7 French), and it was his brief to ease the Turks and Egyptian fleets out of the Peloponnese waters. The allied armada sailed into the Bay of Navarinou, on the 20th October 1827, where were moored some 85-90 warships belonging to the 'other side'. After a bit of 'elbow-shoving' and a demand for the Turks/Egyptians to push off, the Turks, no doubt relying on their superior numbers, fired a salvo or two, as a bit-of-a-frightener. By the following dawn, the Turks had run for open sea, having lost about 55 ships and 6000 men, whilst the Great Powers fleet hadn't lost any ships and only 174 men. As a result, the Turks departed the peninsula and the seal was set on Greek Independence.

To the north of Pilos are *Rooms*, followed by three more, almost side-by-side *Rooms*, one of them being *Angela's*, beyond which is the *Restaurant/Cafe-bar Philip*. To the left is a view over the grand sweep of Navarinou Bay, after which the road drops down almost to sea-level, to a rather marshy, duney seascape, with olive groves on the inland side.

At the outset to the spread-out, bay hugging settlement of **Gialovo**

(104km from Kalamata, tel prefix 0723) are *Tellis Villas* and *Camping Navarino Beach* (Cat C, tel 22761). The road is about 20m from the shoreline, from which it is separated by a thick screen of bamboo, with a large factory on the right. There are two *Rooms/tavernas*, another industrial building, on the right, and oil storage tanks - to left and right. In amongst the almost forest-like thickets of bamboo are some quite smart villas, the *Hotel Villa Zoe* (Class E, tel 22025), with en suite single bedrooms priced at 3890drs & doubles at 5390drs, even more *Rooms*, several filling stations, and a taverna. Towards the north end, the shore is some 100m distant.

With the coastline now about ½km away, the winding, pretty roadside scenery is dominated by marshland and agriculture. At a junction, 12km from Pilos, to the right is the inland village of **Hora**, on the way to which passes by the visually uninteresting archaeological site of **Nestor's Palace** (18km from Pilos). The dig is open daily, but not Mon, between 0830-1500hrs, with admission costing 400drs. The museum is at Hora.

To the left of that 'Hora' junction is the road to **Romanos** (111km) and the very north of Navarinou Bay. On the way, it is possible to turn off, parallel to the coast, past the unattractive, spaced-out, 'Salaminas-island like', 'hut and shack' shanty settlement of **Pestraski**, *en route* to Filiatra.

A side track, signed 'Beach Mati - 500m', threads through tall bamboo to one more Golden Starfish beach, a beautiful sweep of wide sandy shore, backed by gorse covered sand dunes, without a building in sight. To be truthful, there is a chapel to the north, and a couple of single storey structures, well to the south, close to a small headland. This location is a stunner, and where the access 'beaches out', there are a trio of showers. At the top end, where the road angles up to the backshore, there is a small rivulet running into the bay, about where the sand runs out.

Beyond the inland **Gargaliani** town turning, and a sign along a minor track to the coastal located hamlet of **Vromoneri**, is the approach to:

MARATHOPOLI (123km from Kalamata) A way-station of a seaside resort, which, based on the inordinate number of restaurants and tavernas, must be a target for the great Greek, weekend tuck-in.

The panorama is attractive, in the main due to the presence of the offshore **Proti** island, even if the shoreline is rocky.

An inland pointing sign indicates the presence of *Panorama Rooms* 'by the sea'(?), beyond which is a crossroads. To the left leads to the still rocky seafront, (another?) *Panorama Rooms*, and the evidence of a once upon a time, if now shambolic, quayside ferry-boat docking point. In amongst a couple of tavernas and a few shops is the *Restaurant Mouragio*, with a 'We speak German' placard. The rather pathetic, inordinately large main square church appears to have appropriated a few interesting remnants of classical columns.

At the north end is a caique harbour, enclosed by a largish sea wall, and even more restaurants, as well as a very smart zacharoplasteion bread shop. Further on are some surprisingly suburban outskirts, and a sign to the left for *Camping Proti - 500m*.

At an even greater distance, some three or four kilometres on, is a filling station cum disco, set in rather ghastly countryside. In the area of a sign *For Rent Batchelor Apartments*, and the Figaro Disco, an unindicated, unsurfaced track advances towards the coast and a broad, glorious semi-circle strand of dune-backed golden sand. There aren't any 'support facilities', but well set back, in amongst low trees growing on the dunes, is the to-be- expected rubbish, despite the presence of litter bins. An isolated changing-room hut reminds one irresistibly of a French *pissoir*.

The main road countryside becomes prettier, with several glimpses of the beach, and a *Fresh Food Restaurant*. **Langouvardos** (127 km) is nothing more than a hamlet with a caique harbour, 'plastic' agriculture, and at least one *Rooms*. **Filiatra** (133km) has pretensions to grandeur, if the rather ludicrous, certainly unexpected, approximately 15m high, metal fretwork model of the Eiffel Tower and a globe, at the north end of the town, is any indicator. In fact, dusty, suburban Filiatra is laid out on a boring, sterile, grid system of streets. Apart from a baker, to the right, and a 'big town' square, around which the traffic is one-way'd, there is a filling station, National Bank, Post Office and taxi rank.

The route descends on to an olive tree filled plain, with the sea to the left, and over a river bed. For travellers with time on their hands, it may be worth selecting the turning to the west, in the direction of **Agrilos** (140km). There, surrounded by fields of maize, instead of lawns, is the most outlandish, Hellenic idea of a French chateau. Bizarre! Thank goodness the builder had not been inspired by a Bavarian castle. Agrilos 'staggers' about a small, man-made harbour, a little square, and a chapel. On the far side is a roofless windmill and, beyond a rocky river bed, a rocky shore and dirt track road, the latter lined by street lighting - yes, street lighting (which leads to a pleasantly opulent private house), and a grey pebble shoreline. Incidentally, for some obscure reason, the harbour has been awarded a Golden Starfish!

Back on the main road about, 15km north of Filiatra is:
KIPARISSIA (148km from Kalamata) Tel prefix 0761. This settlement is at the end of a branch line from the main Pirgos-Kalamata railway line. The tiny, 'all-up-together' railway station, possessing the usual 'attributables' of a cafe and toilets, is also a terminus for OSE operated buses. They not only connect with Athens, but offer other services, as follows:

OSE Bus timetables
Kiparissia to Pirgos & Patras
Daily   0800, 1030, 1215, 1300, 1645, 2233hrs
Kiparissia to Kalamata
Daily   0542, 0959, 1220, 1522, 1826hrs
Kiparissia to Methoni
Daily   0300, 1240, 1625, 2140hrs
Kiparissia to Hora
Daily   0300, 0610, 1010, 1240, 1530, 1625, 2030, 2140hrs

Train timetables
Kiparissia to Athens

Daily Dep.	2221, 0800, 1007, 1532hrs
Pirgos	2343, 0915, 1146, 1656hrs
Patras	0200, 1118, 1408, 1910hrs
Egio	0246, 1156, 1456, 1952hrs
Diakofto	0304, 1216, 1515, 2014hrs
Xilokastro	0353, 1300, 1607, 2104hrs
Korinthos	0428, 1335, 1646, 2145hrs
Athens	0628, 1523, 1900, 2342hrs

Kiparissia to Kalamata

Daily Dep.	0523, 1007, 1507, 1818hrs
Kalamata	0717, 1210, 1702, 2013hrs

Directly opposite the Railway station is the fairly modern, four storey *Hotel Ionian* (Class C, tel 22511), with en suite singles charged at 4500/6000drs & doubles 5500/8000drs. Half-right (*Railway station behind one*), leaving the Ionian to the left, is the sleazy KTEL Bus station, to the rear of which is a toilet.

Bus timetable
Kiparissia to Athens, via Argos & Korinthos
Daily   0845, 1500hrs
Kiparissia to Gargaliani
Daily   0745, 0830, 1015, 1200, 1400, 1500, 1730hrs
Kiparissia to Platania
Daily   0500, 1430, 1545hrs
Kiparissia to Kalamata
Daily   0730, 1030, 1700hrs
Kiparissia to Pirgos
Daily   0830, 0930, 1430, 1500hrs

Almost opposite the Bus station is the old-fashioned, Athens-like *Restaurant Ninio*, with four square tables and all the walls being windows (rather *Irish*, but watch my pen).

Continuing up the street leads to one of the main squares, whereon a periptero selling English language newspapers and, on the left, a National Bank. The Post Office is the opposite side of the square and the entrance to the OTE is at the far left corner, with the doors only open weekdays between 0730-2200hrs. Left from close by the National Bank, ascends Odhos 25th March, beside or around which are all the shops a traveller could want, as well as a two storey *Rooms*, and leads to a little market area. Left here, on Odhos Mitropolio Christanopolios Germanou, advances towards a baker, on the left, who sells a 'nice line' in pies.

Back at the Railway station, the street ahead (*Railway station behind one*), of course, advances to the referred to 25th March St, and in the second block from the station, on the right, is the modern, four storey, roof-terraced *Hotel Vassilikon* (Class C, tel 22655). This establishment exacts the following scale of charges: single rooms sharing the bathroom facilities 4065/4875drs; singles with en suite bathrooms 5825/6500drs; doubles sharing 4550/5850drs; and doubles en suite 6500/9430drs.

The south-east of the town appears to be hemmed in by mountains, the most easterly being topped by a Byzantine/Frankish ruined castle, around the walls of which radiate the now deserted streets of Old Kiparissia. The town overlooks a bay, but the beach is 3km distant, to the north.

Six kilometres north of Kiparissia is the main west-east road that leads to a junction with the Kalamata/Tripoli road. About 28km along the latter is the village railway halt **Zevgolatio**, where the anticlockwise and clockwise Peloponnese train tracks junction, for the down-leg to Kalamata. The Railway station is a 'standard issue' terminus, even if it would not be a shock to observe the Greek equivalent of John Wayne high-boot along the main street. Apart from a bus stop, there is a cafe-bar, offering a special of the day - in English, and a general store. Not a bit like Crewe, or Swindon...!

Returning to the main coast road, almost immediately on the left is a turning to the left, signed 'Hotel', which should really read 'Beach', which it does later, as the road jinks around the railway line, on the way to the seaside hamlet of **Kalo Nero** (154km, tel prefix 0761). The access road tips out on to a dirt track that runs along the backshore of a wide, sand with pebble beach, and large pebble sea-bed. Interesting, undulating little outcrops of rock are dotted about, here and there. A two storey, pension-like building, next door to a chapel, has *Rooms*. Further to the left are a couple more buildings, and the drab, almost nasty-new, nasty-coloured, two storey *Hotel Akriogiali* (Class E, tel 71345), where an en suite single costs 4020drs & a double 4800/5880drs. Kalo Nero is really in the middle of nowhere, and apart from the nearby railway sidings, the occasional kafeneion, and the *Restaurant Zante*, is a 'watch the coffee grouts settle' location.

The main road, hereabouts, is some 150m distant from the shoreline, down to which branch one or two lanes. The island of land between the two is occupied by agriculture, some 'plastic' greenhouses, houses, homesteads, farmsteads, and olive trees, scattered throughout which are a fair number of mature arethemusa trees.

At **Elea** (165km) yet another side-road plunges off to finish up in a backshore pine tree grove, in the summer months stuffed with camper-vans. And no wonder, for I have mentioned big stretches of beach, once or twice in this book, but this truly is a 'ginormous', 40m wide sweep of golden sand, extending - as far as the eye can see, in either direction. The backshore continues to be attractively edged with pine trees, and there aren't any immediate 'support facilities' - thank goodness. Not even a campsite, but there is a drinking water tap. As is often the case, the first metre or so of sea-bed is pebbly, beyond which it drops, suddenly, to a continuous flow of sand. It is supposedly a turtle nesting shore. For the train travellers, the halt of Epousi is convenient, and well equipped with a kafeneion and toilets.

A kilometre and a half north along the main route, is the hamlet of **Giannitsohori** (166½km), where a *Rooms* and *Camping Apollo* (Cat C, tel (0625) 61200). At **Tholo** (169½km) is another railway halt and a turning down to *Camping Tholo* (Cat C, tel (0625) 61345).

From Tholo, enterprising souls can cut inland for 37km. This route passes by the ancient walls of **Lepreo**, and through the villages of **Nea Figalia**, **Petralona** and **Dragogi**, heading towards **Andritsena**. This attractively picturesque, if rather ramshackle, mountain stream-lush, traditional hillside settlement is largely made-up of timber houses. About 12km prior to Andritsena is the isolated, rocky mountainside, terrace- located, remarkably well-preserved, **Temple of Epikourios** at **Vasses**, probably constructed circa BC 425. I suppose it almost goes without saying that the British Museum has a number of the marble friezes tucked away 'in their vaults'. The really adventurous can continue on from Andritsena, to the medieval, fortress town of **Karitena**, a further 29km.

Back on the west coast, **Neohori** (173km) possesses various beach-pointing signs, indicating this and that.

The unclear if 'at all' signed turning for **Kakovatos** (175km) passes by a *Rooms*, a railway halt, more *Rooms*, and accommodation ('Bed Sitters Flats'), as well as an indicator 'To the Sea'. This side road terminates at a backshore panhandle of a cul-de-sac, flanked by a beach restaurant, a beach taverna, and dunes. The shore here, which is simply a continuation of the Elea beach, despite being narrower and busier, is still super sand, but with tiny pebbles at the sea's edge. A number of local fishing boats are pulled-up on the backshore, and the 'sleazo' beach kafeneion operates on a 'couldn't care less' basis. But all is not lost, for on the way down, on the right, is a most welcoming rural taverna, with an entertaining, 'Irish joker' of a Greek mine host. A repast here, of a 'surfeit' of tzatziki, half a loaf of bread, a very tasty plateful of kalamares and 2 beers, cost 1300drs.

On the approach to **Zaharo** (178km), the beach turning is marked by traffic lights and the *Hotel Nestor* (Class C, tel 31206), where en suite singles are priced at 3400drs & doubles 4600drs. The straight metalled road cruises by the *Hotel Rex* (Class C, tel 31221), with en suite singles costing 3700drs & doubles 5000drs, over the railway line, past a number of *Rooms*, including those of *Evelyn*, *Theodore* and *Olympian*. The street angles right to leave a swathe of 'Canvey island' shacks between it, and the backshore of the still beautifully sandy, golden beach. The high water storm mark is delineated, as elsewhere along this bay, by a trace of seaborne detritus. Beyond a beach bar, alongside the backshore, are showers which 'do'.

North of Zaharo are *Rooms*, with a pine forest to the left, in between the road and the shore, whilst to the right are signposts for the 'Thermal Springs' of **Kaiafa**. The latter are based on a small islet set in a large, 5km long, concrete quay and pine forest edged inland lake, or lagoon, alongside which the road runs. Opposite the lake is a duckboard trail, over the railway line, and dunes, to the continuation of the aforementioned beach. Beyond the lake, the route swings inland for the big one, for:

OLYMPIA (Illus. 26) (220km from Kalamata) Tel prefix 0624.   The signposting for the village of one of the most famous sites in the world, let alone Greece, is poor.

The swept-up, souvenir shop and touristy village is at crossroads.

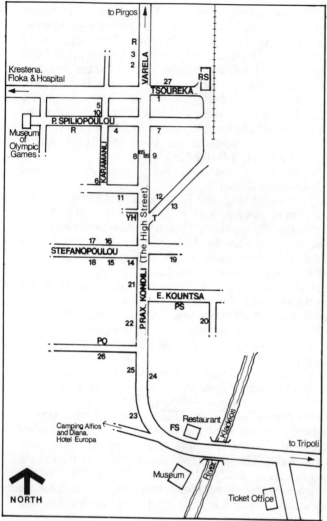

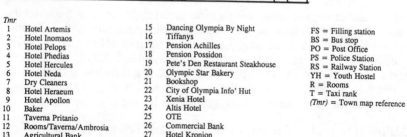

Tmr

1	Hotel Artemis	15	Dancing Olympia By Night	FS	= Filling station
2	Hotel Inomaos	16	Tiffanys	BS	= Bus stop
3	Hotel Pelops	17	Pension Achilles	PO	= Post Office
4	Hotel Phedias	18	Pension Possidon	PS	= Police Station
5	Hotel Hercules	19	Pete's Den Restaurant Steakhouse	RS	= Railway Station
6	Hotel Neda	20	Olympic Star Bakery	YH	= Youth Hostel
7	Dry Cleaners	21	Bookshop	R	= Rooms
8	Hotel Heraeum	22	City of Olympia Info' Hut	T	= Taxi rank
9	Hotel Apollon	23	Xenia Hotel	*(Tmr)*	= Town map reference
10	Baker	24	Altis Hotel		
11	Taverna Pritanio	25	OTE		
12	Rooms/Taverna/Ambrosia	26	Commercial Bank		
13	Agricultural Bank	27	Hotel Kronion		
14	National Bank				

Illustration 26 Olympia Village

Taking the High St as lying north-south, Pirgos is to the north, Krestena to the west and Tripoli to the east.

Approaching from Pirgos, the road sweeps by: filling stations; tavernas; the on stilts, modern *Motel Xenios Zeus* (Class B, tel 22522) with en suite singles priced at 5000drs & a double 7500drs; more tavernas; the older style *Hotel Olympic Torch* (Class C, tel 22668) with en suite singles charged at 3600drs & doubles 5300drs; *Rooms*, on the right, as are the *Hotel Pelops* (*Tmr* 3) (Class C, tel 22543), with en suite singles costing 3500drs & doubles 5500drs, and the *Hotel Inomaos* (*Tmr* 2) (Class C, tel 22056), with en suite singles priced at 3300drs & doubles 4435drs.

At the first crossroads, to the right is the ascending Krestena road, which passes by the Hospital. To the left descends past the *Hotel Artemis* (*Tmr* 1) (Class C, tel 22255) with en suite singles charged at 2900drs & doubles 4000drs, and the *Hotel Kronion* (*Tmr* 27) (Class C, tel 22502) with en suite singles charged at 3500drs & doubles 4800drs. It is about 100m to the Railway station, the toilets of which are in a separate building. Arrivals by train are usually met by a Youth Hostel representative and owners of accommodation, one of whom I have observed 'carting his catch off', along the tracks.

Train timetable
Olympia to Pirgos
Daily Dep.   0750, 1050, 1326, 1544, 2040hrs
One-way fare 120drs; duration ½hr.

Back at and continuing south along the High St, at the next crossroads, to the right and Odhos P. Spiliopoulou ascends by the modern, two storey, roof-terrace'd *Hotel Phedias* (*Tmr* 4) (Class C, tel 22667) with en suite singles charged at 3500drs & doubles 4500drs. At the first lateral junction, to the right (*High St behind one*) is a Baker (*Tmr* 10) and the *Hotel Hercules* (*Tmr* 5) (Class C, tel 22696), where en suite singles cost 4200/4500drs & doubles 4600/5100drs. To the left, and at the far end of Odhos Karamanli, is the *Hotel Neda* (*Tmr* 6) (Class B, tel 22563). Further on up Odhos P. Spiliopoulou is a very smart *Rooms* (*Tmr* R), above a dentist, on the left, whilst at the top of the street is the Museum of the Olympic Games. The latter opens daily 0800-1530hrs (except Mon), with 200drs required for entrance. The other side of the High St crossroads descends past a Dry Cleaners (*Tmr* 7).

Meanwhile, the High St continues south past, on the right, the older two storey *Hotel Heraeum* (*Tmr* 8) (Class D, tel 22539), with double rooms sharing at a cost of 3000drs, and across the street, the more modern, three storey *Hotel Apollon* (*Tmr* 9) (Class B, tel 22522), with en suite singles costing 5600drs & doubles 8600drs. The High St Bus stop for Tripoli (0920, 1320, 1720hrs at 1200drs, for the 4hr trip) is outside the *Heraeum*, and that for Pirgos (9-16 a day costing 240drs, for the 30min journey) is outside the *Apollon*.

The next side street off to the right of the High St ascends past, on the left, the *Taverna Pritanio* (*Tmr* 11), which is recommended and serves reasonably priced meals - for Olympia, that is.

Back on the High St, there are monipos, with, on the left, a Taxi rank

(*Tmr* T) at the junction with a backward angled street. Along this latter are *Rooms/Taverna Ambrosia* (*Tmr* 12), overseen by Mr Spilliopoulos, and, across the street, an Agricultural Bank (*Tmr* 13). Incidentally, a number of Olympia restaurants offer Menus 1, 2, 3, 4, 5, & etcetera. Sample prices: No 1 - fried potatoes and tomato salad 725drs; No 2 - souvlaki with rice & fried potatoes, Greek salad 900drs - with ouzo or red wine 1000drs; No 3 - moussaka or pastachio or spaghetti bolognese, with tzatziki or taramosalata or dolmades 845drs - with ouzo or red wine 995drs; No 4 - souvlaki with rice & fried potatoes, Greek salad, ouzo or red wine, baklava or creme caramel 1395drs; No 5 - moussaka or pistachio or spaghetti bolognese, with souvlaki, rice & fried potatoes, Greek salad, red wine or ouzo 1650drs. Other dishes include: green beans with tomato and onion sauce 450drs; giouvetsi or veal & minestrone cooked in tomato sauce and served with grated cheese 650drs; papout saki, or stuffed eggplant with cheese 580drs; fatsitsio, or layers of macaroni with mincemeat sauce and bechamel sauce on top, baked in the oven 635drs; breakfasts - coffee or tea with milk, jam, butter and bread 500drs; coffee or tea with milk, eggs, bacon, bread 650drs; pizza's with cheese 750drs; a large cheese, ham and green pepper pizza 1150drs; and special pizza's 1375drs.

The opposite side of the High St, to the backward angled street, is an old-fashioned *Youth Hostel* (*Tmr* YH, tel 22580), at No 18 Praxitelous Kondili, which is entered via a flight of steel steps from a narrow alley to the right (*Facing Youth Hostel*). Charges are 600drs per person per night, 120drs for sheets, 120drs for hot showers, and breakfasts 250drs.

Further south is yet another crossroads, whereon a National Bank (*Tmr* 14). To the right ascends Odhos Stefanopoulou, on the left of which is Dancing Olympia By Night (*Tmr* 15), opposite Tiffanys (*Tmr* 16). Further along Stefanopoulou St are *Pension Achilles* (*Tmr* 17) (Class C, tel 22562), on the right, and *Pension Possidon* (*Tmr* 18) (Class C, tel 22567), on the left, where doubles sharing cost 3600drs. The lateral street the other side of the High St houses *Pete's Den Restaurant Steakhouse* (*Tmr* 19).

A High St Bookshop (*Tmr* 21), selling English language newspapers, is opposite the side-street Odhos E Kountsa, on the right of which is the Police Station (*Tmr* PS). Yet another side street off Kountsa St leads to the Olympic Star Bakery (*Tmr* 20).

Bordering the High St is the City of Olympia Information Hut (*Tmr* 22). This is open daily between 0900-2300hrs, and is 'girled' by Thespina, who speaks excellent English, but can only hand out a general leaflet, unless specific questions are asked. Also on sale here are commemorative stamps.

The next side-street branching off to the right of the High St climbs to the Post Office (*Tmr* PO), on the right, and open Mon-Thurs 0730-2000hrs, Fri & Sat 0730-1400hrs, and Sun 0900-1330hrs. Opposite is a Commercial Bank (*Tmr* 26).

Continuing south along the High St, and on the right is an OTE (*Tmr* 25), only open weekdays between 0730-2200hrs. The other side of the main drag is the *Hotel Altis* (*Tmr* 24) (Class B, tel 23101), with en suite singles costing 7400drs & doubles 10400drs. Further on, close to a left-hand curve in the road, and on the right is the *Xenia Hotel* (*Tmr* 23) (Class B, tel 22510), with en suite doubles charged at 4700/6250drs & doubles 5900/7800drs. Along a slip road, just beyond the *Xenia*, are *Camping Alfios* (Cat C, tel 22950), *Camping Diana* (Cat C, tel 22314), and the *Hotel Europa* (Class A, tel 22650), where en suite singles are priced at 9900/11800drs & doubles 13700/16400drs. Ouch! Of the campsites, the *Diana* is the closest. It is shaded, well set out, with a good general store, a swimming pool and washroom block, wherein morning and evening hot showers.

As the extension of the High St continues to swing on round, it passes by a Texaco filling station (*Tmr* FS) and restaurant, on one side, whilst on the right, on a raised hill, is the Archaeological Museum. Once over the River Kladeos, to the right is the entrance to the:

Olympia Archaeological Site (Illus. 27). Open weekdays between 0800-1900hrs, Sat & Sun 0800-1900hrs and holidays 0830-1500hrs. Admission costs 1000drs.

This is the mega-star of the Greek archaeological sites, the only others in the same league being Delphi and Mycenae. It is a pity that the ruins are a jumbled disarray and that, for English speakers, the labelling is poor-to-none existent. Perhaps the aerial views are best. Despite these minor grumbles, the location has to be considered nigh on idyllic, with a verdant valley set between the rivers Kladeos and Alfios, close to the foot of the wooded Kronion hillsides.

Settlement appears to have started in 2800BC. Olympia developed both as a sacred place of worship and as a centre at which were staged athletic events, or games - the latter being the forerunner of the modern-day Olympic Games. The original concept of a simple, localised, strictly amateur competition, started in 1100BC, grew into a more regimented, nationwide, four yearly event, by the 9thC BC. To enable these to proceed without hindrance, a sacred (peace) truce was declared between all the various city states, for the duration of the Games. By the 4thC BC the competitors were almost exclusively professionals, attended by their promoters. After the Romans took over, the degenerative process accelerated, with bribery, corruption and 'fixing' sharing the honours, and podium, with the winners. Even so, the actual demise of the Games only came about due to the Roman Emperor Theodosus being converted to Christianity. As a result, he forbade most existing pagan associated festivities, in AD393.

Thenceforth, the ensuing destruction of the site, was followed by quarrying for stonework, occupation by barbarians, and devastation by earthquakes. If these disasters were not damaging enough, the Rivers Alfios and Kladeos variously flooding the site, leaving it covered with a minimum of a three metre layer of silt, for some thirteen centuries. How the mighty were fallen!

PIRGOS (239km from Kalamata) Tel prefix 0621. This town is a bit of a commercial dump - no, its an absolute dump. But it is a pivotal dump,

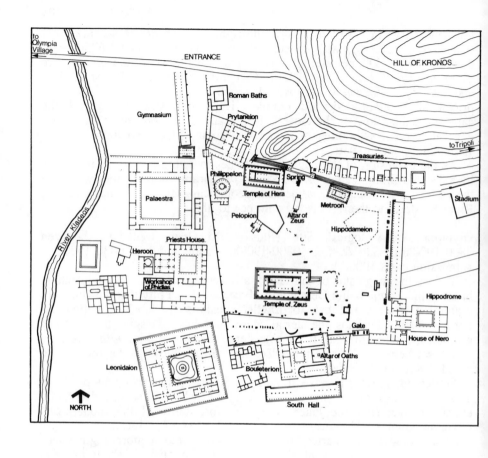

Illustration 27 Olympia Archaeological Site

especially for travellers down the west coast of the Peloponnese - with Olympia in mind.

The Railway station can be used as the starting point.

Train timetables
Pirgos to Athens

Daily Dep.	2343, 0610, 0915, 1146, 1630, 1656hrs
Patras	0200, 0837, 1118, 1408, 1815, 1910hrs
Egio	0246, 0923, 1156, 1456, 1854, 1952hrs
Diakofto	0304, 0944, 1216, 1515, 1909, 2014hrs
Xilokastro	0353, 1035, 1300, 1607, - 2104hrs
Korinthos	0428, 1110, 1335, 1646, - 2145hrs
Athens	0628, 1309, 1523, 1900, 2143, 2342hrs

Pirgos to Kalamata

Daily Dep.	0405, 0835, 0945, 1342, 1655, 1950hrs
Kiparissia	0523, 1007, 1106, 1507, 1818, 2103hrs
Kalamata	0717, 1210, - 1702, 2013, - hrs

Pirgos to Olympia

Daily Dep.	50, 1050, 1326, 1544, 2040hrs
Olympia	0826, 1126, 1403, 1620, 2116hrs

One-way fare Pirgos to Athens 1800drs; duration 5-7hrs
Olympia 120drs;   ½hr.

With the Railway station directly behind one, the street to the fore yields up, along the first turning off to the left, the smart, modern *Hotel Marily* (Class C, tel 28133), with en suite singles costing 4235drs & doubles 5500drs, whilst continuing on, to the left is the *Hotel Kentron*, beyond which and down the next turning to the left is the modern *Hotel Pantheon* (Class C, tel 29746), where en suite singles cost 3600/4000drs & doubles 4800/5300drs.

Back on the main avenue from the Railway station, on the left, some four blocks on is the *Hotel Olympus* (Class C, tel 23650), where en suite singles cost 3800drs & doubles 5000drs. Beside the *Olympus* is a small roundabout. Veering left here leads past a baker, to a short stretch of dual carriageway, where turn right at the large shoe shop (looking like a supermarket) and directly to the front. About 100m down on the left is the Bus terminus office.

Bus timetables
Pirgos to Athens (100 Kifissou St)

Daily	0530, 0730, 0830, 0930, 1030, 1230, 1400, 1530, 1700, 2130hrs

Return journey

Daily	0630, 0730, 0900, 1045, 1230, 1415, 1530, 1700, 1900, 2130hrs

One-way fare 3500drs; duration 5hrs

Pirgos to Patras

Daily	0600, 0730, 0815, 0945, 1115, 1330, 1500, 1700, 1830, 2000hrs
Sun/hols	As above, but no 0600hrs bus.

Pirgos to Kalamata

Weekdays	0945, 1650hrs
Sat/Sun/hol	0845, 1600hrs

Pirgos to Killini
Weekdays   0600, 1030, 1435hrs
Sat/Sun   1030, 1400hrs
 & hols
Pirgos to Zaharo
Daily   0530, 0600, 0640, 0930, 1115, 1200, 1315, 1435, 1600, 1730, 1930hrs
Pirgos to Krestena
Daily   0530, 0600, 0640, 0830, 0930, 1115, 1230, 1300, 1435, 1600,
            1730, 1930hrs
Sat/Sun   0700, 0900, 0930, 1100, 1230, 1500, 1730, 1930hrs
 & hols
Pirgos to Kiparissia
Weekdays   0640, 1315hrs
Sat/Sun   0845, 1600hrs
 & hols
Pirgos to Olympia
Weekdays   16 buses a day, between 0515-2100hrs
Sat   14 buses a day, between 0515-1930hrs
Sun/hols   0515, 0730, 0900, 1100, 1230, 1430, 1600, 1800, 1930hrs
One-way fare 240drs; duration ½hr.
Pirgos to Ag Ilias
Daily   1030, 1315hrs
Pirgos to Amaliada & Varda
Weekdays   0600, 0700, 0800, 0930, 1100, 1200, 1300, 1600, 1800, 1930hrs
Sat/Sun   0700, 0930, 1200, 1600, 1800hrs

Returning to the 'shoe supermarket', forking left, up a hill, leaves the OTE on the left (open daily, between 0700-2400hrs), in front of which is a small triangle of a square and a taxi rank. Continuing by the Commercial Bank, also on the left, turn immediately left on Germinou St, and the Post Office is to the right of the second side street turning off Germinou St.

Back at the Commercial Bank, turning right leads to the Main Square, beside which is a National Bank. To the south-west of this square is a *Levi Jeans* warehouse.

For the heart of the town, continue on past the Commercial Bank, not turning left onto Germinou St, over the crest of the hill, and down the other side.

Beside the Patras road, north from Pirgos, is an ELPA office, whilst the main road to the west passes by the town's Hospital, on the right.

The road for the nearest beach to Pirgos crosses a filthy, rubbish-laden swamp. The beach is of lovely sand, but the surrounds are Greek shanty, with doo-hickey seaside shacks, to left and right.

From the road to the west, in the direction of Katakolo, branches a narrow road that panhandles out at a better class of holiday-home. Here, glorious sand sweeps on 'for ever', to the left, and for a few kilometres to the right. Much of the surrounding countryside is despoiled by industry.

KATAKOLO (251km from Kalamata) Tel prefix 0621. The settlement is sited at the very north of the huge crescent of Kiparissiakos Bay.   The large harbour and concrete evidence of a once working branch railway line, indicate that Katakolo must have been the port of Pirgos.

What was previously an industrially busy place has been skilfully adapted to the more leisurely demands of holidaying Greeks, but is visited by few overseas tourists. The old, low elevation, stone and brick quayside warehouses have been almost thoughtfully adapted, and   converted. For instance, the railway station, rather set aside in a grove of trees, has undergone an adroit metamorphosis, becoming a glitzy cocktail bar, whilst the waterfront buildings have, in the main, been transformed into tavernas and restaurants. The railway lines that routed alongside the wharf wall have been displaced by the tables and chairs, of the various dining establishments. One 'tiny' drawback is the almost permanent smell of drains, emanating from somewhere.

The cul-de-sac of an approach road passes by: a mixture of low-rise old and new housing; the *Hotel Ionio* (Class C, tel 41494), where sharing singles cost 3900drs, doubles sharing 5000drs & doubles en suite 6000drs; the Main Square; and the *Hotel Delfini* (Class D, tel 41214).

The initially messy pre-shore, followed by the outset of a wide beach, curves away to the south, past an also seemingly endless collection of motley, ramshackle bungalows. Behind these is a surfaced access lane, from which branch tracks that edge between the homes. To save on wear and tear, the locals tend to utilise the beach backshore as a road.

The right-hand side of Katakolo is stopped off, if not overshadowed, by an extremely large harbour sea wall. The quayside waterfront is paralleled by a 'sort of' High St. Beside this are: the two storey *Hotel Zefros* (Class A pension, tel 41170), where en suite doubles are charged 4180/4500drs; a *Rooms*; Post Office; the *Hotel Carel* (Class D, tel 41066), with en suite doubles costing 4450/5000drs; and a Rent A Bike business.

A tasty meal, for two, at one of the quayside restaurants, of beef & spaghetti sprinkled with parmesan, a large bottle of kortaki retsina, bread & service, costs about 2250drs.

Probably the most surprising item to note is that an Italy-Patras-Crete-Egypt ferry-boat appears to drop in. Why, and what basis? I think we should be told!

North of the Cape of Katakolo, are a number of tracks down to mainly unmarked coastal sites. One such is **Skourohori**, where a small, boulderous shore edged bay, with a couple of offshore islets, and a rather smart hotel are overlooked by the diminutive remains of a ruined castle.

From Mirtea is a 2km long road, to the south of the Ag Ilias road. Curiously, this route passes by the: *Rooms Katerina*; another *Rooms*; the low, two storey, modernish *Hotel Apollon* (Class E, tel 0621 94380), with en suite doubles priced at 3000/3600drs; and more signs for *Rooms*, the 'wrong' side of the railway track. Once over the lines, there is a *Club Mediterranee* encampment, around which the   access road jinks. Where this emerges on the backshore of a wide, glorious sweep of beach, there are no facilities, that is except for the Club Med 'lump' of seafront, to the left. Away to the right is a sighting of the Ag Ilias headland.

MIRTEA (260km from Kalamata) Tel prefix 0621. Here is the *Hotel Zorbas* (Class D, tel 94233), offering en suite singles for 2180/2760drs & doubles 4200/5400drs, a filling station, and a chemist.

A road advances 4km to **Ag Ilias** (264km). This is a spaced out, tidy, if motley bungalow settlement, grouped around the railway halt. Half a kilometre distant is the backshore of a sandy, if bleak beach. The access spills on to a road paralleling, but a bungalow plot width from the shoreline, alongside a narrow entrance to the beach. To the right is a fish taverna, to the left the shore has some rock and kelp. A faint fishy smell overlays the location. There isn't any accommodation.

North of Mirtea is **Douneika** (263km), where yet another side road turns down to the coast. This choice terminates on a panhandle, just above the backshore, in amongst a disparate collection of shacks, with some fishing boats anchored inshore, close to a sandy run of beach. There is a high-water kelp mark, as well as fishing nets bagged up on the shore. A small, well shaded taverna is the sole business enterprise. Away to the right are dunes.

Amaliada (270km) is a railway halt town, with a bread shop (incidentally, open on Sunday mornings), a filling station, Post Office, and a hospital. Scattered about this 'neck of the woods', in an arc to the west of Amaliada, are a fair number of coastal settlements, in amongst which are a surfeit of camping sites, *Rooms*, pensions and hotels. These seaside locations include, neat and quiet **Kourouta** (270km, tel prefix 0622), the approach to which crosses over the National Highway and between a lovely avenue of trees. The outskirts are heralded by a 'glitter of signs' which include *Pension Kourouta Beach, Camping Kourouta Beach, Restaurant Achillion, Camping Kourouta* (Cat C, tel 28543), and *Municipal Camping Kourouta*. The beach stretches away to the left for a couple of kilometres and undulates to the right, for miles. The access road junctions with an Esplanade that limits the freedom of movement. On the left (*Fsw*) is a water tower and on the right, a natty, circular, modernistic building housing the *Restaurant Strogalo*. Despite the smart, little orange coloured litter boxes, a certain amount of rubbish is scattered about the shore. There is a hint of tiny pebbles in the first step of the sea-bed, but who cares - there is a beach shower. The municipal campsite shuts off the Esplanade to the right, at which end is also the *Hotel Iliakti* (Class C, tel 27311). The expensive *Pension Kourouta* (Class B, tel 22902) has en suite single rooms for 7000/10800drs & doubles for 8000/11400drs.

The turning off to **Savalia Beach** is clearly signed, if unsurfaced and 'interesting' here and there. The last section rushes through groves of bamboo, then sand dunes, prior to spilling on to a vehicle turn-round. This is in amongst the backshore of simply miles of sand, edged by dunes of an even greater width than the beach. The only signs of man are a cluster of three bamboo huts, with some more away in the distance, and a solitary, offshore (oil?) platform.

The unlovely inland village of **Gastouni** (280km), whereat a National Bank, is more a small town, en route to the equally landbound, but pleasant shambles of **Vartholomio** (284km). The countryside around the latter is dominated by the hill-topping **Chlemoutsi Castle**. The fort is actually a few kilometres to the west, at the aptly named village of **Kastro**, was constructed sometime in the 1220s, and occupied by the usual hordes of invading chappies. Vartholomio marks the outset of the signs and hordings declaring that language need not be a barrier to transacting this or that bit of business, as well as those proclaiming the presence of a 'rash' of ferry ticket agencies. This graffiti is due to the proximity of Killini, an adjacency which results in more campsites, than is 'good for girl or boy'.

Glifa (294km, tel prefix 0623), marks the north of the sweep of beach, the southernmost end of which originated at about Skafidia. The glories of the middle of the bay edging shore are not repeated at this end, due to its lack of width and that the sand contains a copious amount of pebble, especially at the sea's edge. In addition, there is a fair amount of middle-shore litter. Glifa is 'a bit of a shambles'. There are few houses, but there is a taverna to the right (*Fsw*), the patio extending out over the water, buoyed up on concrete filled oil drums. Beyond the taverna is a caique harbour, on the way to which are a 'scatter' of seaside shacks. To the left is a beach Cantina. Apart from the to-be-expected campsites (*Ionian Beach & Aginari*), Glifa also offers the two storey, unattractively modern *Hotel Kypriotis* (Class C, tel 96372).

The approach to the busy health spa of **Loutra Killini** (294km, tel prefix 0623) is along a graceful avenue. The resort is pleasantly shaded by gum trees, as well as pines, and the side streets branching off the High St are also 'avenued'. Apart from the *Xenia Hotel* (Class A, tel 96270), with en suite doubles costing 7500/8200drs, there is a campsite. The Esplanade is separated from the shore, by up to 50m wide dunes, which support not only the usual grass and gorse, but pine trees. The pleasantly broad beach is edged by some biscuit rock and a shallow, sandy sea-bed. To the left (*Fsw*), about 3km distant, is a low, sandy, gorse covered headland.

The climb up to the castle dominated village of **Kastro** (300km, tel prefix 0623), is steep and serpentine. The usual services of a taxi rank, a few mini-markets, a 'Sunday opening' bakery, and several tavernas, are augmented by *Rooms*, amongst whose number is *Rooms/Restaurant Maria*, and the *Hotel Chryssi Avgi* (Class C, tel 95224). The hotel offers en suite double bedrooms for a per night fee of 5300drs.

From Kastro, the four kilometre distant **Golden Beach**, is clearly indicated. Why this location, rather than any other, should have been selected for an onslaught of modern, package holiday hotels is not entirely clear. There isn't even a vestigial fishing hamlet or settlement, and the beach is not outstanding. In fact, the immediate countryside bordering the shoreline is a somewhat confusing ramble of large sand dunes, more suited to testing tanks. The approach road passes by the *Paradise Hotel*, *Camping Melissa Beach*, and the massive complex of the *Robinson Club Killini Beach*. The siting of the latter requires those who are not hotel guests to proceed along an unsurfaced track. This bimbles around to the right (*Fsw*), through an all-pervading 'big-potty' (or sulphurous) pong, to a path down to the not overwide, pebble edged, and certainly anything but golden beach. On the other hand, the sea bed is sandy. From this viewpoint, to the left are the terraces of the various hotels (and their hordes of guests), bordering the backshore, whilst to the right, a low cliff edged beach runs on for a couple of kilometres, towards a distant headland.

Probably the most important resort port, for many a mile, is the ferry-boat harbour of Killini.

A Methoni Castle wall

A Geraka chapel

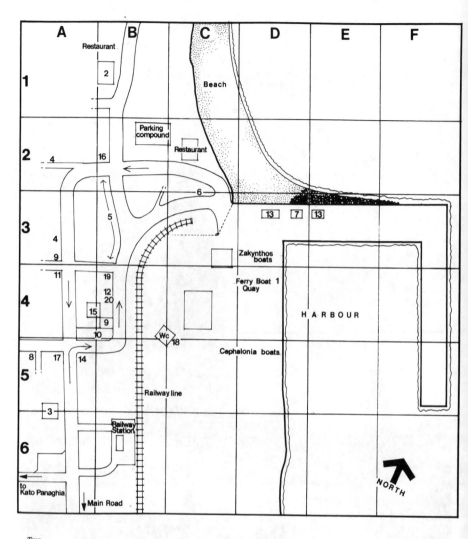

A	**B**	**C**	**D**	**E**	**F**

1 Restaurant — 2 — Beach

2 4 — 16 — Parking compound — Restaurant

6

3 5 — 4 — 9 — 13 · 7 · 13 — Zakynthos boats

4 11 — 19 — 12 20 — 15 — 9 — 10 — Wc 18 — Ferry Boat 1 Quay — HARBOUR

5 8 — 17 — 14 — Cephalonia boats — Railway line

6 3 — Railway Station — to Kato Panaghia — Main Road

NORTH

Tmr
1D3/4	Ferry-boat Quay
2B1	Hotel Ionian
3A5/6	Hotel Glarentza
4	Rooms
5B3	Restaurants, tavernas & cafeterias ('a row of')
6C2/3	Kafeneion 'shed'
7D3	Snackbar hut
8A5	Bakery
9	Butchers
10A/B4/5	General Store
11A3/4	Store
12B4	Fruit & Vegetable store
13D3 & E3	Ferry-boat ticket huts

14A5	Chemist
15A/B4	Petrol station
16A/B2	Police station
17A5	Post Office
18B/C4/5	Toilets
19B4	Kafeneion
20B4	Snackbar

(Tmr) = Town map reference
(Fsw) = Facing seawards
(Sbo) = Sea behind one
(Fbqbo) = Ferry-boat Quay behind one

Illustration 28 Killini

12 KILLINI (Kilini, Kyllini)

Illustration 28

FIRST IMPRESSIONS A scruffy, rather fly-blown, messy, rather port.

SPECIALITIES Ferry-boats.

VITAL STATISTICS Tel prefix 0623.

GENERAL Killini is the major ferry-boat connection to the island of Zakynthos, as well as a link with the better served Cephalonia Island. The harbour, formed by the upside down 'L' shaped quay, not only hosts the ferry-boats, but is the home port for a fair number of medium sized, high-prowed and raised stern fishing boats.

ARRIVAL BY BUS Buses pull up on the Ferry-boat Quay (*Tmr* 1D3/4).

ARRIVAL BY FERRY It is an immense harbour, for the size of the settlement. The Ferry-boats moor stern to the main Quay (*Tmr* 1D3/4).

ARRIVAL BY TRAIN The train journey to Killini requires a change of train at Kavasila junction. For some obscure reason, the latter is rarely detailed on the official, small scale maps.
On descending from the train (*Tmr* B6), it is necessary to take off diagonally to the right (*Train behind one*), across the sandy station environs, left down a short hedgerowed lane, and right along the main road. This spills out on to the sprawling, rather disjointed layout that is Killini port and settlement. To the right is the huge quay, whilst the rest of Killini straggles away to the left. Sometimes the trains proceed all the way to the harbour.

THE ACCOMMODATION & EATING OUT
The Accommodation There are two hotels and a number of simple *Rooms*.

Hotel Ionion (*Tmr* 2B1) (Class C)   Tel 92318
Directions: Towards the far side of Killini, overlooking the broadest section of the beach and backshore (on which a number of vans informally park most summer month nights).
A single room, sharing the bathrooms, costs 3600drs & a double sharing 5000drs, whilst a double room, with an en suite bathroom, costs 5400drs.

Hotel Glarentza (*Tmr* 3A5/6) (Class C)   Tel 92397
Directions: About 200m along the main road south of the port, and on the right (*Port behind one*).
A surprisingly modern, if drab building, with a single room priced at 3300drs & a double room 4900drs, all rooms with en suite bathrooms.

There are a number of *Rooms* set back from the waterfront. The house (*Tmr* 4A2) on the right (*Sbo*) is in a smart building, those to the left (*Sbo*) (*Tmr* 4A3) appear rather ethnic. A number of homes spread along the main road from Killini offer accommodation.

The Eating Out There are a row of restaurants, tavernas and cafeterias (*Tmr* 5B3), parallel to the waterfront, and about 100m from the entrance to the Ferry-boat Quay.

One of the most inexpensive *Kafeneion/snackbars* (*Tmr* 6C2/3) is on the left (*Fsw*) of the final approach to the Ferry-boat Quay, housed in a small shed. Another noteworthy *Snackbar* 'hut' (*Tmr* 7D3) is on the left of the Ferry-boat Quay, from which the patron sells acceptable cheese pies and doughnuts. A fruit & vegetable store is straddled by a *Kafeneion* (*Tmr* 19B4) and a *Snackbar* (*Tmr* 20B4).

THE A TO Z OF USEFUL INFORMATION

BEACHES There is a surprisingly noteworthy sweep of sand. It is at its widest, adjacent to the harbour wall, from whence it stretches away for about 250m. The beach is a dirty grey colour, with quite a lot of kelp spread about, and the sea-bed is sandy. In fact the beach would be very attractive, if it were kept clean of rubbish. There is no excuse, as litter bins are ranged along the length of the backshore.

BREAD SHOP One, a **Bakery** (*Tmr* 8A5) to the far side of the Post Office.

BUSES There are 3 buses a day to Pirgos (500drs, 1hr duration), 1 a day to Patras (720drs, 1½hr), 10 a day to Lehena (390drs, ½hr), and 2 a day to and from Athens.

COMMERCIAL SHOPPING AREA There are sufficient shops, including two **Butchers** (*Tmr* 9A3/4 & 9A/B4); a **General Store** (*Tmr* 10A/B4/5), which also sells milk and cheese, and in which most of the goods are stacked on the floor; another small **Store** (*Tmr* 11A3/4), with very few goods on the simple shelving, but which possesses a metered telephone; as well as a **Store** (*Tmr* 12B4), selling fruit and vegetables.

FERRY-BOATS The port services both the islands of Cephalonia and Zakynthos, but inconveniently this arrangement does not extend to a scheduled ferry-boat running between the two islands. There is a connection, but this is a performed by a smaller, 'private enterprise' craft, only operating a height of summer season schedule.

Ferry-boat timetable

Day	Departure time	Ports/Islands of Call
Daily exc. Sun	1200, 1730, 2130hrs	Poros (Cephalonia)
Daily	0815, 1000, 1300, 1530, 1730, 2045, 2200hrs.	Zakynthos
One-way fares Killini to Poros	1199drs; duration 1½hrs	
Zakynthos	722drs; " 1¼hrs	

FERRY-BOAT TICKET OFFICES Well, in reality huts (*Tmr* 13D3 & 13E3), on the left (*Fsw*) of the Ferry-boat Quay. If not open all day, they certainly 'lift the hatches', prior to a particular craft's departure.

MEDICAL CARE Not a lot, but there is a Chemist (*Tmr* 14A5).

OTE A small Store (*Tmr* 11A3/4) has a metered telephone.

PETROL The filling station (*Tmr* 15A/B4) is located where the main   road swings round towards the waterfront.

POLICE (*Tmr* 16A/B2) The office is beside the corner of a crossroads, and looks out over the ugly shambles of a wire-mesh enclosed vehicle park.

POST OFFICE (*Tmr* 17A5) Alongside the village's major crossroads.

TOILETS A quite clean, 'squatty' block (*Tmr* 18B/C4/5) is plonked down towards the south end of the Ferry-boat Quay.

TRAINS There are some five trains a day to the Kavasila junction. Kavasila is a halt on the main Korinthos/Patras/Pirgos/Kalamata, west-about Peloponnese railway system.

EXCURSIONS TO KILLINI SURROUNDS
Excursion to Lake Pinios (some 30km) Whilst at Killini, the River Pinios Lake may well appear to be worth a visit. That is if the area of trapped water, depicted on most maps, is anything to go by.
The main road proceeds via the agricultural hotchpotch of **Rupaki** (20km) village, past the rather pitiful archaeological remains of **Ancient Ilis**. The latter was the city state that had the 'franchise' to run the ancient Games at Olympia, and was the 'games town', where the athletes   trained   for   a   month,   prior   to   the   actual   event.   The archaeological museum is on the left.
The village of **Ag Dimitrios** (28km) marks the outset of various waterworks associated with the Pinios Dam. But ..., not only would the high hopes of the 1960s planners appear to have been dashed, as the huge basin, stretching 'as far as the eye can see', is almost empty, but the surrounding countryside is rather depressing. Perhaps this detour is not really worth the effort, after all.

ROUTE ELEVEN (Illus. 29)
To Patras (75km) At **Lehena** (13km) main square there is the opportunity to follow the signs for *Camping Panorama Beach* and *Camping Lehena*, but I wouldn't bother. The road is rather tortuous, the flat surrounds are drained marshland, and the wide, soulless sweep of beach is unacceptably rubbish and kelp polluted. In the main, this is due to the prevailing on-shore wind, which relentlessly piles up the detritus. The campsite owners appear to be making valiant attempts to clear up, but...
From **Varda** (29km) it is possible to turn down across much prettier countryside. The village of **Manolas** (33km) is lucky enough to have an old Byzantine church. The settlement marks the onset of a pine tree forest, which marches on as far as the 'indolent', thermal resort of:

LOUTRO KOUNOUPELLI (36km). In direct contrast to Loutro Killini, there is not much 'mud-packing' or 'thermalling' going on at this doo-hickey   location.   Despite   which,   it   is   somehow   attractive,

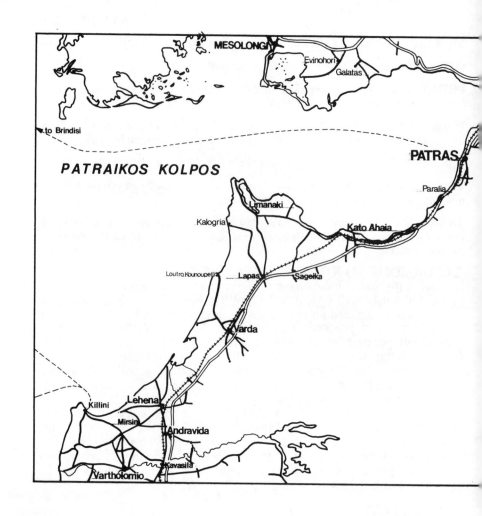

Illustration 29 Route Eleven

and impressive, possibly due to the pleasant, circular bay, and the landmass beyond. Moreover, on a fine day ..., away in the distance to the north, it is possible to glimpse Central Greece mainland. To the far left (*Fsw*) are the old thermal buildings, and to the immediate left a taverna. The mainly pebble, rubbishy shore, on which are haphazardly drawn up a number of small fishing boats, is a bit of a disappointment.

From **Lapas** (38km), and the National Highway, a nine or ten kilometre detour, via **Metohi** (42km), advances to the resort of **Kalogria** (48km). This road passes across heath and marshland, on which are dotted corrugated tin cowsheds. Woodland, a lake, and the headland of Cape Kalogria, make this an interesting choice. At the top end of the lake is a chapel, and to the right are a belt of pine trees, whereabouts the countryside irresistibly reminds one of carefully maintained parkland. A river flows from the lake to the coast, whilst the road passes by a couple of deserted cabins, several tavernas, seemingly in the middle of nowhere, to head straight for the *Hotel Kologria Beach*. Only at the last moment does the road direction change, to swing round past the *Hotel Christina Beach*, as well as several self-service, Spanish-style, restaurant/cafe-bars. All these establishments are low-rise, glitzy and luxuriously expensive. No 'kiss me quick' hats here! Both the *Christina Beach* (Tel 0693 31469) and the *Kalogria Beach* (Tel 31276) are Class B. Their en suite bedrooms cost 5750/8500drs, for a single, & 7500/10500drs for a double.

The road runs out, in amongst dunes, with the river between it and the beach. A foot bridge allows access to the enormously wide, beautiful, if shadeless sweep of beach. The right-hand (*Fsw*) end is stopped off fairly close, by the river mouth and the peninsula headland, whilst the shore continues on to the left, for a long way. The two large, aforementioned hotels ensure this pretty location stays busy. Water sports encompass pedaloes and a ski-run. Some camper vans might be 'lurking', gaining access to the back- shore from a left-hand fork. A bus from Metohi shuttles back and forth.

Returning to the main route, the airfield at Lapas is not used by civil craft. The National Highway heads past Kato Ahaia, for Patras.

From Cape Kalogri, east along Karavostasi Bay are a number of disjointed, dissimilar, pebble beach coastal resorts, villages and settlements. The small, 'suburban' town of **Kato Ahaia** (53km, tel prefix 0693) is pivotal to gain access to them. None are outstanding, though each has a conventional mix of a campsite, one or two hotels, and three or four taverna/restaurants. Without doubt, the panoramas, to the north, across the straits, in the direction of Messolongi, are   most impressive. Kato Ahaia can own-up to the *Hotel Achaia* (Cat C, tel 22678), where en suite singles cost 4000drs & doubles 6000drs, and the railway allows a fairly easy link with 22km yonder Patras.   About 3km from the town is the well recommended *Camping Kato Achaia* (Tel 22400).

Symbols, Keys & Definitions Below are some notes in respect of the few initials and symbols used in the text, as well as an explanation of the possibly idiosyncratic nouns, adjectives and phrases, to be found scattered throughout the book.

Readers must accept that judgements of this or that location are carried out on whimsical grounds and are based purely on personal observation. The absence of any mention, has no detrimental significance and might, indicate that I did not personally inspect a particular establishment.

Keys The key *Tmr*, in conjunction with grids, is used as a map reference to aid easy identification of this or that location on port and town plans. Other keys used in the text include *Sbo* - 'Sea behind one'; *Fsw* - 'Facing seawards'; *Fbqbo* - 'Ferry-boat quay behind one'; *BPTs* - 'British Package Tourists' and *OTT* - 'Over The Top'.

GROC's definitions, 'proper' adjectives & nouns: These may require some elucidation, as most do not appear in 'official' works of reference and are used with my own interpretation, as set out below.

Backshore: the furthest strip of beach from the sea's edge. The marginal rim separating the shore from the surrounds. *See* **Scrubbly.**

Chatty: with pretention to grandeur or sophistication.

Dead: an establishment that appears to be 'terminally' closed, and not about to open for business, but... who knows?

Donkey-droppings: as in 'two donkey-droppings', indicating a very small hamlet. *See* **One-eyed.**

Doo-hickey: an Irish based colloquialism, suggesting an extreme lack of sophistication and or rather 'daffy' (despite contrary indications in the authoritative and excellent *Partridges Dictionary of Slang!*).

Ethnic: very unsophisticated, Greek indigenous and, as a rule, applied to hotels and pensions. *See* **Provincial.**

(Ships) Galley Cooking: used to describe 'tired' rows of metal trays 'lurking' under the glass counters of tavernas, containing the exhausted, dried up, overcooked remnants of the lunch-time fare.

Gongoozle: borrowed from canal boat terminology, and indicates the state of very idly and leisurely, but inquisitively staring at others involved in some busy activity.

Graze: Dine out or eat.

Great unwashed: the less attractive, modern-day mutation of the 1960s hippy. They are usually Western European, inactive loafers and layabouts 'by choice', or unemployed drop-outs. Once having located a

desirable location, often a splendid beach, they camp under plastic and in shabby tents, thus ensuring the spot is despoiled for others. The 'men of the tribe' tend to trail a mangy dog on a piece of string. The women, more often than not, with a grubby child or two in train, pester cafe-bar clients to purchase items of home-made jewellery or trinkets.
Note the above genre appears to be incurably penniless (but then who isn't?).

Grecocilious: necessary to describe those Greeks, usually bank clerks or tour office owners, who are making their money from tourists but are disdainful of the 'hand that feeds them'. They appear to consider holiday-makers are some form of small intellect, low-browed, tree clambering, inferior relation to the Greek homo-sapiens. They can usually converse passably in two or three foreign languages (when it suits them) and habitually display an air of weary sophistication.

Grelish: Greco-English accented chat.

Grine: Expatriate Greeks who have lived a number of years in Australia, and thus have a Greek-Australian, or 'Grine' accent.

Hillbilly: similar to 'ethnic', but applied to describe countryside or a settlement, as in 'backwoods'.

Hippy: those who live outside the predictable, boring (!) mainstream of life and are frequently genuine, if sometimes impecunious travellers. The category may include students, or young professionals, taking a sabbatical and who are often 'negligent' of their sartorial appearance.

Hose down: Have a shower.

Independents: vacationers who make their own travel and accommodation arrangements, spurning the 'siren calls' of structured tourism, preferring to step off the package holiday carousel and make their own way.

Kosta'd: used to describe the 'ultimate' in development necessary for a settlement to reach the apogee required to satisfy the popular common denominator of package tourism. That this state of 'paradise on earth' has been accomplished, will be evidenced by the 'High St' presence of cocktail or music bars, discos, (garden) pubs, bistros and fast food. 'First division' locations are pinpointed by the aforementioned establishments offering inducements, which may include wet T-shirt, nightdress or pyjama bottom parties; air conditioning; space invader games and table top videos; as well as sundowner, happy or doubles hours.

Local prices: *See* **Special prices.**

Mr Big: a local trader or pension owner, an aspiring tycoon, a small fish trying to be a big one in a 'small pool'. Despite being sometimes flashy with shady overtones, his lack of sophistication is apparent by his not being Grecocilious!

Noddies or nodders: the palpable, floating evidence of untreated sewage being discharged into the sea.

One-eyed: small. *See* Donkey-droppings.

Poom: a descriptive noun 'borrowed' after sighting on Crete, some years ago, a crudely written sign advertising accommodation that simply stated POOMS! This particular place was basic with low-raftered ceilings, earth-floors and windowless rooms, simply equipped with a pair of truckle beds and rickety oilcloth covered washstand - very reminiscent of typical Cycladean cubicles of the 1950/60s period.

Provincial: usually applied to accommodation and is an improvement on Ethnic. Not meant to indicate, say, dirty but should conjure up images of faded, rather gloomy establishments, with a mausoleum atmosphere; high ceilinged, Victorian rooms with worn, brown linoleum; dusty, tired aspidistras, as well as bathrooms and plumbing of unbelievable antiquity.

Pump ship: To 'ablute'.

Richter scale: borrowed from earthquake seismology and employed to indicate the (appalling) state of toilets, on an 'eye-watering' scale.
Rustic: unsophisticated, unrefined.

Schlepper: vigorous touting for customers by restaurant staff. It is said of a skilled market schlepper that he can 'retrieve' a passer-by from up to thirty or forty metres beyond the stall.

Scrubbly: usually applied to a beach or countryside, and indicating a rather messy, shabby area.

Special prices: A phrase employed to conceal the fact that the price charged is no more, no less than that of all the other bandits! No, no - competitors.

Local prices: is a homespun variation designed to give the impression that the goods are charged at a much lower figure than that obtainable elsewhere. Both are totally inaccurate, misleading misnomers.

Squatty: A Turkish (or French) style ablution arrangement. None of the old, familiar lavatory bowl and seat. Oh, no, just two moulded footprints edging a dirty looking hole, set in a porcelain surround. Apart from the unaccustomed nature of the exercise, the Lord simply did not give us enough limbs to keep a shirt up and control wayward trousers, that constantly attempt to flop down on to the floor, awash with goodness knows what! All this has to be enacted whilst gripping the toilet roll in one hand and wiping one's 'botty', with the other hand. Impossible! Incidentally, ladies should (perhaps) substitute blouse for shirt and skirt for trousers, but then it is easier (I am told) to tuck a skirt into one's waistband! A minor defect in the transition from Turkey, is that the close-to-the-floor tap, installed to aid flushing a squatty, is noticeable by its absence, in Greece. Well, it would be wouldn't it?

Way-station: mainly used to refer to an office or terminus in the sticks, and cloaked with an abandoned, unwanted air.

And this little seaside shanty town had been awarded a 'Golden Starfish'!

Methoni Castle

Old Monemvassia

Artwork: Ted Spittles &
 Geoffrey O'Connell
Packaging: Willowbridge Publishing
Plans & Maps: Graham
 Bishop & Geoffrey O'Connell
Typeset: Disc preparation
 Viv Grady & Willowbridge
 Publishing
Cover Preparation & Printing:
 FotoDIRECT Ltd
Printers: The Bath Press

GROC's Terra Firma Guides...

The definitive onshore guides ...to the ports and harbours of

The Solent
and
The Channel Islands
& adjacent French Coast

GROC's Terra Firma Guide to the
Ports & Harbours
of the
CHANNEL ISLA...
GROC's Terra Firma Guide to the
Ports & Harbours
of the
SOLENT

These two books are the first of a planned series of some twelve 'Terra Firma' guides to the coastal ports and harbours of the United Kingdom, Channel Islands, France and Southern Ireland. Each one covers some 20-25 locations and includes the most detailed information in respect of each, with unique, all-encompassing A to Z, as well as a comprehensive description of local excursions.

The author, Geoffrey O'Connell, already has three successful nautical books to his credit, as well as nine titles in his inimitable series of GROC's Candid Guides to Greece and the Greek Islands.

GROC's Terra Firma Guides to the Ports and Harbours of:

The Solent
192 pages, paperback, full colour laminated cover, size 254mm x 158mm.
Publication date April 1993

£14.95

The Channel Islands & adjacent French Coast
192 pages, paperback, fullcolour laminated cover, size 254mm x 158mm.
Publication date May 1993

£14.95

Ashford, Buchan & Enright,
31 Bridge Street,
Leatherhead, Surrey KT22 8BN
Tel: 0372 373355 Fax: 0372 363550

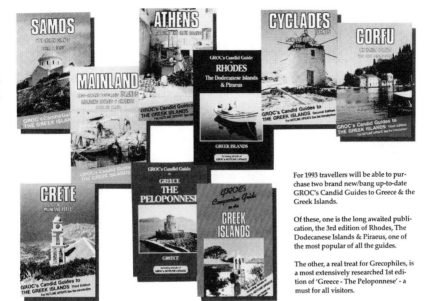

For 1993 travellers will be able to purchase two brand new/bang up-to-date GROC's Candid Guides to Greece & the Greek Islands.

Of these, one is the long awaited publication, the 3rd edition of Rhodes, The Dodecanese Islands & Piraeus, one of the most popular of all the guides.

The other, a real treat for Grecophiles, is a most extensively researched 1st edition of 'Greece - The Peloponnese' - a must for all visitors.

GROC's Candid Guides

to

Greece

and the

Greek Islands

by
Geoffrey O'Connell

GROC's Candid Guides are just that - candid, frank, honest and unbiased. Besides good, solid information, they also answer the basic questions that every holiday-maker asks and needs to have answered: Where are the toilets? Is the beach pebbly? Is the sea clean? What is the Greek word for doctor? Where is the local hospital?

Samos and the North East Aegean Islands, Athens & Piraeus
1st Edition £11.95 paperback

The Mainland Islands, Argo-Saronic & Sporades, including Spetses & Skiathos. Athens & Piraeus
1st Edition £11.95 paperback

Athens and Travelling the Greek Islands
1st Edition £7.95 paperback

Crete & Mainland Ports
3rd Edition £11.95 paperback

Cyclades Islands, Mainland Ports & Piraeus incl. Mykonos, Naxos, Paros & Santorini
2nd Edition £11.95 paperback

Corfu, The Ionian Islands & West Coast Ports
3rd Edition £11.95 paperback

Companion Guide to the Greek Islands
1st Edition £11.95 paperback

NEW for 1993:

Greece - The Peloponnese
1st Edition £14.95 paperback

Rhodes, The Dodecanese Islands & Piraeus
3rd Edition £14.95 paperback

"research is extensive, detailed and practical...recommendations are invaluable...judgements are invariably fair, fun and functional." World Magazine

"idiosyncratic style but up-to-date and meticulously researched" Financial Times

"Even if you never intended visiting (Greece) the books make an interesting and amusing read." The Greek Review

"essential reading" Sunday Times Magazine

"We use your guide as a Greek bible." M.G. of Keighly, W. Yorkshire

"Your guides helped enormously. Thanks for an excellent and informative book." D. & C.E. of Kingston Upon Thames

"Congratulations on producing the best guides to the Greek Islands. I would be unable to travel without them. I also love your humour." C.D. of London, E9

"Your book was very accurate. Thank you very much for your help.. E.L. of Southampton

Ashford, Buchan & Enright,
31 Bridge Street,
Leatherhead, Surrey KT22 8BN
Tel: 0372 373355 Fax: 0372 363550